WORLD WAR II DATA BOOK

THIRD REICH

1933–1945

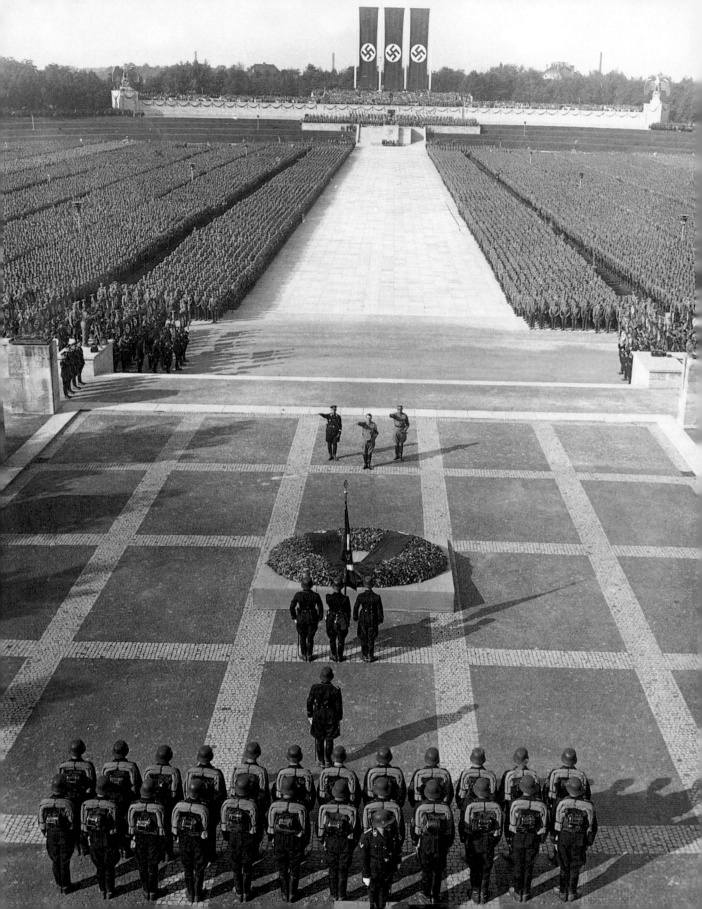

WORLD WAR II DATA BOOK

THIRD REICH

1933–1945

THE ESSENTIAL FACTS AND FIGURES FOR HITLER'S GERMANY

CHRIS McNAB

First published in 2009 by
Amber Books Ltd
Bradley's Close
74–77 White Lion Street
London N1 9PF
www.amberbooks.co.uk

ISBN: 978-1-906626-51-8

Project Editor: Michael Spilling
Design: Colin Hawes
Picture Research: Terry Forshaw

Printed in Thailand

PICTURE CREDITS

Art-Tech/MARS: 16/17, 20, 52/53
Cody Images: 2, 28/29, 74/75, 90/91, 103, 108/109, 138/139, 151,
    152/153, 155, 166/167, 179
U.S. Department of Defense: 6/7, 95, 175

All maps by Patrick Mulrey (© Amber Books) except pages 9,
10/11, 36, 39 and 41 by Cartographica (© Amber Books)

CONTENTS

CHAPTER 1

History of the Reich

The history of the Third Reich is an undeniably epic story of regeneration, hubris and final, utter disaster. Ultimately dominated by the vision and personality of one man, Adolf Hitler, Germany emerged from the social chaos and political turmoil of the Weimar Republic into a new world governed by Nazi ideology and propagandist politics. By early 1939, furthermore, the country was also on the road to another world war.

Hitler's militaristic ambitions for expansion, beginning against Poland in September 1939, brought undeniable successes. By the end of 1941, almost the whole of Western Europe, the Balkans and much of the western Soviet Union and Ukraine were under German control. Yet the storm of growing Allied resistance intensified, and by April 1945 the last flames of the Third Reich were snuffed out, doused by Allied offensives from both east and west. Hitler had taken his people on a journey of victory and then defeat, and in so doing created one of the most violent periods in all of human history.

◄ **Hitler accepts the ovation of the *Reichstag* after announcing the 'peaceful' annexation of Austria, March 1938.**

New World Order, 1918–33

In the aftermath of its defeat in World War I, Germany was a socially and politically divided nation, humiliated by severe international reparations treaties. The conditions of these treaties partly laid the groundwork for the Nazi rise to power.

The German defeat in 1918 brought the *Kaiserreich* (German Empire) down in flames, and left a bruised nation wracked by social disorder. Nor did the establishment in January 1919 of the Weimar Republic, a constituent assembly with its seat at Weimar, calm the country's turbulence. Anti-democratic political parties were gathering influence – they attracted 35 per cent of electoral support in the 1920 elections – and literally fought amongst themselves in vigorous street battles.

Many nationalist Germans believed that defeat in the war came from a 'stab in the back' from the politicians, not from military failure, and Allied reparations plans saddled the nation with a debt of 150 billion marks. The Versailles Treaty's terms seemed to crush Germany's future capability for military redevelopment. Adding further to Germany's woes, the

▶ **MAP: Under the terms of treaties after World War I, Germany became strategically squeezed in Europe. East Prussia was separated from the rest of the German state by the Polish-controlled Danzig corridor, while Alsace-Lorraine, Saarland and Eupen-Malmedy in the west were transferred to France or Belgium. The Rhineland remained a German possession, but no military deployment was permitted here.**

THE THREE GERMAN REICHS

Reich	Date	Description
First	800–1806	Heiliges Römisches Reich Deutscher Nation (Holy Roman Empire of the German Nation). Founded with crowning of Charlemagne (Charles the Great) and dissolved with abdication of Franz II in August 1806.
Second	1870–1919	Hohenzollern Germany, from unification of Germany to abdication of Wilhelm II in 1919 following World War I.
Third	1933–45	Germany under the leadership of Adolf Hitler, from his ascension to the chancellorship in 1933.

POLITICAL PARTIES, GERMANY, 1918–33

Major Party	Translation	Orientation
Nationalsozialistische Deutsche Arbeiterpartei (NSDAP)	National Socialist German Workers Party	Nationalist/Fascist
Deutschnationale Volkspartei (DNVP)	German National People's Party	Nationalist
Deutsche Volkspartei (DVP)	German People's Party	Right-wing Liberal/Anti-Republic
Zentrum	Centre Party	Catholic/Workers
Bayerische Volkspartei (BVP)	Bavarian People's Party	Catholic (Bavarian wing of Zentrum)/Anti-Democratic
Deutsche Demokratische Partei (DDP)	German Democratic Party	Left-wing/Liberal
Sozialdemokratische Partei Deutschlands (SPD)	Social Democratic Party of Germany	Left-wing/Socialist

Minor Party	Translation	Orientation
Kommunistische Partei Deutschlands (KPD)	Communist Party of Germany	Communist
Bayerischer Bauernbund (BBB)	Bavarian Farmers' League	Republican/Agrarian
Christliche Volkspartei (CVP)	Christian People's Party	Rhineland offshoot of Zentrum
Konservative Volkspartei (KVP)	Conservative People's Party	Conservative/Nationalist
Landbund	Agricultural League	Agrarian
Bund der Polen	Polish League	Polish/minority interests
Völkische-Nationaler Block (VNB)	People's Nationalist Party	Nationalist
Wirtschaftspartei	Business Party	Middle-class interests

GERMANY'S SITUATION IN EUROPE, 1920–21

Germany's situation in Europe,
1920–21

- - - Poland's treaty
boundary 1921
Western Allies
New States created 1919–20
Neutral States

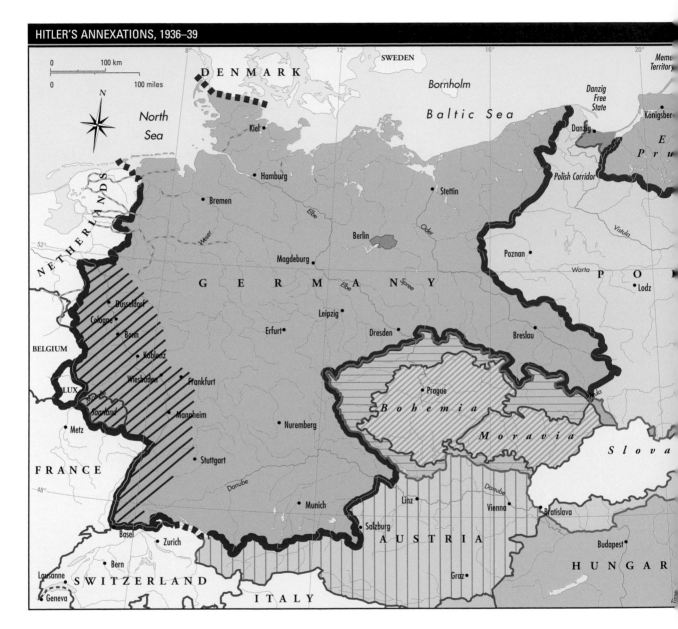

HITLER'S ANNEXATIONS, 1936–39

French and Belgian occupation of the Ruhr area in January 1923 precipitated a catastrophic collapse in the value of German currency, plunging the nation into financial desperation. The former Allies finally reacted, introducing economic measures that stabilized the German economy and injected some economic growth back into Germany between 1924 and 1928. Yet the German people remained volatile and dissatisfied, and hence were vulnerable to any kind of demagogue who promised to rejuvenate the nation at home and renew its standing abroad.

The Nazi phenomenon

Into this political landscape emerged the *Nationalsozialistische Deutsche*

◀ **RECLAIMING TERRITORY**
Compared with the map on page 9, this map graphically illustrates how important territorial expansion became to Hitler as he sought to exorcise the ghosts of defeat during the late 1930s. The remilitarization of the Rhineland, in particular, beginning in March 1936, sent a message to the world that Germany was no longer subservient to conditions imposed by foreign powers.

Hitler's Annexations
1936–39

■	Germany after 1919
▨	Troops into demilitarized Rhineland March 1936
▥	*Anschluss* (union with Austria) March 1938
▦	Occupation of Sudetenland October 1938
—	Original Czechoslovak border
▨	Formerly Czechoslovakia occupied March 1939
▬	Moravian territory to Poland October 1938
▬	Memel territory to Germany March 1939
▬	Protectorate of Slovakia territory to Hungary Nov 1938
▬	Czechoslovak territory to Hungary March 1939

Arbeiterpartei (NSDAP), at first simply one of the many right-wing nationalist organizations vying for power in post-war Germany. Growing out from its Bavarian roots, the NSDAP increased in popularity, propounding an initial anti-capitalist and anti-Semitic programme developed in part by a rising political star – Adolf Hitler. Hitler became the Party chairman in July 1921, and two years later the NSDAP launched its 'Beer Hall Putsch' in Munich, an attempted military coup that ended in failure for the Party and imprisonment for Hitler. During his nine months in Landsberg prison, Hitler had a change of political heart, expressed partly through the first volume of his political work

Mein Kampf (My Struggle). Once released from prison, Hitler committed himself to the legal pursuit of power, albeit a pursuit framed by the muscle of the *Sturmabteilung* (SA), the NSDAP's paramilitary wing.

Although NSDAP support increased amongst both working-class and middle-class voters, electoral returns were disappointing during the late 1920s. Fortunes changed, however, from 1930, partly due to the German people looking for strong solutions to the dreadful conditions of the Great Depression, and partly through skilful NSDAP propaganda and campaigning. The NSDAP had a particularly strong powerbase amongst Germany's rural population, but it expanded its focus to bring in middle-class business owners and state officials – people of influence, in short.

Taking the reins
The early 1930s saw the NSDAP expand from a party that was locally powerful to one that was nationally powerful, directly through the ballot box. Ironically, defining NSDAP ideology remains complicated, as Hitler's views were a largely unoriginal mish-mash of nationalist and racial ideas with long historical roots in European society. An awkward label to the NSDAP philosphy is 'Racial Social Darwinism', as Hitler saw the battle between superior and, in his view, inferior races as a fight for national survival. At the top of his racial tree were the Aryan *Herrenvolk* (master race), and at the bottom were the negroes, Slavs, gypsies and, above

ELECTIONS FOR THE REICHSTAG, 1930–33 (SEATS WON)

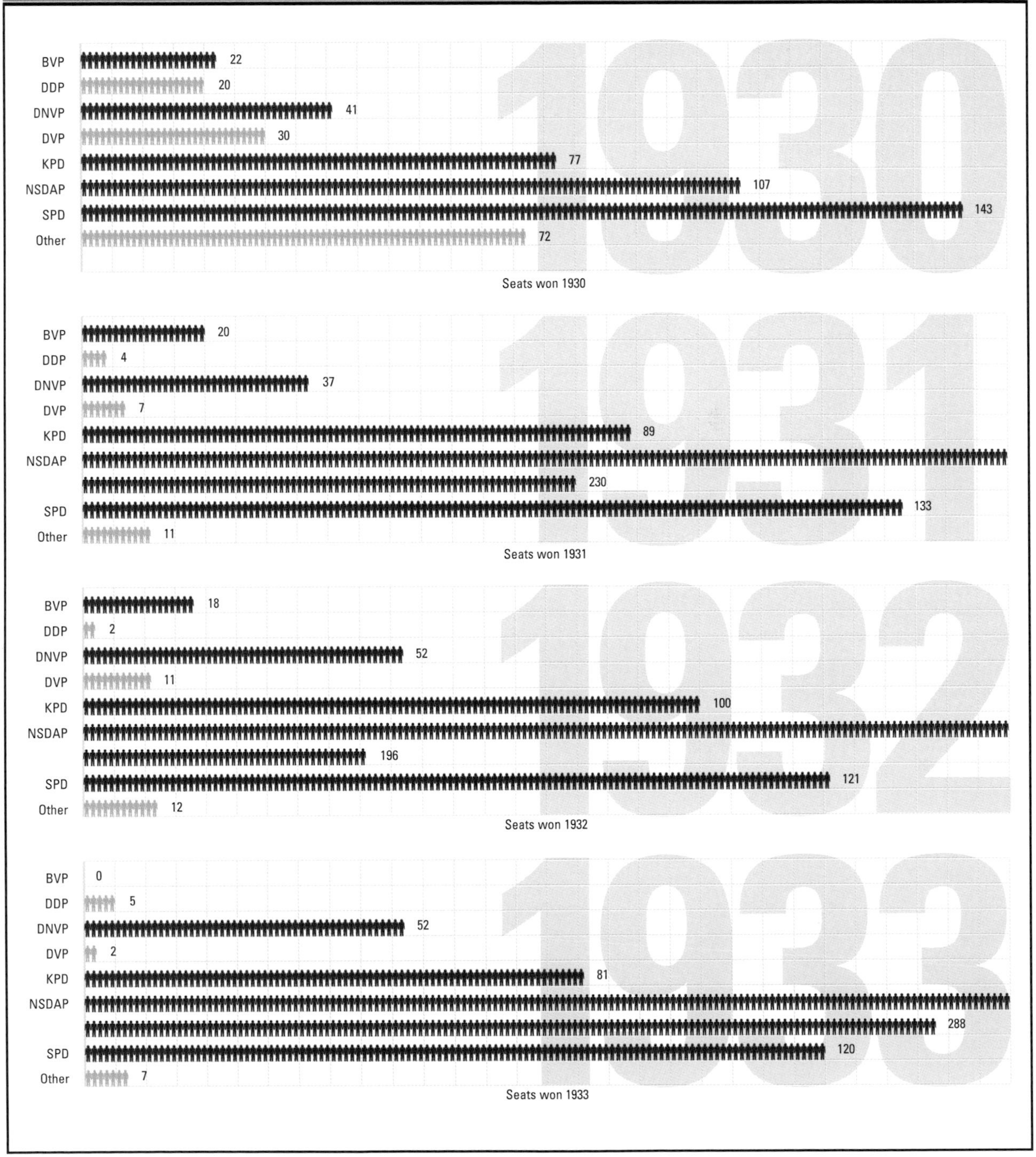

1930

BVP	22
DDP	20
DNVP	41
DVP	30
KPD	77
NSDAP	107
SPD	143
Other	72

Seats won 1930

1931

BVP	20
DDP	4
DNVP	37
DVP	7
KPD	89
NSDAP	230
SPD	133
Other	11

Seats won 1931

1932

BVP	18
DDP	2
DNVP	52
DVP	11
KPD	100
NSDAP	196
SPD	121
Other	12

Seats won 1932

1933

BVP	0
DDP	5
DNVP	52
DVP	2
KPD	81
NSDAP	288
SPD	120
Other	7

Seats won 1933

all, the Jews. There were three other key ingredients to his political outlook:

1) *Volksgemeinschaft* (People's Community) – This rather nebulous concept evoked a sense of traditional community and values that transcended class, and which bonded the German people together in nationalist unity.

2) *Führerprinzip* (Leadership Principle) – Although Hitler rose to power via democratic activity, he

actually saw multi-party states as weak and vacillating. The *Führerprinzip* embodied an authoritarian view of government, in which a single, uncontested leader would rule Germany with iron resolve, and self-interests would defer to nationalist purpose.

3) *Lebensraum* (Living Space) – Hitler argued that it was the inexorable right for Germany to commit itself to territorial expansion, bringing the nation the food, labour and materials to grow. The concept of *Lebensraum* was, in effect, the ideological engine behind the future world war.

Seizing opportunity

Even as the NSDAP swelled in power, the government of the Weimar Republic entered new forms of crisis, opening the door just enough for the Nazi foot. The lack of a true majority

party in the *Reichstag* meant that much policy-making was achieved through intimidation and presidential decrees, rather than consensual government. In the spring of 1930, President Paul von Hindenburg appointed Heinrich Brüning (leader of the Centre Party) as the German Chancellor. It was Brüning's failure to push through an emergency economic decree that led to his calling of the September 1930 election, in which the Nazis made significant gains.

Brüning's resignation was forced in May 1932, and he was replaced by Franz von Papen, also of the Centre Party, who was helped into the position by *Generalmajor* Kurt von Schleicher, who represented Army interests. More disorder followed, and Papen gave Hitler two important concessions as he attempted to ally himself with the increasingly popular

GERMAN LABOUR FRONT (DAF) MEMBERSHIP, 1933–45	
Date	
December 1933	9.36 million
June 1934	about 16 million
April 1935	about 21 million
September 1939	about 22 million
September 1942	about 25 million

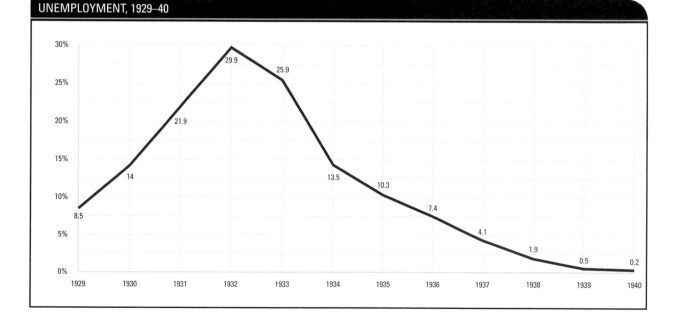

UNEMPLOYMENT, 1929–40

Nazis. First, Papen agreed to the dissolution of the *Reichstag* and the calling of a new election. Second, the ban on the Nazi *Schutzstaffel* (SS) and *Sturmabteilung* (SA) paramilitary organizations was lifted. Both of these actions proved to be historically fatal mistakes.

Two elections were held in 1932 (July and November), and although the Nazi Party lost some votes in the second round, it gained and retained its position as Germany's largest political party. Now Hitler had serious muscle. From the July election, Hitler had attempted to force his ascension to Chancellor, a goal that Papen seemed to resist successfully (such was part of the reason behind a dip in Nazi morale, and the poorer electoral results in November). Schleicher, meanwhile, had manoeuvred Hindenburg against Papen, and in early December Papen resigned and Schleicher himself took over as Chancellor. In revenge, Papen secretly negotiated with Hitler regarding a return to power, this time with the assurance that Hitler would be Chancellor, while Papen would act as Vice-Chancellor. (Papen believed that Hitler's influence in office would be overwhelmed by more conservative presences.) Hindeburg once again shifted allegiances under pressure, and on 30 January 1933 Adolf Hitler was appointed Chancellor. He had come a long way since the 1920s.

Absolute Power, 1933–39

Once he was Chancellor, Hitler could begin to centralize power upon himself. Over a period of six years, Hitler transformed the national spirit while at the same time using his popularity to extirpate opposition and give himself dictatorial powers.

From 1933 to 1939, Hitler rapidly centralized power in his own hands through the process of *Gleichschaltung* (coordination) – essentially the concentration of social control in NSDAP hands. The months following Hitler's appointment to the chancellorship brought rapid change. An election on 5 March confirmed Nazi popularity, as the Party took nearly 44 per cent of the vote. That same month, Hitler coerced the *Reichstag* into passing the Enabling Act, a law that essentially gave Hitler dictatorial powers over legislation. (Hitler had already given his government emergency powers following the *Reichstag* arson in February 1933.) As the year progressed, Hitler steadily saw to the banning or disbandment of rival political parties, and trade unions came under Nazi control. On 14 July, in a landmark piece of legislation, the *Reichstag* passed the Law Against the Establishment of Parties, and political opposition to the Nazis was now prohibited.

Choosing sides

Hitler had effectively wrought a revolution in German politics, but there were consequences. Conservative, but influential, elements of German society – businesses, the German Army, the civil service and so on – were rightly troubled by the more violent extremes of the Nazi Party, particularly the SA under Ernst Röhm, which gravitated towards a more radical shake-up of German society. Hitler had to take sides, and in June 1934 made his choice clear by launching his SS bodyguard against the SA leadership, arresting and murdering Röhm and dozens of other key figures. By doing so, Hitler also removed the potential threat of the SA turning against him.

With the SA out of the way, *Gleichschaltung* continued apace. With the death of Hindenburg in

LEADERS OF THE STURMABTEILUNG (SA)	
Name	Date
Emil Maurice	1920–21
Hans Ulrich Klintzsche	1921–23
Hermann Göring	1923
(Position vacant)	1923–25
Franz Pfeffer von Salomon	1926–30
Adolf Hitler	1930–31
Ernst Röhm	1931–34
Viktor Lutze	1934–43
Wilhelm Scheppmann	1943–45

August 1934, Hitler merged the offices of President and Chancellor. He also made the armed forces swear loyalty to him as *Führer* – the first step in his steady gathering of military command powers. Also in 1934, Hitler brought all the regional governments of Germany under his administrative umbrella via the Law for the Reconstruction of the Reich.

At the same time as these political changes were taking place, Hitler appointed Hjalmar Schacht, widely considered a safe pair of financial hands by the German business community, as Economics Minister, and wage control measures stabilized relations between business and the German workforce. Prosperity and security began to return to Germany, aided by massive public works projects such as the construction of the *Autobahnen*. From the mid-1930s, Hitler also began a rapid process of rearmament.

Total power

In 1937, Schacht was effectively supplanted by Hitler's then right-hand man, Hermann Göring. Many people would have recognized that Hitler was putting Germany on the path to war. He broke free from the shackles of the Versailles Treaty, and on 4 February 1938 assumed supreme command of the German armed forces. Any opposition was ruthlessly crushed by a Nazi-controlled police and justice system, backed by the predatory SS and delivered via units such as the *Gestapo*. Yet a large percentage of the German population saw only the benefits Hitler appeared to have brought, and followed him into a war greater than any other.

SA RANKS

Military

- Oberster SA-führer (OSAF) *(Supreme SA Leader)*
- Stabschef der SA *(Chief of Staff of the SA)*
- SA-Obergruppenführer *(SA Senior Group Leader)*
- SA-Gruppenführer *(SA Group Leader)*
- SA-Brigadeführer *(SA Brigade Leader)*
- SA-Oberführer *(SA Senior Leader)*
- SA-Standartenführer *(SA Regiment Leader)*
- SA-Obersturmbannführer *(SA Senior Storm Unit Leader)*
- SA-Sturmbannführer *(SA Storm Unit Leader)*
- SA-Hauptsturmführer *(SA Storm Unit Captain)*
- SA-Obersturmführer *(SA Senior Storm Leader)*
- SA-Sturmführer *(SA Storm Leader)*
- SA-Haupttruppführer *(SA Head Troop Leader)*
- SA-Obertruppführer *(SA Senior Troop Leader)*
- SA-Truppführer *(SA Troop Leader)*
- SA-Oberscharführer *(SA Senior Squad Leader)*
- SA-Scharführer *(SA Squad Leader)*
- SA-Rottenführer *(SA Section Leader)*
- SA-Obersturmmann *(SA Senior Storm Trooper)*
- SA-Sturmmann *(SA Storm Trooper)*

Medical

- Sanitäts-Obergruppenführer *(Medical Senior Group Leader)*
- Sanitäts-Gruppenführer *(Medical Group Leader)*
- Sanitäts-Brigadeführer *(Medical Brigade Leader)*
- Sanitäts-Oberführer *(Medical Senior Leader)*
- Sanitäts-Standartenführer *(Medical Regiment Leader)*
- Sanitäts-Obersturmbannführer *(Medical Senior Storm Unit Leader)*
- Sanitäts-Sturmbannführer *(Medical Storm Unit Leader)*
- Sanitäts-Hauptsturmführer *(Medical Head Storm Leader)*
- Sanitäts-Obersturmführer *(Medical Senior Storm Leader)*
- Sanitäts-Sturmführer *(Medical Storm Leader)*
- Sanitäts-Führer-Antwärter *(Medical Leader Candidate)*

Administrative

- Gruppengeldverwalter *(Group Financial Officer)*
- Reichszeugmeister *(Reich Armoury Master)*
- Untergruppengeldverwalter *(Assistant Group Financial Officer)*
- Zeugmeister *(Armoury Master)*
- Standartengeldverwalter *(Regimental Financial Officer)*
- Sturmbanngeldverwalter *(Storm Unit Financial Officer)*
- Sturmgeldverwalter *(Storm Financial Officer)*

OBERSTE SA-FÜHRUNG (SUPREME SA LEADERSHIP), 1932

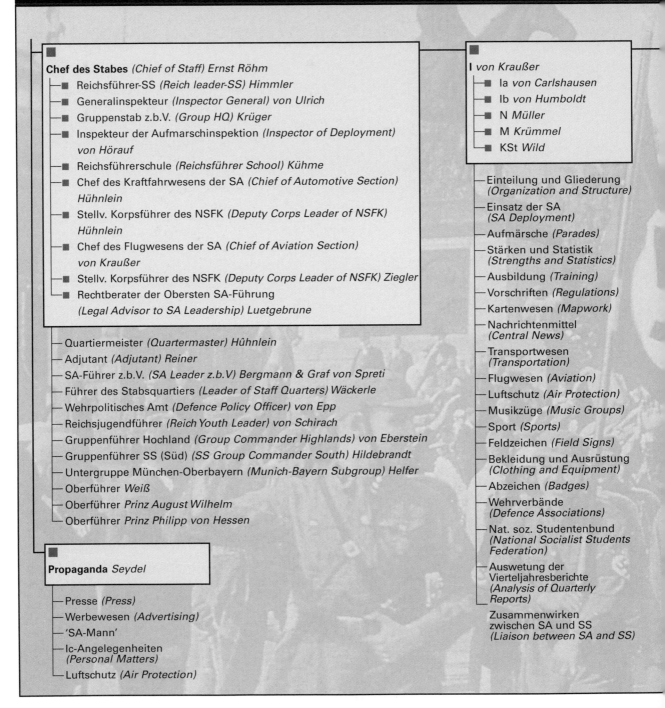

Chef des Stabes *(Chief of Staff) Ernst Röhm*
- Reichsführer-SS *(Reich leader-SS) Himmler*
- Generalinspekteur *(Inspector General) von Ulrich*
- Gruppenstab z.b.V. *(Group HQ) Krüger*
- Inspekteur der Aufmarschinspektion *(Inspector of Deployment) von Hörauf*
- Reichsführerschule *(Reichsführer School) Kühme*
- Chef des Kraftfahrwesens der SA *(Chief of Automotive Section) Hühnlein*
- Stellv. Korpsführer des NSFK *(Deputy Corps Leader of NSFK) Hühnlein*
- Chef des Flugwesens der SA *(Chief of Aviation Section) von Kraußer*
- Stellv. Korpsführer des NSFK *(Deputy Corps Leader of NSFK) Ziegler*
- Rechtberater der Obersten SA-Führung *(Legal Advisor to SA Leadership) Luetgebrune*

- Quartiermeister *(Quartermaster) Hühnlein*
- Adjutant *(Adjutant) Reiner*
- SA-Führer z.b.V. *(SA Leader z.b.V) Bergmann & Graf von Spreti*
- Führer des Stabsquartiers *(Leader of Staff Quarters) Wäckerle*
- Wehrpolitisches Amt *(Defence Policy Officer) von Epp*
- Reichsjugendführer *(Reich Youth Leader) von Schirach*
- Gruppenführer Hochland *(Group Commander Highlands) von Eberstein*
- Gruppenführer SS (Süd) *(SS Group Commander South) Hildebrandt*
- Untergruppe München-Oberbayern *(Munich-Bayern Subgroup) Helfer*
- Oberführer *Weiß*
- Oberführer *Prinz August Wilhelm*
- Oberführer *Prinz Philipp von Hessen*

Propaganda *Seydel*

- Presse *(Press)*
- Werbewesen *(Advertising)*
- 'SA-Mann'
- Ic-Angelegenheiten *(Personal Matters)*
- Luftschutz *(Air Protection)*

I *von Kraußer*
- Ia *von Carlshausen*
- Ib *von Humboldt*
- N *Müller*
- M *Krümmel*
- KSt *Wild*

- Einteilung und Gliederung *(Organization and Structure)*
- Einsatz der SA *(SA Deployment)*
- Aufmärsche *(Parades)*
- Stärken und Statistik *(Strengths and Statistics)*
- Ausbildung *(Training)*
- Vorschriften *(Regulations)*
- Kartenwesen *(Mapwork)*
- Nachrichtenmittel *(Central News)*
- Transportwesen *(Transportation)*
- Flugwesen *(Aviation)*
- Luftschutz *(Air Protection)*
- Musikzüge *(Music Groups)*
- Sport *(Sports)*
- Feldzeichen *(Field Signs)*
- Bekleidung und Ausrüstung *(Clothing and Equipment)*
- Abzeichen *(Badges)*
- Wehrverbände *(Defence Associations)*
- Nat. soz. Studentenbund *(National Socialist Students Federation)*
- Auswetung der Vierteljahresberichte *(Analysis of Quarterly Reports)*

Zusammenwirken zwischen SA und SS *(Liaison between SA and SS)*

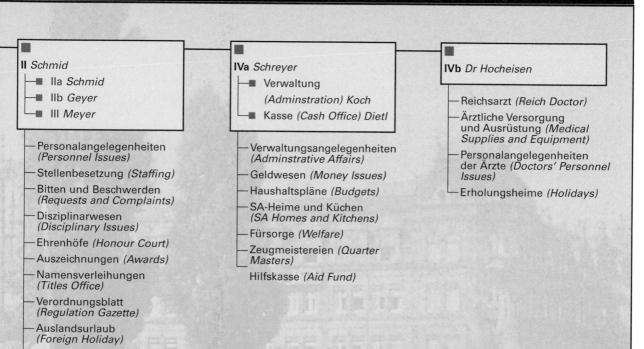

II *Schmid*
- IIa *Schmid*
- IIb *Geyer*
- III *Meyer*

- Personalangelegenheiten
  (Personnel Issues)
- Stellenbesetzung *(Staffing)*
- Bitten und Beschwerden
  (Requests and Complaints)
- Disziplinarwesen
  (Disciplinary Issues)
- Ehrenhöfe *(Honour Court)*
- Auszeichnungen *(Awards)*
- Namensverleihungen
  (Titles Office)
- Verordnungsblatt
  (Regulation Gazette)
- Auslandsurlaub
  (Foreign Holiday)
- Rechtswesen *(Legal)*

IVa *Schreyer*
- Verwaltung
  (Adminstration) Koch
- Kasse *(Cash Office) Dietl*

- Verwaltungsangelegenheiten
  (Adminstrative Affairs)
- Geldwesen *(Money Issues)*
- Haushaltspläne *(Budgets)*
- SA-Heime und Küchen
  (SA Homes and Kitchens)
- Fürsorge *(Welfare)*
- Zeugmeistereien *(Quarter
  Masters)*
- Hilfskasse *(Aid Fund)*

IVb *Dr Hocheisen*

- Reichsarzt *(Reich Doctor)*
- Ärztliche Versorgung
  und Ausrüstung *(Medical
  Supplies and Equipment)*
- Personalangelegenheiten
  der Ärzte *(Doctors' Personnel
  Issues)*
- Erholungsheime *(Holidays)*

The *Oberste SA-Führung* was the
headquarters command for the SA,
separated into central management
divisions and sub-offices, each
dedicated to a different aspect of
the organization. Note that the SA
never developed foreign affairs
offices, unlike the SS.

KNOWN INDIVIDUALS EXECUTED AS CONSEQUENCE OF 'NIGHT OF THE LONG KNIVES', 29/30 JUNE 1934

Name	Position held (where known)	Name	Position held (where known)
Otto Ballerstadt	Diplomat	Hans Hayn	SA-Gruppenführer, NSDAP Reichstag deputy.
Fritz Beck	Director	? Heck	SA-Standartenführer
Karl Belding	SA-Standartenführer	Edmund Heines	SA-Obergruppenführer, NSDAP Reichstag deputy
Erwald Kuppel Bergmann			
Veit Ulrich von Beulwitz	SA-Sturmführer	Oskar Heines	SA-Obersturmbannführer
Alois Bittman	SA-Scharführer	Robert Heiser	
Franz Blasner	SA-Truppführer	Hans Peter von Heydebreck	SA-Gruppenführer, NSDAP Reichstag deputy
Herbert von Bose	Secretary to Franz von Papen		
Ferdinand von Bredow	Generalmajor in Reichswehr	Anton Freiherr von Hohberg und Buchwald	SS-Reiter and Obertruppführer
A. Charig		Edgar Julius Jung	Journalist, speech writer
? von der Decken		Gustav Ritter von Kahr	Former Staatskommissar for Bavaria
Georg von Detten	SA-Gruppenführer, SA political chief, NSDAP Reichstag deputy	? Kamphausen	City Engineer
? Ender-Schulen	SA-Sturmbannführer	Eugen von Kessel	Hauptman Polizei
Kurt Engelhardt	SA-Sturmbannführer	? Kirschbaum	
Werner Engels	SA-Sturmbannführer, acting Police President of Breslau	Dr Erich Klausener	Head of Preußisch Ministerie Polizei, Centre Party, Catholic Action
? Enkel	SA-Standartenführer	Willi Klemm	SA-Brigadeführer
Karl Ernst	Freikorps Roßbach, SA-Gruppenführer, NSDAP Reichstag deputy	Hans Karl Koch	SA-Brigadeführer
		Heinrich Konig	SA-Oberscharführer
Ernst Martin Ewald	Leiter der ND Gau Sachsen	Ewald Koppel	Communist
Hans Joachim von Falkenhausen	SA-Oberführer	? Krause	SA-Sturmbannführer
Gustav Fink	SS-Mann	Fritz Ritter von Kraußer	SA-Obergruppenführer, NSDAP Reichstag deputy.
Dr Walter Förster	Lawyer		
? Gehrt	SA-Sturmbannführer	Friedrich Karl Laemmermann	HJ Führer
Fritz Gerlich	Journalist	Gotthard Langer	SA-Obertruppführer.
Daniel Gerth	SA-Obersturmführer	Dr Lindemann	
Dr Alexander Glaser		Karl Lipinsky	SA-Reiter-Sturmführer
Freiherr von Guttenberg		? Max	Röhm's chauffeur
Dr Haber		? Marcus	SA-Standartenführer

Riding the Wave, 1939–42

Although Hitler was undoubtedly an unstable and an unpleasant personality, he was equally a military commander of genuine insight and daring, at least in the early years of his reign and the opening campaigns of World War II.

Nazi expansionism pre-dated the German invasion of Poland in September 1939. In 1935, the Saar region returned to German control by popular mandate, and in March the same year German forces remilitarized the Rhineland and became more deeply involved in assisting Franco's fascists in the Spanish Civil War (1936–39). Two years later, in March 1938, German troops occupied Austria as the two countries united in the *Anschluss*, Hitler supporting pro-Nazi Austrian factions against the established

Name	Position held (where known)	Name	Position held (where known)
Dr Hermann Mattheis	SA-Standartenführer	August Schneidhüber	SA-Obergruppenführer, Munich Police Chief, NSDAP Reichstag deputy
Walter von Mohrenschildt			
? Muhlert		Walter Schotte	
Edmund Neumeier	SA-Rottenführer	Konrad Schragmüller	SA-Gruppenführer, NSDAP Reichstag deputy
Heinrich Nixdorf	SA-Oberst Feldjagerei		
Dr Ernst Oberfohren	Nationalist Reichstag deputy?	Dr Joachim Schroder	SA-Obersturmführer
Lambeardus Ostendorp	SA-Oberst Feldjager	Max Walter Otto Schuldt	SA-Sturmführer
Otto Pietrzok	SA-Sturmbannführer	Walter Schulz	Stabschef der SA Gruppe Pommern
Fritz Pleines	SS-Mann	Max Schulze	SA-Obersturmführer
Adalbert Probst	Catholic youth leader in Munich, former Bavarian Landtag deputy	Hans Schweighardt	SA-Standartenführer
		Emil Sembach	SS-Oberführer
Hans Ramshorn	SA-Brigadeführer, Police president of Gleiwitz	Hans Graf von Spreti-Weilbach	SA-Standartenführer, SA-Führer zur besonderen Verwendung
Robert Reh	Communist	Oskar Stable	Freikorps Maercker, Freikorps Roßbach, NSDAP/NSDStB
Ernst Röhm	Stabschef SA, NSDAP Reichstag deputy		
Paul Röhrbein	Frontbahn	Father Bernhard Stempfle	Catholic priest
Wilhelm Sander	SA-Stabsführer	Gregor Strasser	Gauleiter of Niederbayern-Oberpfalz; Reichsorganisationsleiter
Emil Saasbach			
Wilhelm Sander	SA-Brigadeführer	Otto Stucken	SA-Obersturmführer
Martin Schätzl	SA-Standartenführer	? Surk	SA-Standartenführer
Gaiseric Scherl	SA-Standartenführer, NS Studentenbund	? Thomas	SA-Standartenführer
		Ottmar Toifl	SS-Truppführer; Polizei kommissar
Erich Schieweck	SA-Obertruppführer	Dr Erwin Villain	SA-Standartenartzt
Elisabeth von Schleicher	Wife of General von Schleicher	Max Vogel	SA-Obersturmführer
Kurt von Schleicher	Chancellor of Germany (1932–33)	Gerd Voss	Attorney to Strasser
Hans W. Schmidt	SA-Obersturmführer	Karl Eberhard von Wechmar	SA-Gruppenführer
Theodor Schmidt	SA-Gruppenführer	Udo von Woyrsch	
Dr Wilhelm Schmidt	Music critic; mistaken for SA-Gruppenführer Schmidt	Karl Zehnter	Associate of Röhm and Heines
		Ernestine Zoref	
Wilhelm Eduard Schmidt	SA-Gruppenführer	Alex Zweig	
		Jeanette Zweig	

government. Czechoslovakia, which contained a large ethnic German population, was his next target for incorporation. Now the international community started to react. Protests from France and Britain resulted in compromise – Germany occupied the Sudetenland as part of a negotiated settlement. Yet far from bringing 'peace for our time', as British Prime Minister Neville Chamberlain famously declared, the Sudetenland settlement was just a stepping stone for Hitler, and in March 1939 German forces occupied Bohemia-Moravia and turned Slovakia into a puppet state. Taken with Germany's relentless rearmament, it should have been obvious to all nations that Germany's territorial ambitions were unlikely to stop.

Poland and the West
The German victories of 1939 and 1940 are rightly held up as object lessons in military brilliance. The German armed forces had developed combined-arms tactics to a much higher degree than many of their opponents, and had forged an extremely professional officer class. Yet we must not overlook the risks in Hitler's commitment of Germany to war. While it was confidently assumed that Poland would fall with little trouble, the same could not be said of France and Britain. German reserve forces were limited, and not suited to fighting a long war of

ADOLF HITLER

Birth:	20 April 1889
Death:	30 April 1945
Place of birth:	Braunau am Inn, Austria-Hungary
Parents:	Alois Hitler and Klara Pölzl
Siblings:	Gustav (1885–87); Ida (1886–88); Otto (1887–?); Edmund (1894–1900); Paula (1896–1960)
Half-siblings:	Alois (1882–1956); Angela (1883–1949)
Place of death:	Berlin, Germany
Height:	1.75m (5ft 9in)
Weight:	79.5kg (175lb)
Military service:	16th Bavarian Reserve Regiment (1914–20) Commander-in-Chief of the Wehrmacht (1938–45)
Decorations:	Iron Cross, Second Class (1914); Iron Cross, Second Class (1918); Wound Badge (1917)
Criminal record:	Convicted of treason in 1923. Served nine months of a five-year sentence in Landsberg prison.
Major political positions:	1919 – Member of Deutsche Arbeiter Partei (DAP) 1921 – Chairman of Nationalsozialistische Deutsche Arbeiterpartei (NSDAP) 1933 – Chancellor of Germany 1934 – Declares himself Führer and Reich Chancellor

■ **Hitler was rightly known for his powers of oratory, which were carefully crafted for public effect.**

attrition. In the event, a combination of poor Allied responses and a daring and fast-moving German strategy brought a level of victory that even Hitler could have hardly believed.

Germany invaded Poland on 1 September 1939, Poland's strategic isolation worsened by the German-Soviet Non-Aggression Pact signed on 23 August – Soviet forces invaded from the east on 17 September. Germany's five-army force steadily crushed Polish opposition (although not as easily as history often claims), and the last pockets of Polish resistance were forced to surrender on 28 September. Following the victory, Hitler carved up Poland to

suit German exploitation, and Poland set out on an appalling five-and-a-half years of occupation.

The Allies in the West were finally scalded into action, and both Britain and France declared war on Germany on 3 September 1939. Yet from October 1939 to April 1940, there was little war to speak of, as the opposing sides eyed each other warily. Hitler, meanwhile, was preparing to launch his most audacious campaign. The opening shots of this campaign came on 9 April 1940, with the German invasion of Denmark and Norway. Denmark fell within hours, but the Norwegian campaign brought German forces into a direct clash

with the British and French, and showed up weaknesses – in naval engagements at Narvik, for example, the *Kriegsmarine* (German Navy) lost 10 destroyers. Yet German determination, plus distractions for the Allies in new theatres, meant that Norway succumbed to German occupation in June.

Events in Scandinavia were soon eclipsed by those in France, Belgium and the Netherlands, all of which faced German invasion on 10 May. While two German army groups punched into the Low Countries, a third launched an offensive through the supposedly impassable Ardennes forest into France, neatly bypassing

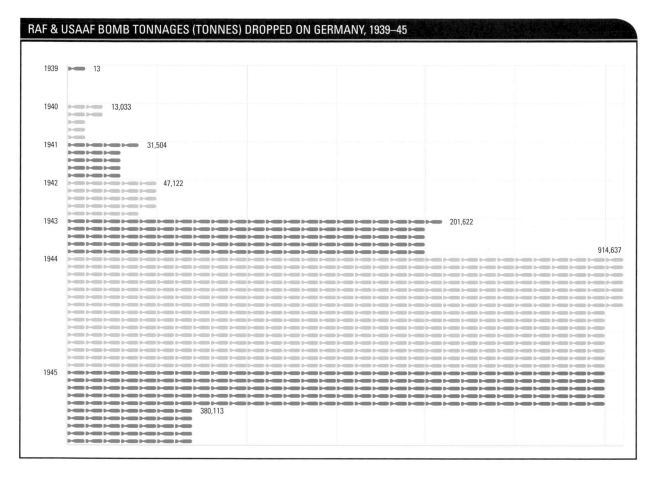

RAF & USAAF BOMB TONNAGES (TONNES) DROPPED ON GERMANY, 1939–45

Year	Tonnage
1939	13
1940	13,033
1941	31,504
1942	47,122
1943	201,622
1944	914,637
1945	380,113

the French Maginot Line border fortifications. Armoured spearheads were quickly across the Meuse and slicing across the French countryside, throwing the Allies into disarray. The surviving elements of the British Expeditionary Force (BEF) were squeezed out of France from the beaches at Dunkirk between 27 May and 4 June, leaving France to its inevitable fate – complete surrender on 22 June. In only six weeks, Hitler's forces had brought three nations under German control and humbled a fourth, Britain. Germany had seized more territory in

a matter of weeks than it had done in the whole of World War I.

Turning east
The conquest of much of Western Europe gave Hitler a surge of popularity, although he was soon to suffer his first setback. Göring, in preparation for the proposed invasion of Britain, promised to crush the Royal Air Force (RAF) with his *Luftwaffe* (Air Force). Although what became known as the Battle of Britain was certainly a close-run thing, by September 1940 it was clear that the German air campaign had

failed. Furthermore, by this point Hitler had turned his attentions elsewhere.

The Soviet Union was the ultimate objective of German *Lebensraum*. Not only did it offer seemingly limitless expanses of space and huge volumes of raw materials, it also embodied the primary ideological fears of National Socialism – Communism and Judaism. Hitler's plans to invade the Soviet Union were hindered somewhat by obligations to help out his Italian allies in the Balkans and North Africa, but on 22 June 1941 a massive Axis army, three million men

KEY FIGURES IN THE THIRD REICH GOVERNMENT

Name	Dates	Key position(s) held
Axmann, Artur	1913–96	Reich Youth Leader
Backe, Herbert	1896–1947	Minister of Food and Agriculture
Blomberg, Werner von	1878–1946	Minister of War
Bormann, Martin	1900–45	Hitler's private secretary and Head of Party Chancellory
Bouhler, Philipp	1899–1945	Head of Nazi Euthanasia Programme
Buch, Walter	1883–1949	President of Nazi Supreme Court
Canaris, Wilhelm	1887–1945	Head of Counter-intelligence Service
Diels, Otto	1900–57	First Head of the Gestapo
Dorpmüller, Julius	1869–1945	Transport Minister
Eichmann, Adolf	1906–62	Head of 'Office for Jewish Emigration'
Esser, Hermann	1900–81	Co-founder of Nazi Party
Fritzsche, Hans	1900–53	Head of Radio Broadcasting
Funk, Walther	1890–1960	Economics Minister
Goebbels, Paul Joseph	1897–1945	Minister of Public Enlightenment and Propaganda; Plenipotentiary for Total War
Göring, Hermann	1893–1946	Aviation Minister; Plenipotentiary for the Four-Year Plan; Reichstag President; Prime Minister and Interior Minister of Prussia
Gürtner, Franz	1881–1941	Justice Minister
Hess, Walther Richard Rudolf	1894–1987	Deputy Party Leader; Führer's Deputy for Party Affairs
Heydrich, Reinhard	1904–42	Head of Reich Security Head Office (RSHA)
Himmler, Heinrich	1900–45	Reichsführer SS; Minister of the Interior; Head of Gestapo and Police; Commissar for the Consolidation of German Nationhood
Hitler, Adolf	1889–1945	Chairman NSDAP; Chancellor of Germany; Führer of the Third Reich
Keppler, Wilhelm	1882–1960	Reich Commissioner for Economic Affairs
Kerrl, Hanns	1887–1941	Minister for Churches
Lammers, Hans Heinrich	1879–1962	Head of Reich Chancellory; Minister without Portfolio
Ley, Robert	1890–1945	Reich Organization Leader; Leader of German Labour Front (DAF)
Müller, Heinrich	1901–45	Head of the Gestapo
Nebe, Arthur	1894–1945	Head of the Criminal Police (Kripo)
Neurath, Constantin Freiherr von	1873–1956	Foreign Minister
Ribbentrop, Joachim von	1893–1946	Reich Commissar for Disarmament; Foreign Minister
Röhm, Ernst	1887–1934	Leader of Sturmabteilung (SA)
Rust, Bernhard	1883–1945	Education Minister
Saukel, Fritz	1894–1946	Plenipotentiary General for Labour Mobilization
Schacht, Hjalmar	1877–1970	President of the Reichsbank; Economics Minister; Plenipotentiary General for the War Economy
Schellenberg, Walter	1910–52	Supreme Head of Military and SS Intelligence
Schirach, Baldur von	1907–74	Reich Youth Leader
Scholtz-Klink, Gertrud	b.1902	Leader of Nazi Women's League; Reich Women's Leader
Schwarz, Franz Xaver von	1875–1947	NSDAP Treasurer
Schwerin von Krosigk	1887–1952	Finance Minister
Seldte, Franz	1882–1952	Minister of Labour
Speer, Albert	1905–81	Minister for Armaments and War Production
Todt, Fritz	1891–1942	Minister for Armaments and Munitions

strong, drove over the Soviet borders in Operation *Barbarossa*. An ill-coordinated and recklessly costly Soviet response brought German victories on a scale never before seen, on a front that stretched from the Gulf of Finland down to the Black Sea. The advance took more than two million Soviet prisoners in three months, as well as capturing most of the major industrial zones in western Russia and the Ukraine. Yet just a day's drive from Moscow, the Russian winter and a major Soviet counter-offensive brought the German offensive to a grinding halt.

Germany now began to experience the war of attrition it had wanted to avoid, and the vast distances of the Soviet hinterland made logistics a nightmare. Nevertheless, in June 1942 the Germans launched Operation *Blue*, which aimed to conquer the Crimea and consolidate the Ukraine, then drive down into the Caucasus to capture vital Soviet oilfields. Once again, the world witnessed huge German advances and appalling Soviet losses. In the south the Red Army was driven back into Stalingrad, on the River Volga, by September 1942. Here was the high point of the German advance, a remarkable military achievement by any reckoning. Yet from the end of 1942, everything would change.

Defeat and Collapse, 1942–44

The Third Reich had reached its greatest territorial extent by the winter of 1942. Yet the Soviet Union was now resurgent, and the Sixth Army's total defeat at Stalingrad was the point at which World War II turned irrevocably against Nazi Germany.

The story of the Third Reich is characterized by hubris at the highest levels. As the war progressed through 1942, Hitler seemed to buy into a growing myth of German invincibility. Nowhere is this better illustrated than in the *Führer*'s declaration of war against the United States back in December 1941, bringing Germany directly into conflict with the world's industrial powerhouse. Hitler committed his country to the ultimate military nightmare – war on multiple fronts. The true implications of this policy began to reveal themselves in 1942.

First defeats
In 1942, Germany's problems began in all theatres. In the Atlantic, the hunting ground of the *Kriegsmarine*'s U-boats, improved Allied tactics and technology slowly forced the submarines onto the defensive, and during 1943 killed the underwater hunters in unsustainable numbers. In North Africa, Mongomery's El Alamein offensive, launched on 23 October, began the final push of German forces back to Tunis, who were then squeezed against the Anglo-American invasion of Morocco and Algeria on 8 November. During 1943, the Germans were forced out of North Africa, defeated on Sicily, and began a brutal, protracted defensive retreat up mainland Italy.

Yet the most serious setback undoubtedly came at Stalingrad in the winter of 1942/43. In a battle of apocalyptic proportions, the Soviets hung onto the city, then on 19–20 November launched a pincer-like counteroffensive that closed a trap on the German Sixth Army holed up within the city. An attempt by *Generalfeldmarschall* Erich von Manstein's Eleventh Army to break a relief corridor through the Soviet trap failed, and on 31 January 1943 the bloodied remnants of the German Sixth Army surrendered.

Dwindling resources
For a nation fighting on multiple fronts with stretched resources (Hitler's limited appreciation of logistics was one of his critical failures in strategic thinking), the loss of an entire army was a critical blow, both to practical operations and to national morale. Furthermore, the Soviets were now building up a juggernaut-like momentum, partly through their new material stength via US Lend-Lease aid. With the failure of Operation *Citadel* – the Battle of Kursk – in July–August 1943, the German capacity to stop steady

Soviet advances was practically exhausted, although the remarkable capacities of the German Army at a tactical level meant that the Red Army would fight for every centimetre of ground on its way to Germany. Throughout 1943 and 1944, the Soviets pushed forwards, crossing the Dnieper at the end of 1943 and cutting off the German Seventeenth Army in the Crimea. Leningrad's nightmarish 900-day siege was finally broken in January 1944, and by April the Soviets were pushing up towards the Polish and Hungarian borders.

Home travails

Within Germany itself, the realities of war came to visit in the form of an increasingly effective US and British air campaign. British bombers, flying from English airfields, maintained heavy night-time raids against key industrial areas, with the US bombers concentrating on daylight raids. For the Allies, the air attacks cost them dear in terms of pilots and aircraft, but the scale of destruction was impressive. On 31 May 1942, for example, Britain launched the first of its 1000-bomber raids, target Cologne. The German death toll was relatively light, but some 40,000 people were made homeless. In February 1944, the city of Dresden was virtually erased in a firestorm raid, killing anything up to 100,000 people.

Almost every major city in the Reich was targeted during 1943 and 1944, some being reduced to little more than skeletal, charred frames. German fighter defence was progressively overwhelmed, particularly when the Allies introduced long-range fighters in

spring 1944, after which *Luftwaffe* fighter losses climbed to around 25 per cent every month. Yet remarkably, we cannot say that the Allied air campaign either crushed the German defensive spirit or destroyed the country's production capacity, both of which stayed strong until the very last months of the war.

Closing in

The final act in Germany's defeat surely began in June 1944, when the Allied forces opened a new front in Western Europe through the D-Day landings in Normandy. Having failed to crush the invasion at the outset, the *Wehrmacht* and SS were unable to prevent the expansion of the Allied beachheads and the progressive advances into the French interior. In August Paris was liberated, and by mid-September the US, British and other Allied forces were pressed against the borders of Germany itself. Still the Germans displayed a remarkable ability to fight back, destroying the Allied airborne operation around Arnhem in September 1944 and launching the impressive but futile Ardennes offensive in December 1944, Hitler's last and deluded attempt to take the lead once again in the West.

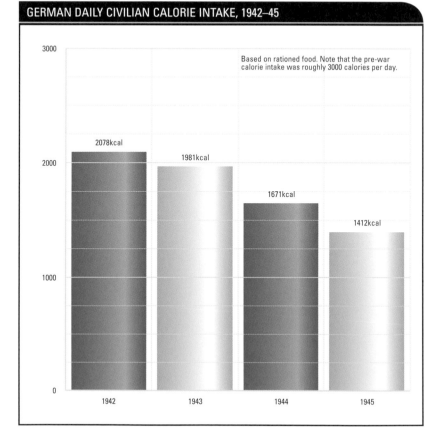

GERMAN DAILY CIVILIAN CALORIE INTAKE, 1942–45

Based on rationed food. Note that the pre-war calorie intake was roughly 3000 calories per day.

1942	1943	1944	1945
2078kcal	1981kcal	1671kcal	1412kcal

In the East, there were new horrors for Germany. Operation *Bagration*, a Soviet offensive to clear Belorussia and eastern Poland, drowned the German defenders under two million men, 4000 armoured fighting vehicles and 24,000 artillery pieces. The momentum of the attack carried the Red Army all the way to the outskirts of Berlin by February 1945, even as the Western Allies pushed into Germany from the opposite direction.

The Reckoning: 1945 and Beyond

The final defeat of the Third Reich brought scenes of almost unimaginable horror. It is estimated that some 300,000 refugees from East Prussia alone died during their panicked flight from the Red Army during the winter months of early 1945.

During the glory days of his reign, Adolf Hitler had been fond of declaring the foundation of a '1000-year Reich'. His intention was that the German Third Reich, like the Holy Roman Empire, would endure for centuries. As it was, the Third Reich lasted for just 12 years (dating it from the start of Hitler's chancellorship), and it ended in destruction.

When the end came, it was brutal up to the very last moments. On 31 March 1945, the Soviets launched their final, epic assault on Berlin, delivering millions of artillery shells onto a city already smashed by Allied air raids. Incredibly, the German people continued to defend their capital, motivated in part by the sheer terror of falling to the Soviets, plus the fear of the predatory security units that moved through the city, executing those who showed glimmers of defeatism.

On 30 April 1945, Hilter shot himself in the *Führerbunker* under the Chancellery as the Soviets closed in, his body, and that of his lover Eva Braun, being incinerated in a pit in the Chancellery garden. It was a sordid end to a man who had brought the world down around him in flames. On 7 May, German forces officially surrendered, and the war in Europe came to a close. Hitler's ambitions had cost the German people more than three million dead and nearly five million wounded.

Discoveries

In the last few months of World War II, Allied forces and intelligence agencies began to lift the lid on some of the darkest aspects of the Nazi regime. On 27 January 1945, Red Army soldiers entered and liberated the Auschwitz-Birkenau extermination camp in Poland. What they discovered there horrified the world, and over subsequent months the reality of the Holocaust emerged into the public domain (although the Allies knew about the plans for genocide back in 1942, and were aware of the gassing operations at Auschwitz-Birkenau by early 1944).

Some six million Jews and hundreds of thousands of gypsies, homosexuals, political 'criminals' and Soviet prisoners of war died under the Nazis, either through systematic mistreatment or outright execution. In the Soviet Union, German *Einsatzgruppen* (task forces), staffed mostly by the *Waffen-SS*, aided by local anti-Semitic and police units, worked as mobile killing squads, murdering 1.2 million Jews on top of the 230,000 killed in the Baltic states. The fact is that Hitler's ambition for a 'Jew-free Reich' came perilously close to being realized.

The shock at Nazi crimes against humanity steadily gave way to a desire for retribution. While much of this retribution was enacted at a local level by Allied combatants (particularly by Soviet troops paying Germany back for their 25 million war dead), it also found expression in high-profile war crimes trials. The most important were the Nuremberg Trials between 1945 and 1949.

Those accused of war crimes included some of the Nazi regime's most high-profile figures, including Hermann Göring (who cheated a death sentence through suicide), Rudolf Hess, Alfred Jodl, Joachim von Ribbentrop, Karl Dönitz, Albert Speer, Martin Bormann (tried and sentenced in absentia) and Wilhelm Keitel. The trials also spread out to include key members of the *Einsatzgruppen* and SS leaders involved in the horrors of racial engineering experiments.

Many of those brought to trial were sentenced to death or long prison sentences. Other culpable individuals, such as the 'architect of the Holocaust' Adolf Eichmann (later captured by Israeli agents in Argentina, taken back to Israel, tried and executed), remained as fugitives. Meanwhile, the United States and the Soviet Union raced to acquire Germany's scientists for use in rocket, space and weapons programmes – after all, World War II had proved the ingenuity of Germany's inventors and engineers.

Nevertheless, now, more than anything, the Allies had to decide what to do with Germany.

New beginning

In the immediate aftermath of its defeat, Germany was carved up into various Allied zones of occupation (see map opposite). Each Allied nation stripped German industrial plants of useful equipment and assets, but in the West at least there was to be no repeat of the crushing reparations treaties seen in the aftermath of the previous war. In fact, financial imperatives (the occupation was extremely costly) and political motives (the West did not want dictatorial Communism to replace

Nazism) meant that from 1947 US aid began to pour into West Germany, promoting rapid economic development. A total of $3.1 billion of

NUREMBERG TRIALS, INDICTMENTS	
Count	Description
Count I	Conspiracy to Wage Aggressive War
Count II	Waging Aggressive War, or 'Crimes Against Peace'
Count III	War Crimes
Count IV	Crimes Against Humanity*

* Count III focused on 'traditional' types of war crimes such as mistreatment of prisoners and use of slave labour, while Count IV was more concerned with genocidal activity, principally the Holocaust.

NUREMBERG TRIALS, VERDICTS & SENTENCES ON MAJOR FIGURES

Defendant	Count I	Count II	Count III	Count IV	Sentence
Martin Bormann	Not Guilty	–	Guilty	Guilty	Death by hanging
Karl Dönitz	Not Guilty	Guilty	Guilty	–	10 years' imprisonment
Hans Frank	Not Guilty	–	Guilty	Guilty	Death by hanging
Wilhelm Frick	Not Guilty	Guilty	Guilty	Guilty	Death by hanging
Hans Fritzsche	Not Guilty	–	Not Guilty	Not Guilty	Acquitted
Walther Funk	Not Guilty	Guilty	Guilty	Guilty	Life imprisonment
Hermann Wilhelm Göring	Guilty	Guilty	Guilty	Guilty	Death by hanging (Göring committed suicide before his sentence could be delivered)
Rudolf Hess	Guilty	Guilty	Not Guilty	Not Guilty	Life imprisonment
Alfred Jodl	Guilty	Guilty	Guilty	Guilty	Death by hanging
Ernst Kaltenbrunner	Not Guilty	–	Guilty	Guilty	Death by hanging
Wilhelm Keitel	Guilty	Guilty	Guilty	Guilty	Death by hanging
Erich Raeder	Guilty	Guilty	Guilty	–	Life imprisonment
Alfred Rosenberg	Guilty	Guilty	Guilty	Guilty	Death by hanging
Fritz Sauckel	Not Guilty	Not Guilty	Guilty	Guilty	Death by hanging
Hjalmar Schacht	Not Guilty	Not Guilty	–	–	Acquitted
Arthur Seyss-Inquart	Not Guilty	Guilty	Guilty	Guilty	Death by hanging
Albert Speer	Not Guilty	Not Guilty	Guilty	Guilty	20 years' imprisonment
Julius Streicher	Not Guilty	–	–	Guilty	Death by hanging
Constantin von Neurath	Guilty	Guilty	Guilty	Guilty	15 years' imprisonment
Franz von Papen	Not Guilty	Not Guilty	–	–	Acquitted
Joachim von Ribbentrop	Guilty	Guilty	Guilty	Guilty	Death by hanging
Baldur von Shirach	Not Guilty	–	–	Guilty	20 years' imprisonment

Marshall Aid funding helped propel Germany out of its post-war despair and into a new future.

East Germany's destiny was different, lived under the shadow of Communism. Indeed, Germany almost became the flashpoint for another world war between the superpowers. Hitler's dreams of a united, racially homogeneous state were gone.

▼ **THE COST OF WAR** At the end of World War I, apart from some reasonably minor territorial losses on its fringes, Germany essentially remained a separate nation state, governing its own affairs. At the end of World War II, by contrast, such was the Allied desire to crush Germany completely (fuelled by Germany's continuing reckless resistance) that the entire nation was eventually carved up between various Allied administrations. The British, Americans, French and Soviets divided up the country into major adminstrative zones, with the city of Berlin a microcosm of these divisions and a future thorn in the side of international relations. Poland received German territory via the Potsdam Agreement.

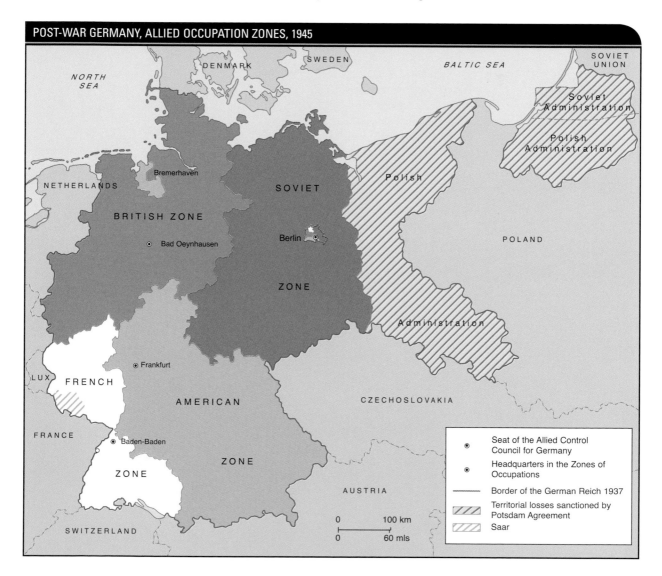

POST-WAR GERMANY, ALLIED OCCUPATION ZONES, 1945

Legend:
- ⊙ Seat of the Allied Control Council for Germany
- ⊙ Headquarters in the Zones of Occupations
- —— Border of the German Reich 1937
- ▨ Territorial losses sanctioned by Potsdam Agreement
- ▨ Saar

0 — 100 km
0 — 60 mls

CHAPTER 2

Geography

Geography was central to the ideology of the Third Reich. Even during the early days of his rise to power, Hitler realized that re-engineering German territory would be key to Germany's future.

There were three main movements in the territorial ambitions of the Third Reich between 1933 and 1945. First, Hitler wanted to reconfigure the internal governmental divisions of Germany so that they supported his centralized Nazi administration, rather than older localized loyalties. Second, he aimed to reclaim those territories lost to the Versailles Treaty, and add to the Reich those border states with strong ethnic German presences or allegiances.

Finally, Hitler sought direct expansion through military conquest, looking both east and west to fulfil this ambition, and provide his people with Lebensraum.

└ **Hitler parades in a motorcade through the Austrian capital of Vienna following the *Anschluss*, or merger, of the two countries in March 1938.**

Consolidation and Expansion

The Allied-enforced treaties in the aftermath of World War I reshaped Germany's borders and limited the country's economic opportunities. A key objective of the Nazi regime, therefore, was to throw off these shackles.

The Versailles Treaty, signed on 28 June 1919, cut deep into Germany's territorial power. Alsace-Lorraine went to France, Eupen-Malmédy to Belgium, North Schleswig to Denmark, and Posen, West Prussia and Upper Silesia to Poland. (East Prussia was now separated from the rest of Germany by the so-called Danzig Corridor.) Austria's independence from Germany was set as irrevocable. The Allies also tightened their grip over Germany's major industrial areas – the Saarland, a mining centre, was placed under League of Nations control, while the Rhineland, which included the Ruhr industrial centre, was demilitarized. The Ruhr itself was occupied in 1923 by France and Belgium, on the basis that Germany had failed to keep the terms of its war reparations.

All of Germany's overseas colonies, such as German West Africa, Samoa and the Marshall Islands, were relinquished, and major German rivers such as the Elbe, Oder and Rhine were to be opened to international traffic. The scale of the Allied management of German territory was deeply humiliating to the German people, and it was little wonder that Hitler made overturning this situation a central priority.

Looking at the economic map of post-1918 Germany, it is easy to see the method in the rearrangement of the country by the Allies. German industrial might, the engine house of war, was heavily concentrated in the western parts of the country bordering the Rhine river, while northern and central parts of Germany were more dominated by agriculture. For this reason, the Allies imposed a more direct grip over western Germany.

Repossession

Hitler's first major act of forcible reintegration was the remilitarization of the Rhineland on 7 March 1936, a feat achieved with little fuss from the international community – France in particular was dealing with its own social problems. (Note that Germany had already officially rejected the disarmament clauses of the Versailles Treaty, on 16 March 1935.) The Saarland was already back in the German fold, since a plebiscite held on 13 January 1935 had resulted in more than 90 per cent of the population voting in favour of a return to German control.

As Hitler's acquisitive momentum built, the issue of Austria became more pressing. A reunion with Austria was critical to Hitler's future plans for the Reich – apart from its manpower and industrial output, its strategic location in relation to the Balkans and Czechoslovakia was excellent.

POPULATIONS OF MAJOR GERMAN CITIES, 1933

City	Population	City	Population
Altona	242,000	Halle	209,000
Augsburg	177,000	Hamburg	1,129,000
Berlin	4,243,000	Hanover	444,000
Bochum	315,000	Kassel	175,000
Bremen	323,000	Kiel	218,000
Breslau	625,000	Königsberg	316,000
Chemnitz	351,000	Leipzig	714,000
Cologne	757,000	Magdeburg	307,000
Dortmund	541,000	Mannheim	275,000
Dresden	642,000	Munich	735,000
Duisburg	440,000	Nuremberg	410,000
Düsseldorf	499,000	Oberhausen	192,000
Essen	654,000	Stettin	271,000
Frankfurt/Main	556,000	Stuttgart	415,000
Gelsenkirchen	333,000	Wuppertal	409,000

EXPANSION, 1938–40

NORTH SEA

BALTIC SEA

Königsberg

Kiel

Danzig

Ostpreußen

Schleswig-Holstein

Schwerin

Pommern

Hamburg

Mecklenburg

Stettin

Danzig Westpreußen

Oldenburg

Lüneburg

Weser-Ems

Ost-Hannover

Mark Brandenburg

Berlin

Auslands-Organization

Posen

Munster

Hahm

Süd-Hannover

Magdeburg

Wartheland

Westfalen Nord

Braun-schweig

Magdeburg

Essen

Bochum

Halle-Mersebg.

Nieder-Schlesien

General Government

Düsseldorf

Westfalen-Süd

Kassel

Halle

Breslau

Köln-Aachen

Köln

Kurhessen

Weimar

Sachsen

Reichenberg

Koblenz

Messen-Massau

Thüringen

Ober-Schlesien

Katowitz

Frankfurt

Main-Franken

Sudeten-Land

Prague

Krakau

Moselland

Würzburg

Bayreuth

Protektorat Böhmen Und Mähren

Saarbrücken

Westmark

Nürnberg

Karlsruhe

Franken

Bayrisch Ostmark

Niederdonau

Straß

Stuttgart

Würdemberg Hohenzollern

Augsburg

München

Krems

Wien

(Elsaß)

Baden

Schwaben

München-Oberbayern

Linz

Oberdonau

Salzburg

Steiermark

Innsbruck

Salzburg

Graz

Tiral-Vorarlberg

Kärnten

Klagenfurt

0   200 km
0   120 mls

——— Pre-war border 1939

Austria had a sizeable population group that desired integration with Germany and, combined with a highly volatile Austrian politics, this group meant that Hitler was able to wield increasing influence over the country's affairs. From July 1936, Germany was virtually dictating policy to the Austrian government.

▲ **TERRITORIAL INCREASE The orange line here represents Germany's pre-1939 border, but even within this we can see the evidence of German expansionism. The Sudetenland has been shaved off what was western Czechoslovakia, and Austria is fully incorporated into the Third Reich. Rolling the clock forward to 1940, we see how Germany consolidated even more land through conquest. The principal administrative unit of the new territory was the *Reichsgau*: Austria was divided into seven *Reichsgaue*, the Sudetenland formed another one, while what were western and northern Poland became the *Reichsgaue* of Wartheland and Danzig-West Prussia.**

POPULATION OF THE REICH, 1918–39 (MILLIONS)

Year	Population
1918	66.8
1919	62.9
1920	61.7
1921	62.4
1922	62.0
1923	62.4
1924	62.5
1925	63.1
1926	63.6
1927	64.0
1928	64.3
1929	64.7
1930	65.0
1931	65.4
1932	65.7
1933	66.0
1934	66.4
1935	66.8
1936	67.3
1937	67.8
1938	75.3
1939	86.9

Includes the *Anschluss* with Austria (March 1938), the occupation of the Sudetenland (September 1938), and the occupation of Czechoslovakia (March 1939).

Forced to act by a planned referendum on Austrian independence, Hitler installed a National Socialist chancellor in Austria on 11 March 1938, and the next day sent in occupying forces totalling 100,000 troops. On 13 March, the *Anschluss* of Austria and Germany was officially announced.

Sudetenland
Inspired by events in Austria, ethnic Germans in Czechoslovakia pressed harder for reunion with Germany. In 1921, Czechoslovakia had more than three million Germans living within its territory (more than 23 per cent of the population), with a particularly high conentration in the Sudetenland regions bordering Germany. The Nazis funded separatist German political parties in the country, leading to riots and, on 29 November 1937, the secession of the Sudeten Germans from the Czech parliament. It became apparent to the international community that Czechoslovakia was a powder keg, with Hitler poised to invade the entire republic to enforce what he saw as the rights of ethnic Germans. Britain intervened, headed by Prime Minister Neville Chamberlain, and opened negotiations between Germany and the Czechs. The odds were stacked against the Czech government, which resigned after Hitler announced his intention to invade on 22 September.

More frantic diplomacy produced the Munich Agreement of 30 September 1938, which formally ceded the Sudetenland to Germany.

REICHSGAU POPULATION, AUGUST 1941

Territory	Population
Carinthia	449,000
Danzig-West Prussia	2,228,000
Lower Danube	1,697,000
Salzburg	257,000
Styria	1,116,000
Sudetenland	2,943,000
Tyrol	486,000
Upper Danube	1,034,000
Vienna	1,929,000
Wartheland	4,583,000

EXTENT OF REICHSGAU TERRITORIES (AREA SQ. KM)

Reichsgau	Area (sq. km)
Carinthia	11,553,000
Danzig-West Prussia	26,057,000
Lower Danube	23,502,000
Salzburg	7,153,000
Styria	17,384,000
Sudetenland	22,608,000
Tyrol	13,126,000
Upper Danube	14,216,000
Vienna	1,216,000
Wartheland	43,905,000

POPULATIONS OF PRINCIPAL GERMAN STATES, AUGUST 1941	
State	Population
Anhalt	431,000
Baden	2,502,000
Bavaria	8,222,000
Bremen	450,000
Brunswick	603,000
Hamburg	1,711,000
Hesse	1,469,000
Lippe	187,000
Mecklenburg	900,000
Oldenburg	578,000
Prussia	45,328,000
Saarland	842,000
Saxony	5,231,000
Schaumburg-Lippe	53,000
Thuringia	1,743,000
Württemberg	2,896,000

Yet Hitler was just getting into his stride, and on 15 March 1939 he occupied the rest of Czechoslovakia. While the Sudetenland became a directly administered *Reichsgau*, the remainder of the country was reshaped into the Protectorate of Bohemia and Moravia, essentially a Nazi puppet state.

Open conquest

Hitler's conquests between 1933 and 1939 were bloodless affairs, albeit ones that ran the risk of open conflict. In September 1939, such restraint was discarded with the invasion of Poland. Hitler's geographical ambitions for Poland were twofold. First, Hitler was determined to reclaim control of the Danzig Corridor, the separation of East Prussia from the rest of Germany being an affront to his nationalism. Second, and taking in the broader picture, the occupation of Poland was essential for providing a future jumping-off point for the invasion of the Soviet Union, Hitler's ultimate territorial ambition.

The conquest of Poland added by far the largest chunk of directly administered territory to the Reich, as the tables on the previous pages indicate. The occupation of Wartheland and Danzig-West Prussia brought an extra 6.8 million people under German control, with the rich potential therein for economic exploitation and slave labour. Hitler was building the foundations of an empire.

The Reconstruction of Poland

Poland was a special case in the history of German occupation policy. While large portions of the country, confined to the west, were integrated directly into the Reich, a special zone was established in central Poland, named the General Government.

The General Government (in German, *Generalgouvernement*) was a pure expression of Germany's racial prejudices conveyed through geographical means. Essentially the territory was a massive slave colony, in which the Nazi overlords were allowed to do as they pleased with a literally captive population. In total, the General Government covered 96,000sq km (37,000 square miles), and by including major cities such as Warsaw and Crakow it had a population of 12 million people. It was governed by Hans Frank and was divided up into four territorial districts – District Cracow (Cracow was the capital), District Warsaw, District Lublin and District Radom. Note also that the German offensive against the Soviet Union from June 1941 captured East Galicia, which was in turn incorporated in the General Government as District Galicia.

The population of the General Government was exploited with ruthless disdain. By 1944, when the territory was liberated by the Soviets, some four million people from the pre-war population were dead.

▶ **DIVIDED NATION The map clearly shows how Poland was carved up by the Nazis in the period 1939–42. Also note how, following the invasion of the Soviet Union, Germany administered the eastern territories as *Reichskommissariate* (Reich Commissions). Here we see *Reichskommissariat Ostland*, which included eastern Poland, the Baltic states, plus western Russia, Belorussia and parts of Ukraine, while *Reichskommissariat Ukraine* covered much of western Ukraine, with plans to extend eastwards.**

OCCUPIED POLAND, 1939–42

SWEDEN

BALTIC SEA

Riga

LATVIA

LITHUANIA

Klaipéda
(Memel)

REICHSKOMMISSARIAT OSTLAND

Danzig

Kaliningrad
(Königsberg)

Kaunas
(Kovono)

Vilnius
(Vilno)

REICHSGAU
DANZIG-
WEST
PRUSSIA

EAST PRUSSIA

Minsk

GERMANY

Olsztyn

Grodno

BIALYSTOK

Bydgoszcz
(Bromberg)

Bialystok

Inowroclaw
(Hohensalza)

Zichenau

Poznan
(Posen)

ZICHENAU

REICHSGAU
WARTHELAND

Warsaw

REICHSKOMMISSARIAT
UKRAINE

Kalisz

Lódź
(Litzmannstadt)

WARSAW DISTRICT

LITZMANNSTADT

GENERAL GOVERNMENT

Radom

Lublin

LUBLIN DISTRICT

RADOM
DISTRICT

Zamosc

Dubno

Katowice

KATOWICE

Cracow

CRACÓW DISTRICT

Lvov
(Lemberg)

CZECHOSLOVAKIA

GALICIA

Polish boundary before 1 September 1939

German–Soviet line

Under German civil administration

To Upper Silesia

Annexed by Germany

To Slovakia November 1939

To Poland 1938. To Upper
Silesia October 1939

0   150 km

0   75 mls

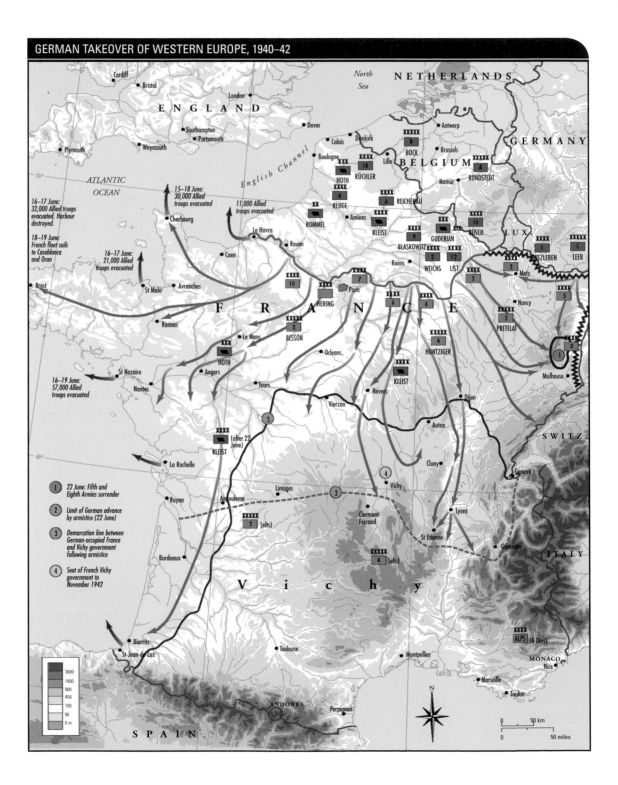

GERMAN TAKEOVER OF WESTERN EUROPE, 1940–42

15–18 June:
30,000 Allied
troops evacuated.

11,000 Allied
troops evacuated

16–17 June:
32,000 Allied troops
evacuated. Harbour
destroyed.

18–19 June:
French fleet sails
to Casablanca
and Oran

16–17 June:
21,000 Allied
troops evacuated

16–19 June:
57,000 Allied
troops evacuated

1 **22 June:** Fifth and
Eighth Armies surrender

2 **Limit of German advance**
by armistice (22 June)

3 **Demarcation line between**
German-occupied France
and Vichy government
following armistice

4 **Seat of French Vichy**
government to
November 1942

Occupation of Western Europe, 1940–44

Although there was no doubt as to who was in charge, the German occupiers in Western Europe often permitted the previous administrations to continue in some form or another, in contrast to the brutal policies used in the East.

Hitler's attitude to Western Europe differed from that towards Eastern Europe for several distinct reasons. First, although his hostility towards the Jews remained implacable, Hitler placed most Western Europeans outside the category of *Untermenschen* (sub-humans) in which he placed many Eastern peoples. Indeed, Hitler regarded many Western Europeans as Aryans by ancestry, particularly the Scandinavians, and hence permitted large foreign contributions of manpower to his SS formations as the war progressed.

Administrations

As a rule, the German occupiers in the West took over countries that

◀ **SWALLOWING EUROPE Here we see the impressive range of German control over Western Europe achieved between 1940 and 1942. The territorial extent of the Vichy-ruled 'free zone' was significant, although there was little doubt that its independence was conditional and could be taken away by the Germans at any time – as was proved in November 1942. Germany governed Western Europe through a mix of indigenous, military and Reich administrations, the military administrations taking priority in strategically sensitive areas.**

already had sophisticated civil services in place, and hence there was often a general reluctance to change their practical structure. In Denmark, for example, King Christian X retained his throne, and the country was administered by a Nazi-approved coalition government. A powerful *Reichsbevollmächtigter* (Reich Plenipotentiary) acted as the German power behind the throne, however, and as the war progressed German interference in Danish politics and industry left little illusion as to who were the true masters.

In Norway, the established government fled following the invasion, becoming the government-in-exile in the United Kingdom. In its place, the Germans permitted the Norwegian Nazi Vidkun Quisling to become Minister President on 1 February 1942, but real power lay in the hands of German ministers and Josef Terboven, the *Reichskommissar* to Norway.

In other parts of Europe, the Geman occupiers made more drastic rearrangements, or imposed a militaristic form of rule. In Belgium, the districts of Eupen, Malmédy and St Vith were taken into the Reich itself by special decree on 18 May 1940, while the remainder of the country and the French departments of Nord and Pas-de-Calais were ruled by a *Militärverwaltung* (Military

Administration). This policy reflected strategic realities – any attempt by the Allies to open up the Western Front would come through the French or Belgian coastal regions, and hence these areas required *Wehrmacht* governorship.

In the case of France, the northern and western parts – making up two-thirds – of the country were under military governance as the 'occupied zone', while Alsace and Lorraine were directly incorporated into the Reich and were administered by *Gauleiter*. The Nazis permitted southern France to exist as a 'free zone' of sorts. The Vichy regime here (so-called because of its seat at the town of Vichy in central France), under Marshal Philippe Pétain, became a byword for collaborationism. Nevertheless from 11 November 1942 Hitler ordered his forces to occupy all of France, believing that it was becoming too strategically important to leave in the hands of the French.

As for the Netherlands, it became the *Reichskommissariat Niederlande*, headed by the Austrian National Socialist politician Arthur Seyss-Inquart. The Netherlands was roughly handled by the German administration, which stripped the country of many of its assets and also deported 104,000 Dutch Jews to the concentration camps.

Invasion of the Soviet Union

The invasion of the Soviet Union offered Nazi Germany the greatest potential for territorial expansion. As well as seemingly limitless tracts of land, the territory tempted Hitler with rich natural resources and millions of potential slave labourers.

As we have already seen, there were multiple psychological and territorial imperatives driving Hitler's decision to invade the Soviet Union in 1941. Following the conquest of Poland, the continuation of eastwards acquisition was made possible, and its rationale was encapsulated by Professor Dr O. Reche, an intellectual advisor to the North-East German Research Community, in a paper entitled 'Basic Principles of the Demographic-Political Securing of the German East'. Although Reche's paper was written at the end of September 1939, the statements were pertinent to future ambitions:

1) Acquisition of *Raum*
1. Only land won through settlement remains secure in possession of a people for a millennium.
2. The German people must secure in Europe – and certainly now after the crushing of Poland – a large, contained, settlement area adequate for a greater German nation (150,000,000) in the future. The German *Volk* will have to become so large since only large peoples in a secure, state *Raum* will survive the struggles of the future. [...]

2) Ethnic Settlement
1. The *Raum* to be won shall exclusively serve German people and the German future; German blood has been spilled for this goal only. The newly acquired lands must be made empty of all foreign ethnic elements; all foreign race, foreign peoples are to be resettled.

(Trans from Burleigh, 2002)

Within these statements, we see a clear belief that German territorial expansion was held as an almost natural right by some German intellectuals. Combined with the fear that Soviet Communism, and indeed any sort of non-Germanic culture, might 'infect' National Socialism, the ideological drive to invade Stalin's empire was strong. Practical motivation came from the post-Great Purge Soviet Army's poor performance against the Finns in the Winter War, which convinced Hitler that the 'mighty' Soviet forces were in fact a house of cards.

Total war

Operation *Barbarossa* was on a scale never before seen in military history. The scale was necessary, as in terms of geography the Soviet Union was unlike anything experienced in the West. The initial invasion line would be more than 1600km (1000 miles) long, from the Baltic Sea, down along the eastern borders of East Prussia, Poland, Hungary and Romania to the Black Sea in the south. Moscow alone lay 1300km (800 miles) to the east along the Moscow Highway, while objectives in the Ukrainian territories involved even greater distances. The German-Soviet War would not be a *Blitzkrieg* war, but a war of logistics.

To manage the unnerving dimensions of the new theatre, the German commanders had divided the armies into three huge army groups. Army Group North would attack from East Prussia, primarily pushing north-eastwards through Lithuania, Latvia and Estonia, with its main objective the distant city of Leningrad. Army Group Centre would launch outwards from Poland to strike through Belorussia into Russia, aiming for Moscow via Smolensk. The southern prong of the invasion, formed by Army Group South, would thrust into the Ukraine towards Kiev and Kharkov, with long-term objectives of taking the Caucasus and Crimea.

Launched on 22 June 1941, Operation *Barbarossa* came close to achieving all of its major objectives within just six months of apocalyptic operations. The western Soviet Army had incurred massive losses (though as history proved, these losses were not unsustainable), German forces were nibbling at the Moscow suburbs, Leningrad was under siege, and Kiev and Kharkov were in German hands.

Yet Operation *Barbarossa*'s

success was significantly compromised. The Russian winter locked down the German advance under arctic conditions in December 1941, and vigorous Soviet counter-attacks pushed the Germans back by a significant depth along most of the front. Although the counter-attacks ran out of steam fairly quickly, they had saved Moscow, inflicted deep losses on the German forces and stabilized the front line until the German offensives of 1942.

A new empire

The high point of the German invasion of the Soviet Union, as earlier noted, came during the offensives of 1942, when the forces of Operation *Blue* drove deep through

the Ukraine to the city of Stalingrad, where the Germans met their

nemesis. Yet up to that point, in addition to carrying out military

▶ **BARBAROSSA The scale of Operation *Barbarossa* is apparent here. In terms of geographical challenge, the *Wehrmacht*'s greatest issue was simple distance, much of the terrain consisting of vast plains, grasslands and tundra, pockmarked intermittently by major urban centres and criss-crossed by lake and river systems. Southern Belorussia and northern Ukraine were also dominated by the Pripet Marshes, a large area of swamp that later became a major operating region for Soviet Partisans. Every German advance brought a lengthened supply line.**

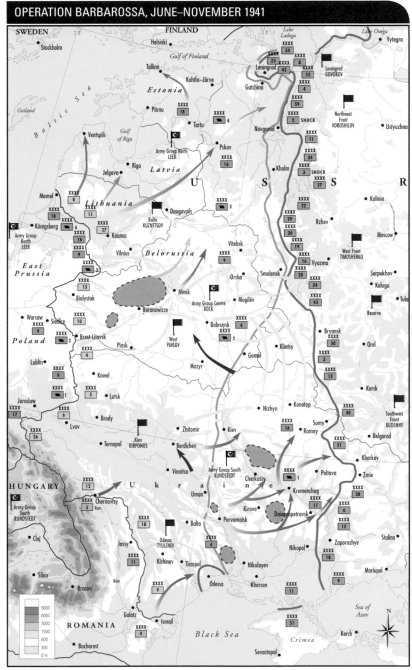

OPERATION BARBAROSSA, JUNE–NOVEMBER 1941

Operation *Barbarossa*
22 June–November 1941

German attack		German front line, end of August	
Soviet positions, 22 June		German front line, October	
Soviet units encircled		Soviet positions, October	
Soviet counter-attacks			

operations, the Nazis had to adjust to administering the vast swathes of Soviet territory now at their disposal, and handling the populations living therein.

The *Reichskommissariate*

The conquered Eastern territories were divided up into two *Reichskommissariate* civil administrations: *Reichskommissariat Ostland* and *Reichskommissariat Ukraine*. Both of these territorial entities fell under the overall jurisdiction of the *Reichsminister für die besetzten Ostgebiete* (Reich Ministerium for the Occupied Eastern Territories), headed by *Reichsleiter* (Reich Leader) Alfred Rosenberg, and they were seen as foundations of the new *Großdeutsches Reich* (Greater Germany) being constructed by German conquests.

Reichskommissariat Ostland consisted of the Baltic states, much of eastern Poland and western parts of Belorussia, East Prussia and the Ukraine, and was created by the *Führer*'s decree on 17 July 1941. Head of the territory was *Der Reichskommissar für das Ostland* Hinrich Lohse. To make government of such a massive region more manageable, it was subdivided into four *Generalbezirke* (General Regions) – *Generalbezirk Estland* (Estonia), *Generalbezirk Lettland* (Latvia), *Generalbezirk Litauen* (Lithuania) and *Generalbezirk Weißruthenien* ('White Russian'; Belorussia) – each of these led by a *Generalkommissar*. In turn, these four regions were sub-divided into smaller administrative units known as *Kreisgebiete* (Districts), each

governed by a *Gebietskommissar*, then into *Hauptgebiete* (Main Districts), each ruled appropriately by a *Hauptkommissar*.

Note that although this structure was ostensibly a civil administration, the military realities of war in the East meant that authority on the ground was often dispersed between military and civil authorities. The SS in particular held a great deal of unilateral authority within their own areas of operation, particularly relating to the handling of the local population and in anti-Partisan operations.

Crucially, the SS *Einsatzgruppen* operating in *Reichskommissariat Ostland* set about murdering the large Jewish population with impunity. Such dreadful actions were simply the most grotesque part of German resettlement proposals for the *Ostland*, a plan which included settling the three Baltic states with *Volksdeutsche* (ethnic Germans), at which point those countries would be asborbed directly into the Reich.

Reichskommissariate Ukraine

Reichskommissariat Ukraine, as its name described, covered German-conquered territories within the Ukraine. By the beginning of 1943, this German-controlled region was very substantial indeed – it covered 347,042sq km (130,994 square miles) and had a population of more than 17 million people. Governed by *Reichskommissar* Erich Koch, the territory was divided administratively in a similar way to *Reichs-kommissariat Ostland*, using a system of *Generalbezirke*, *Kreisgebiete* and

Hauptgebiete. There were six *Generalbezirke* in total: Kiev, Dniepropetrovsk, Zhitomir, Nikolayev, Volhynia and Podolia, and the Crimea.

As with *Reichskommissariat Ostland*, governmental life in the Ukraine was in reality divided between various different authorities. The *Wehrmacht* wielded much influence, even introducing some religious tolerance reforms in early 1942, while less empathetically the SS *Einsatzgruppen* continued their work of killing or deporting all the Jews they could find.

As we will explore in greater detail below, these two new territories were essentially reservoirs of forced labour and stolen resources, ruled with ideological disdain. They incorporated some of the Soviet Union's greatest industrial centres, although through Herculean efforts the Soviets still managed to save many industrial facilities and ship them east beyond German control, where they would produce the armaments for future liberation.

▶ **CLOSE VICTORY The German penetrations of 1942 were every bit as great as those of 1941, and took the German Army deep into the Caucasus. Yet once the Red Army managed to defeat the Germans at Stalingrad in early 1943, its westwards advance essentially left the Germans in the Caucasus trapped. The Soviet oilfields, critical to the German war effort, remained out of reach, and the German Army was forced into a slow retreat of attrition back towards *Barbarossa*'s invasion start lines.**

INTO THE SOUTHERN SOVIET UNION, JUNE–NOVEMBER 1942

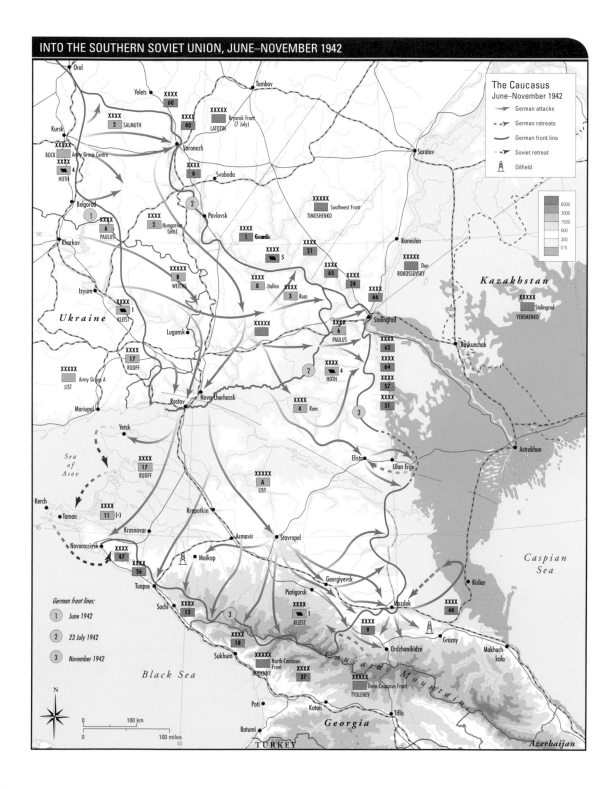

The Caucasus
June–November 1942

→ German attacks
-→ German retreats
→ German front line
-→ Soviet retreat
⚒ Oilfield

6000
3000
1500
600
300
0 ft

Orel
Yelets
XXXX 60
Tambov
Saratov

XXXX 2 SALMUTH
XXXX 40
XXXXX Bryansk Front (7 July) LATOTIN

Kursk
XXXXX BOCK Army Group Centre
XXXX 4 HOTH
Voronezh
XXXX 6 Svoboda

Belgorod
1
XXXX 6 PAULUS
XXXX 2 Hungarian (elts)
2 Pavlovsk
XXXXX Southwest Front TIMOSHENKO

Kharkov
XXXXX 8 WEICHS
XXXX 1 Guards
Kamishin

XXXX 5
XXXX 21
XXXX 65
XXXX Don ROKOSSOVSKY

Izyum
XXXX 1 KLEIST
Lugansk
XXXX 8 Italian
XXXX 3 Rom
XXXX 24
XXXX 66
Kazakhstan

Ukraine
XXXXX
XXXX 6 PAULUS
Stalingrad
XXXX Stalingrad YEREMENKO
Baskunchak

XXXX 17 RUOFF
XXXXX Army Group A LIST
Rostov Novo-Cherkassk
XXXX 2 HOTH 4
XXXX 4 Rom
3
XXXX 62
XXXX 64
XXXX 57
XXXX 51

Mariupol
Yetsk
Sea of Asov
XXXX 17 RUOFF
XXXXX A LIST
Elista
Ulan Erge
Astrakhan

Kerch
Taman
XXXX 11 (-)
Krapotkin
Caspian Sea

Novorossiysk
XXXX 47
XXXX 56
Krasnovar
Maikop
Armavir
Stavropol
Georgiyevsk
Mozdok
Kisliar
XXXX 44

Tuapse
Sochi
XXXX 12
XXXX 3
Piatigorsk
XXXX 1 KLEIST
XXXX 9
Ordzhonikidze
Grozny
Makhach-kala

German front lines:
① June 1942
② 23 July 1942
③ November 1942

XXXX 18
Sukhum
XXXXX North-Caucasus Front BUDENNY
XXXX 37
Caucasus Mountains

Black Sea
XXXXX Trans-Caucasus Front TYULENEV
Poti
Kutais
Tiflis

N
0   100 km
0   100 miles

Georgia
Batumi
TURKEY
Azerbaijan

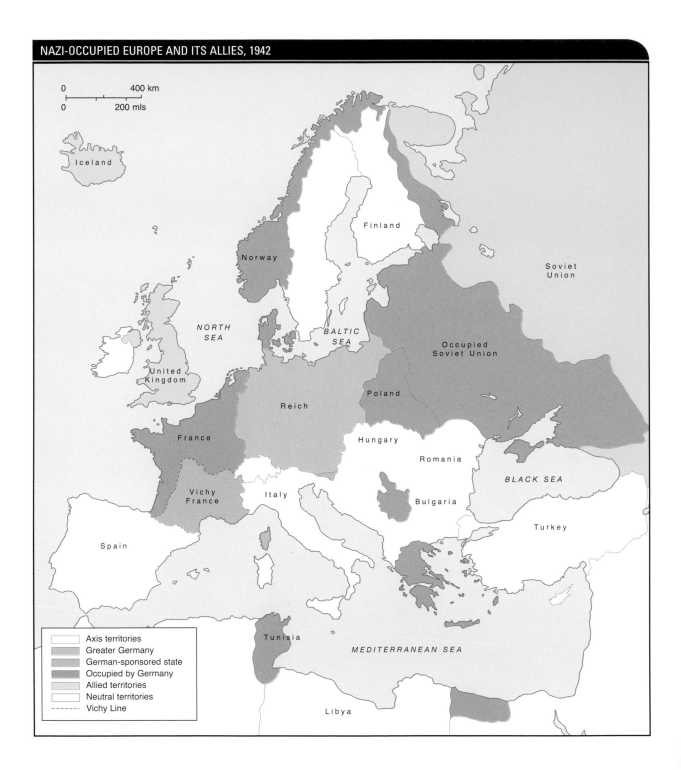

NAZI-OCCUPIED EUROPE AND ITS ALLIES, 1942

0   400 km
0   200 mls

Iceland

Norway

Finland

Soviet Union

NORTH SEA

BALTIC SEA

Occupied Soviet Union

United Kingdom

Reich

Poland

France

Hungary

Romania

Vichy France

Italy

Bulgaria

BLACK SEA

Spain

Turkey

Tunisia

MEDITERRANEAN SEA

Libya

Axis territories
Greater Germany
German-sponsored state
Occupied by Germany
Allied territories
Neutral territories
------- Vichy Line

The Centralized State

By the end of 1942, Germany controlled an empire, albeit a beleaguered one, stretching from Norway to North Africa, and from France to the eastern shores of the Black Sea. Germany itself had also been rearranged by the Nazis in their rise to power.

While we have been focusing on the territorial expansion of Germany through conquest, it is worth taking a step back to explore how Germany itself had been reshaped by Hitler's takeover. Hitler emerged onto the German political scene amidst times of great social division and upheaval, and the territorial divisions of Germany added to the troubles.

Centralization

Historically, Germany had been more a collection of independent states and provinces (*Länder*) than a unitary country, and this situation largely continued under the Weimar Republic. The *Länder* governed their own affairs through *Landtage* (Provincial Parliaments),

◀ **CONTROLLING THE REICH**
A governmental issue for any empire is how to govern far-flung territories from the centre. In the Third Reich, this was achieved through a mixture of policies. Some states or regions were governed simply via military occupation, while others were directly incorporated into Germany, principally the German-speaking territories (indigenous or settled) that became *Reichsgaue*. Note also how the alliances made by Germany created important security buffer zones around the Reich in the south, southeast and north.

organizations that were elected and hence reflected local powerbases and special interests. Furthermore, strong class divisions ran through Germany by region. For example, much of the agrarian northeast (i.e. (Brandenburg, Mecklenburg, Pomerania, East Prussia, Saxony, Silesia) was dominated by the traditional *Junker* aristocratic landowning class, which also had a central presence within the Army leadership and within the German civil service. In the industrial central and western parts of the country, the working classes naturally had a major influence.

When Hitler came to power as Chancellor in 1933, the social structure of Germany no longer suited his interests. What Hitler needed was a Germany that centred itself on the National Socialist leadership, not on its own local interests; otherwise Germany would remain fractured and impotent.

Hitler achieved his aim through three key pieces of legislation. The first two laws – the First Law for the Coordination of the Federal States (31 March 1933) and the Second Law for the Coordination of the Federal States (7 April 1933) – allowed NSDAP state authorities to enact legislation without referring to the *Landtage*, aided by the creation of 18 powerful *Reichstatthalter* (Reich

FOREIGN POPULATIONS UNDER DIRECT GERMAN RULE, SEPTEMBER 1941	
Territory	*Population*
Alsace	1.3 million
General Government	about 17 million
Lorraine	about 700,000
Luxembourg	290,000
Lower Styria, South Carinthia and Upper Carniola	about 700,000
TOTAL:	20 million

Governors) who would oversee regional policy. Yet the most significant change in the nature of the German state came with the Law for the Reconstruction of the Reich on 30 January 1934. In this highly targeted piece of legislation, the *Landtage* were effectively abolished and all local legislatures were placed in a dependent relationship to the central Nazi government.

The principal NSDAP unit of regional administration in Germany during the Third Reich was the *Gau*, each *Gau* being headed by a *Gauleiter*. The system of *Gaue* was established by the Nazis in 1926, and the *Gaue* were typically coterminous with existing *Länder*, although their number changed over time – there were 32 *Gaue* during the early years of the Nazis, but by 1945 there were 42. Although Nazi policy reflected the

POPULATION OF NAZI PARTY *GAUE/REICHSGAUE*, 1939 (MILLIONS)

Gau	Population
Baden	2.5
Bayerische Ostmark	2.3
Berlin	4.4
Danzig-West Prussia	2.3
Düsseldorf	2.3
Essen	1.9
Franconia	1.1
Halle-Merseburg	1.6
Hamburg	1.7
Hesse-Nassau	3.1
Carinthia	0.5
Cologne-Aachen	2.4
Kurhessen	1.0
Magdeburg-Anhalt	1.8
Main-Franconia	0.8
Mark Brandenburg	3.0
Mecklenburg	0.9
Moselland	1.4
Munich-Upper Bavaria	1.9
Lower Danube	1.7
Lower Silesia	3.3
Upper Danube	1.1
Upper Silesia	4.3
East Hanover	1.1
East Prussia	3.3
Pomerania	2.4
Saxony	5.2
Salzburg	0.3
Schleswig-Holstein	1.6
Swabia	0.9
Styria	1.1
Sudetenland	2.9
South Hanover-Brunswick	2.1
Thuringia	2.4
Tyrol-Vorarlberg	0.5
Wartheland	4.6
Weser-Ems	1.8
North Westphalia	2.8
South Westphalia	2.7
Westmark	1.9
Vienna	1.9
Württemberg-Hohenzollern	3.0

need for regional government, Hitler rooted out federalism in favour of dictatorial centralism.

Local control

The rearrangement of the Reich meant that Hitler could now exercise much greater territorial and political control across Germany. The desire for centralization extended beyond the bounds of Germany into the new acquisitions made from the late 1930s. Austria, for example, had the same form of federal government and *Länder* system as Germany, but following the *Anschluss* these were also compromised by the new political structures. Austria was divided into seven *Reichsgaue:* Vienna, Lower Danube, Upper Danube, Styria, Carinthia, Salzburg and Tyrol-Voralberg. (Note that in a clear signal concerning its new political status, Austria even lost its name, and the old provinces of Upper and Lower Austria were replaced by the provinces Lower and Upper Danube.) The Sudetenland formed

▶ **RESTRUCTURING GERMANY: The map shows the *Gaue* system as it had evolved by 1944, although Germany was soon to lose the easternmost territories to the Soviet advance. Such losses were to deprive the Third Reich of large populations – note how the population of Wartheland alone back in 1939 totalled 4.6 million people, being exceeded at the time only by Saxony. East Prussia also had a large population base, but by early 1945 much of this was on the move, fleeing the Soviets on the basis of justifiable fear.**

NAZI PARTY *GAUE*, 1944

NORTH SEA

BALTIC SEA

29

9

17

26

4

25

37

24

38

14

3

16

36

33

6

5

39

8

21

12

13

27

18

34

23

10

15

32

40

7

2

1

42

20

30

22

41

19

35

28

31

11

0   200 km
0   120 mls

1. Baden	13. Kurhessen	24. East Hanover	35. Tyrol-Vorarlberg
2. Bayreuth	14. Magdeburg-Anhalt	25. East Prussia	36. Wartheland
3. Berlin	15. Main-Franconia	26. Pomerania	37. Weser-Ems
4. Danzig-West Prussia	16. Mark Brandenburg	27. Saxony	38. North Westphalia
5. Düsseldorf	17. Mecklenburg	28. Salzburg	39. South Westphalia
6. Essen	18. Moselland	29. Schleswig-Holstein	40. Westmark
7. Franconia	19. Munich-Upper	30. Swabia	41. Vienna
8. Halle-Merseburg	Bavaria	31. Styria	42. Württemberg-
9. Hamburg	20. Lower Danube	32. Sudetenland	Hohenzollern
10. Hesse-Nassau	21. Lower Silesia	33. South Hanover-	
11. Carinthia	22. Upper Danube	Brunswick	
12. Cologne-Aachen	23. Upper Silesia	34. Thuringia	

another *Reichsgau*, and two more were constructed from the dismemberment of Poland following the military campaign of 1939.

Population effects

The German incorporation and conquest of foreign territories naturally brought with it population implications, and helped fill out gaps in the native German workforce (either through willing relocation or through slave labour). In August 1941,

GERMAN MALE POPULATION, 1939	
Age Group	Population
15–20	3,137,429
21–34	8,885,775
35–44	5,695,510
45–65	6,902,034

the population of Germany stood at just over 73 million people. Yet add the populations of the *Reichsgaue*, and that total 'usable' population climbed to just under 90 million.

The addition was an important one for the Third Reich's future, for although there was population growth in Germany during the first half of the twentieth century, the percentage of people aged 30 and under appears to have been in noticeable decline.

For example, in 1910 people aged between 10 and 20 constituted 20.3 per cent of the total population, but by 1939 that figure had dropped to 16.8 per cent (although this was a slight recovery from the 1934 figure of 15.8 per cent). Figures for the 0–10 age group show a similar decline.

The tremendous social and economic disruption of the post-World War I years explains much of this decline, but for Hitler it may have been a cause for concern in plans for a 1000-year Reich.

Another significant population factor in the Third Reich was the increasing urbanization of the populace. If we look back to 1871, 5.4 per cent of the total population was living in cities containing more than 100,000 inhabitants. By 1925 that figure had risen to 26.6 per cent, and by 1939 to 31.6 per cent. On the basis of such growth, Hitler ensured that he targeted many of his employment regeneration schemes within the large towns and cities, thus creating a major support base amongst urban workers and businesses.

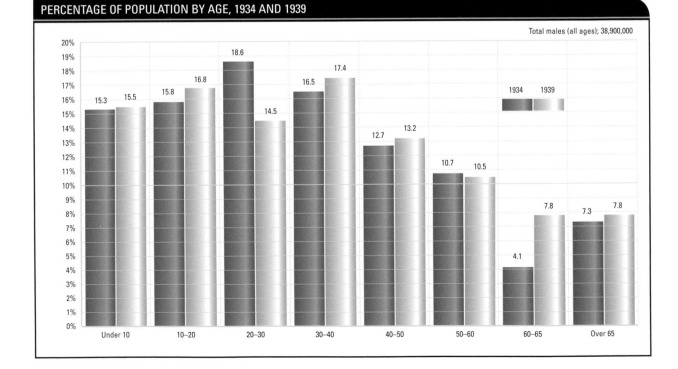

PERCENTAGE OF POPULATION BY AGE, 1934 AND 1939

Total males (all ages); 38,900,000

1934   1939

Age	Under 10	10–20	20–30	30–40	40–50	50–60	60–65	Over 65
1934	15.3	15.8	18.6	16.5	12.7	10.7	4.1	7.3
1939	15.5	16.8	14.5	17.4	13.2	10.5	7.8	7.8

Occupation and Slavery, 1939–45

Between 1939 and 1945, millions of people had to adjust to life under German occupation. For some this meant little more than new sets of paperwork, while for others it brought slave labour conditions.

The challenge of administering 'Greater Germany' was perfectly summarized by Hitler himself during a meeting of the High Command on 16 July 1941, by which time large swathes of Soviet territory were also falling under German control:

In principle we now have to face the task of cutting the giant cake according to our needs, in order to be able, first, to dominate it, second, to administer it, and third, to exploit it.

The 'giant cake' under German control would, ultimately, be used to fulfil the third of Hitler's criteria – exploitation – as its peoples, industrial resources and raw materials were channelled into feeding the German war machine.

Living conditions

The experience of living under German occupation depended on many variables – the part of the world (almost universally, Slavs and Eastern Europeans were treated with contempt when compared with Western Europeans), the German forces encountered (such as the Army as opposed to the SS), religious affiliation and perceived value to the regime. Yet even in a country such as France, the inequities of occupation were clear. When France was occupied, the German soldiers were given an occupation currency with extremely preferential buying power, the Germans clearing out shops of meat, vegetables, leather goods and alcohol, and inflating the prices for French citizens. Gasoline in particular became very scarce or non-existent for domestic use, as the Germans redirected supplies into military or industrial applications. It is notable that in Paris the Germans issued only 7000 driving permits to the whole city – even those issued with permits were generally unable to run their machines. In Athens, taxis became little more than hand carts pulled by a 'driver', who wouldn't even be able to work in the evening because of strict curfew hours.

One notable effect of the German occupation on most subject peoples was a significant reduction in the average number of calories consumed each day. Before the occupation, a French adult would typically consume an average of 2500 calories a day. By 1941 that figure had dropped to around 1500 calories a day, and would go down further in the later war years, when the infrastructure began to suffer under the effects of Allied bombing.

SLAVE LABOUR WORKING IN GERMANY, JANUARY 1945

Nationality	Workers	POWs	Political	Total
Balts	130,000	–	–	130,000
Belgians	183,000	63,000	8900	254,900
Bulgarians	2000	–	–	2000
Czechoslovaks	140,000	–	–	140,000
Dutch	274,000	–	2300	276,300
Greeks	15,000	–	–	15,000
Hungarians	10,000	–	–	10,000
Italians	227,000	400,000	–	627,000
Luxembourgers	14,000	–	1000	15,000
Poles	851,000	60,000	–	911,000
Romanians	5000	–	–	5000
Russians	1,900,000	600,000	11,000	2,511,000
Ukrainians	764,000	750,000	–	1,514,000
Yugoslavs	230,000	–	–	230,000
Others	50,000	–	–	50,000
Totals	4,795,000	1,873,000	23,200	6,691,200

In some territories, however, the occupation brought outright malnutrition and starvation. In Greece, for example, German occupying forces stripped the country of 14 million livestock and thousands of tonnes of crops, resulting in a famine and epidemic of disease that killed more than 200,000 Greeks in the winter of 1941/42. (The conditions were exacerbated by the naval blockade around Greece

TERRITORIAL ADMINISTRATION, THIRD REICH, DECEMBER 1942

Civil Administration

- District Bialystok
- Alsace (Strasbourg)
- Carinthia and Carniola (in Klagenfurt)
- Lorraine (Metz)
- Luxembourg
- Styria (Graz)

Military Administration

- Festungskommandantur Kreta;
  Fortress Commandant Crete
- Kommandant des Heeresgebiets Südfrankreich;
  Commander of the Army Territory Southern France
  (in Lyon)
- Militärbefehlshaber Belgien und Nordfrankreich;
  Military Commander, Belgium and Northern France
  (in Brussels)
- Militärbefehlshaber Frankreich; Military Commander,
  France (in Paris)
- Militärbefehlshaber Saloniki-Ägäis;
  Military Commander, Salonika-Aegean
- Militärbefehlshaber Serbien; Military Commander,
  Serbia (in Belgrade)
- Militärbefehlshaber Südgriechenland;
  Military Commander, Southern Greece

Reichsgaue

- Alpine and Donaureichsgaue
- Danzig-Westpreußen (in Gdansk)
- Sudetenland (in Liberec)
- Wartheland (in Posen)
- Westmark (in Saarbrücken)

States

- Anhalt
- Baden (in Karlsruhe)
- Bayern
- Brunswick
- Bremen
- Hamburg
- Hesse (in Darmstadt)
- Lippe
- Mecklenburg (in Schwerin)
- Oldenburg
- Preußen
- Saxony (in Bückeburg)
- Thuringia (in Weimar)
- Württemberg

Reichskommkissariate

- Reichskommissariat Niederlande;
  Reich Commission Netherlands (in The Hague)
- Reichskommissariat Norwegen;
  Reich Commissarion Norway (in Oslo)
- Reichskommissariat Ostland;
  Reich Commission East (in Riga)
- Reichskommissariat Ukraine;
  Reich Commission Ukraine (in Rovno)

Other

- Generalgouvernement; General Government
  (in Cracow)
- Protektorat Böhmen und Mähren;
  Protectorate of Bohemia and Moravia (in Prague)

imposed by the Royal Navy.) During the later stages of the war, starvation in occupied Holland killed around 30,000 people.

Out in the East, in Poland, Belorussia, western Russia and the Ukraine, the local populations were generally treated with utter inhumanity. Even in the dead of the Russian winter, local peoples were turned out of their homes to make space for German occupiers, or destroyed in reprisal, 'anti-Partisan' or extermination actions. In Belorussia, for example, between 5000 and 9000 settlements were destroyed by the Nazis, and the populations of some 600 villages murdered. Note that the *Wehrmacht*, and not just the SS, were complicit in

these activities. An instruction book issued to German soldiers on 1 June 1941, which explained the conduct of the future war in the East, stated as one of its clauses: 'There will be no prosecution for actions against enemy civilians, committed by *Wehrmacht* military men or civilians, even in case of a crime or misdemeanour.'

Exploitation

A critical element of Germany's Eastern settlement policy was the intention to clear local populations from entire regions, leaving only sufficient indigenous personnel to service the occupiers' needs. Long-term plans involved settling German citizens in special urban zones with a

ratio of two local people for every German. For example, Minsk was to have 50,000 German colonists, supported in their lifestyles by 100,000 locals. Note, however, that such calculations did not allow for surpluses – the excess population would be either exterminated, exiled or effectively murdered through the wastage of starvation and associated disease. Although these policies did not reach their full expression because of the development of the war, they still inflicted a horrifying death toll on the local peoples. In Belorussia alone, for example, perhaps as many as one in three of the entire population died under German occupation between 1941 and 1945. The occupation of

STRUCTURE OF THE GENERAL GOVERNMENT, 1940

District	District Leaders	City Leaders	District	District Leaders	City Leaders
Distrikt Galizien (Galicia)	Brzezany	Lemberg	District Lublin	Biala-Podlaska	Lublin
	Czortkow			Bilgoraj	
	Drohobycz			Chelm	
	Gorodenka			Hrubieszow	
	Kalusz			Janow-Lubelski	
	Kamionka-Strumilowa			Krasnystaw	
	Kolomea			Lublin-Land	
	Lemberg-Grodek			Pulawy	
	Lemberg-Land			Radzyn	
	Rawa-Ruska			Zamosc	
	Sambor		District Radom	Busko	Kielce
	Stanislau			Jedrzejow	Radom
	Stryj			Ilza (in Starachowice)	Tschenstochau
	Tarnopol			Kielce	
	Zloczow			Konskie	
Distrikt Krakau (Cracow)	Debica	Krakau		Opatow	
	Jaroslau (Jaroslaw)			Petrikau (Piotrkow)	
	Krakau-Land			Radom-Land	
	Krosno			Radomsko	
	Miechow			Tomaschow	
	Neumarkt (Nowy Targ)		Distrikt Warschau (Warsaw)	Garwolin	Warschau
	Neu-Sandez (Nowy Sacz)			Grojec	
	Przemysl			Lowicz	
	Reichshof (Rzeszow)			Minsk	
	Sanok			Ostrow	
	Tarnow			Siedlce	
				Sochaczew	
				Sokolow	
				Warschau-Land	

Yugoslavia cost some one million lives, mostly civilian.

Furthermore, Germany was a country with limited raw materials of its own, so its conquests also brought war-critical opportunities to plunder foreign natural resources. France provided extensive coalfields in its central and southern regions, and major deposits of iron ore in the east. Poland offered coal, iron ore, lead and zinc, plus oil and synthetic oil plants. Bohemia-Moravia was rich in manganese. The Soviet Union promised not only coal, oil, steel, copper and zinc but also major food resources, such as cattle, pigs, sheep, barley, wheat, maize and oats. In addition to raw materials, the Germans took over industrial plants and merchant shipping – France handed over more than one million tonnes of shipping for German use.

The exploitation of people was as much a part of German policy as the acquisition of materials. The German use of slave labour to support its domestic economy and its war effort rose to prodigious levels. Nor did this policy simply involve putting the subject peoples to work in situ – rather, millions of workers from all across the occupied territories were shipped back to Germany itself.

Workers for the Reich

As more and more territories fell under Reich control, Nazi Germany expanded its pool of subordinate populations, and in so doing opened up major reserves of forced labour. By 1944, Germany was using 5.3 million civilians and 1.8 million POWs as workers in industry and agriculture, by which time 24 per cent

of the entire German workforce was composed of slave labour. Looking across the entire duration of the war, the Germans employed around 12 million people in forced labour roles, their duties ranging from manual labour such as mining and construction through, although more rarely, to specialist scientific and engineering roles.

Fremdarbeiter (foreign workers) were typically placed into one of four groups. At the top of the tree were the *Gastarbeitnehmer* (guest workers), privileged and respected Germanic workers from either occupied states (such as Norway or Denmark) or other Axis countries. These constituted a tiny percentage of total foreign labour. The major groups were *Militärinternierte* (military internees; POWs), *Zivilarbeiter* (civilian workers) and *Ostarbeiter* (Eastern workers; mainly Soviet civilians). The treatment of these workers could be quite dreadful, depending on their masters in Germany or in the camps in Poland; indeed, forced labour was used as a virtual method of execution for millions of Jews and other Nazi enemies of the state. Some three million Soviet POWs would die working for the Nazis, and labour in the I.G. Farben factory near Auschwitz killed 30,000 workers. (Other major German corporations that benefited from forced labour included Siemens, BMW, Daimler-Benz and Messerschmitt.)

Nationality was an important ingredient in the treatment of foreign workers. Those workers who came from Western Europe were generally paid for their labours, sometimes at

▶ **RAW MATERIALS: The Germans accessed a broad spectrum of raw materials through their conquests, in addition to the manpower derived from occupied populations, although acquiring enough oil always presented a challenge. European countries made a sizeable financial contribution to the German war effort, either directly through liquidated financial assets or through labour costs, contributions of raw materials and through the German use of industrial plants and machinery. Many of the major industrial plants were run by the state-owned Reichswerke 'Hermann Göring' company.**

the same levels as German workers. These individuals would also be taxed on their earnings. Labourers from the East, by contrast, could expect half German earnings at the very most, while millions of them received no pay whatsoever and suffered brutal treatment.

Drain on resources

We must not present the occupied territories as an unequivocal blessing to Germany. The fact remained that active resistance movements in many countries demanded large German military deployments that would have been better used elsewhere. The protracted fight against Yugoslav Partisans, for example, tied down 35 German divisions, and similar numbers fought against the Soviet Partisans, who numbered 150,000 in 1943. Indeed, over time, multiple occupations of restless countries became a drain the Third Reich could scarcely afford.

NATURAL RESOURCES – GERMANY AND AXIS OCCUPIED TERRITORIES, 1940–45

NORWAY
1278
951.8

FINLAND
126

SWEDEN
(Neutral)

NORTH
SEA

DENMARK
488.1

BALTIC
SEA

Königsberg

USSR
8,883
10.6

GREAT
BRITAIN
99.9

HOLLAND
7716
417.2

Hamburg

EAST
PRUSSIA

Smolensk

London

Amsterdam

Berlin

POLAND

Poznan

Warsaw

4517
75.8

BELGIUM

Brussels

Leipzig

Lille

Frankfurt am Main

GERMANY

Prague

Kracow

Rouen

BOHEMIA-MORAVIA

Paris

SLOVAKIA

Munich

Vienna

FRANCE
25,848
1047.7

SWITZ.
(Neutral)

AUSTRIA

Budapest

HUNGARY
51

ROMANIA
12

Lyon

Padua

Bologna

YUGOSLAVIA
678
46.1

Bucharest

SPAIN

MEDITERRANEAN
SEA

BULGARIA

Sofia
27

Rome

ITALY
1432

ALBANIA
29

TURKEY
(Neutral)

GREECE
3758
170

Athens

Legend

Axis and Axis occupied areas (1942)

Coalfields and industrial regions

Other industrial regions

⊙ Crude oil plants

◉ Synthetic oil plants

7716 Cost of German war effort borne by occupied
or allied states (in RM million)

170 Tonnage of merchant shipping seized
(in thousand tons)

Mineral resources

Lead

Chrome

Zinc

Iron Ore

Bauxite

Magnesite

Zinc

Oil

Copper

Manganese

0   400 km

0   200 mls

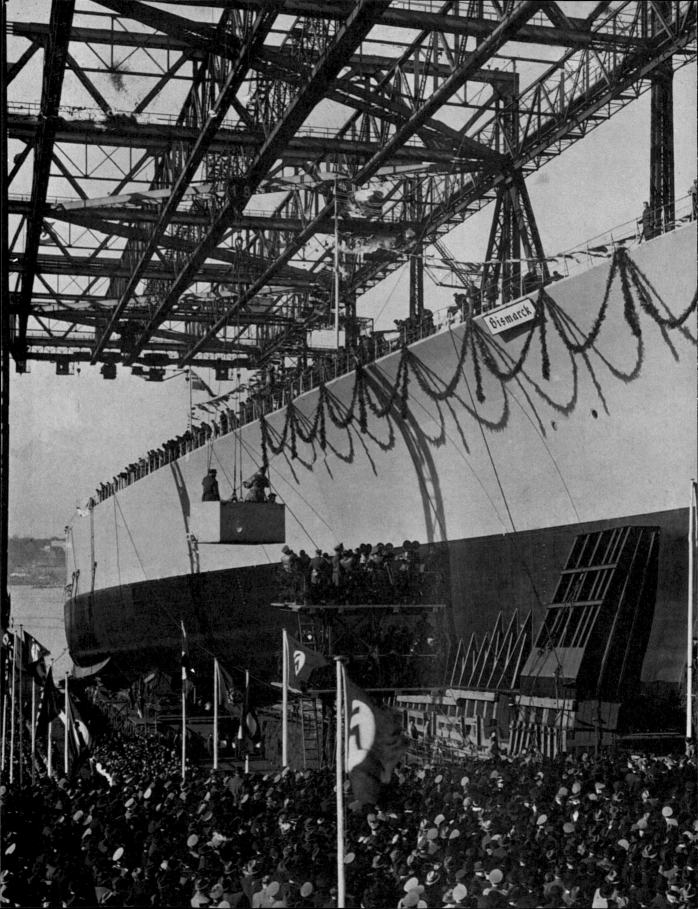

CHAPTER 3

The Nazi Economy

A cornerstone of Hitler's popularity was undoubtedly the economic transformation of Germany. When he took power in January 1933, some six million Germans were unemployed, trapped in the destructive aftermath of the Great Depression. Six years later, unemployment stood at only 302,000.

Unlike many social and fiscal issues, unemployment is one that ordinary citizens actually see, experience and fear, so Hitler's gift of nearly full employment created a tangible bond of affection between the Führer and his people. Yet at the same time, the economic conditions of the Third Reich were those of a centralized dictatorship, where workers' rights were subordinated to national ambitions, and sound fiscal policy was twisted by the creation and maintenance of a war economy.

The mighty battleship *Bismarck* is launched amidst great fanfare from the Blohm & Voss shipyard in Hamburg, 1936.

Economy and Employment, 1933–39

The economic transformation of Germany in the 1930s was held up at the time as a masterpiece of NSDAP policy. Yet it was as much to do with a general global upturn than with Hitler's fiscal acumen.

Germany's economic situation at the beginning of the 1930s was dire. Unemployment stood at a hefty six million people. The agricultural sector was in desperate financial straits, and problems in banking meant that obtaining venture capital to fund new major projects was almost impossible. Germany's balance-of-trade deficit seemed insurmountable, as it imported far more goods than it exported, and was steadily running out of available credit to buy goods and raw materials on the international market. The people of Germany were desperate for a new economic beginning.

Schacht's reforms

We must be careful when attempting to define a 'Nazi economic policy'. While there are definite ingredients to Hitler's fiscal planning, in many ways the economic transformation of Germany came through the multiple policies of different economic leaders, plus the good fortune of a general upturn in the global economy. Yet Hitler was undoubtedly aware that the economy was the foundation of all his future plans for Germany (particularly its militarization), and its restoration was urgent.

Hitler's first major financial decision was the appointment of a new *Reichsbank* president, Dr Hjalmar Schacht, in 1933; Schacht was also appointed as the Economics Minister the following year. Although he was not an NSDAP member (a fact that made him vulnerable in the future), Schacht was an extremely competent economist, and he had been critical in stabilizing Germany's currency and inflation during the 1920s and early 1930s.

In the early days of his new appointments, Schacht pursued policies in line with his belief in the free market. His creation of the Organization of Industry led to a renewed flow of venture capital into Germany, backed by fixed, low interest rates to encourage investment. The establishment of an equitable and more business-focused taxation system brought confidence back to many corporations. Local authorities who were short of cash were given debt rescheduling, meaning that they had a sudden influx of money to inject into the local economy. The government also made major share purchases, revitalizing the share market.

Tackling unemployment was another obvious priority, and Schacht set the tone by initiating his 'New Plan' of 1934. Huge investment was made in public works projects (there was a 70 per cent increase in government expenditure between 1933 and 1936), millions of Reichsmarks being sunk into public building projects, road construction and repair, forestry development and similar programmes. The effect of this investment was rapid and significant. A total of 1.7 million workers were involved in public works projects in 1934, and autobahn construction projects created 84,000 jobs in their first year alone.

Reductions in unemployment were also supported by the efforts of the *Deutsche Arbeitsfront* (German

WORKING DAYS LOST TO INDUSTRIAL DISPUTES, 1918–32			
Date	*1918*	*1919*	*1920*	*1921*
Days	1453	33,083	16,755	25,874
Date	*1922*	*1923*	*1924*	*1925*
Days	27,734	12,344	36,198	2936
Date	*1926*	*1927*	*1928*	*1929*
Days	1222	6144	20,339	4251
Date	*1930*	*1931*	*1932*	
Days	4029	1890	1130	

AVERAGE WORKING HOURS EACH WEEK, 1932–42				
Date	*1932*	*1933*	*1934*	*1935*	*1936*
Hours	42	43	45	44	46
Date	*1937*	*1938*	*1939*	*1942*	
Hours	46	47	47	50	

Labour Front; DAF), created in 1933 and headed by Robert Ley. The DAF was essentially the replacement for all the Weimar-era trade unions banned by Hitler. Being an official Party-associated organization, however, meant that its efforts were more directed towards ensuring worker productivity than workers' rights per se, but there were benefits to joining. Membership of the DAF was voluntary, but getting a job without membership was difficult. The DAF set reasonable wage rates, regularized working hours, opened workers' leisure facilities and canteens and provided greater job security, in return for which the workers were committed to more productive labour.

Another important labour organization in Hitler's Germany was the *Reichsarbeitsdienst* (Reich Labour Service; RAD). Formed in 1934, the RAD was an official state labour service, divided into sections for men and women. The RAD was structured by *Arbeitsgaue* (Divisional Work Districts), with each district having military-style units of labourers. (During the war, the RAD often provided auxiliary combat support, or actually fought in roles such as anti-aircraft gunners.) Its effect on unemployment was also significant, as all men aged between 18 and 25 had to complete six months' service in the organization.

Autarky and the war economy

There was no doubt that Schacht's policies were integral to the major reduction in unemployment in Germany during the early years of the Nazi reign. By January 1934, unemployment had fallen to 3.3 million, and to 2.5 million by January 1936. And yet by the mid-1930s the honeymoon period for Schacht was coming to an end, as his fiscal planning ran into Hitler's overarching and contrasting economic ambitions for Germany.

A central pillar of Hitler's economic demands was the concept of

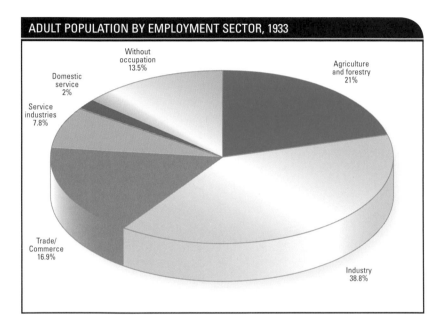

ADULT POPULATION BY EMPLOYMENT SECTOR, 1933

- Without occupation 13.5%
- Domestic service 2%
- Service industries 7.8%
- Trade/Commerce 16.9%
- Industry 38.8%
- Agriculture and forestry 21%

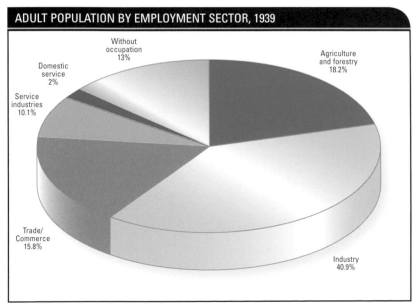

ADULT POPULATION BY EMPLOYMENT SECTOR, 1939

- Without occupation 13%
- Domestic service 2%
- Service industries 10.1%
- Trade/Commerce 15.8%
- Industry 40.9%
- Agriculture and forestry 18.2%

AVERAGE WAGE PER HOUR INDEX, 1925–40

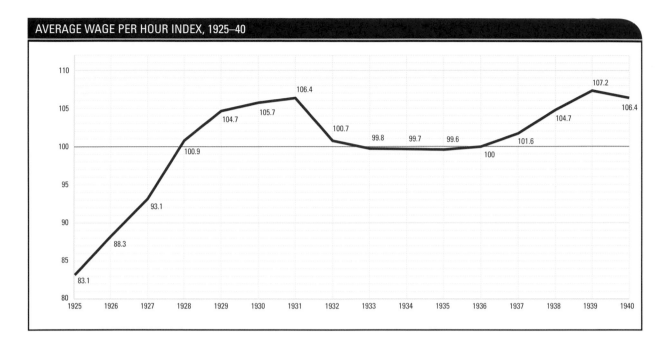

AVERAGE WAGE PER WEEK INDEX, 1925–40

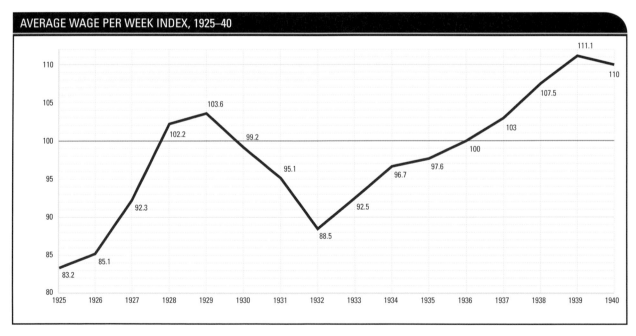

'autarky' – self-sufficiency. Hitler recognized that a dependency on imports made a country vulnerable (as had been proved by British naval blockades of Germany during World War I). Through achieving autarky, Hitler intended that Germany would produce or source all essential raw materials and services from within itself, or, crucially, from within German-controlled territories. As Germany did not have self-sufficiency in raw materials, autarky and *Lebensraum* went hand in hand – Germany would have to conquer territories that would provide its fundamental needs.

Proceding logically from autarky and *Lebensraum* was Hitler's demand that Germany establish a *Wehrwirtschaft* – a war economy. A memorandum written by Hitler in August 1936 indicates how central militarism was to the *Führer*'s economic thinking: 'If we do not succeed in bringing the German Army as rapidly as possible to the rank of the premier army in the world, then Germany will be lost.'

Economic conflict

Increasingly, Schacht – a free-market economist at heart – came into conflict with the centrally planned expectations of Hitler, and also began to argue that the costs of rearmament were not sustainable. By 1936, 19.4 per cent of the net domestic product was being spent on rearmament, up from 6.3 per cent in 1933. Furthermore, investments in industrial autarky, such as synthetic oil plants, were hugely expensive and were not having the significant impact on reducing foreign imports that Hitler desired. Schacht warned Hitler that Germany's deficit spending was getting out of control, and that more investment should be channelled into consumer products and international trade.

This message was not one Hitler wanted to hear, and Schacht's days of influence were coming to an end.

In October 1936, Hitler's associate Hermann Göring, a man not known for his economic expertise, was appointed 'Plenipotentiary for the Four-Year Plan'.

The Four-Year Plan

The Four-Year Plan was an official Nazi economic programme for the years 1936 to 1940. It emphasized autarky and rearmament to the core, and the goal of transforming Germany into a true *Wehrwirtschaft*. Schacht was not out of a job, but he was now effectively sidelined. The winner in the 'guns or butter' debate – Schacht advocated increased investment in food fats, while Göring wanted weapons – was emphatically the guns. (In 1936 Göring had commented, 'Would you rather have butter or guns? Should we import lard

WARTIME GERMAN WORKFORCE BY EMPLOYMENT SECTOR, 1939–45 (MILLIONS)

Sector	1939	1940	1941	1942	1943	1944
Agriculture	11.1	10	9.3	9.3	9	8.7
Industry and Transport	18.5	15.9	15.2	13.8	13.3	12.5
Commerce	4.6	3.7	3.4	3.1	2.9	2.7
Service Industries/Admin	2.7	2.6	2.6	2.4	2.3	2.2
Armed Forces Admin	0.7	0.7	0.8	1.2	1.3	1.3
Domestic Workers	1.6	1.5	1.5	1.4	1.4	1.4

FEMALE LABOUR FORCE IN AGRICULTURE AND INDUSTRY, 1925–44

Date	Agriculture	Industry	All sectors (total)
1925	4,970,000	2,988,000	11,478,000
1933	4,649,000	2,758,000	11,479,000
1939	4,880,000	3,310,000	12,701,000
1940	5,689,000	3,650,000	14,386,000
1941	5,369,000	3,677,000	14,167,000
1942	5,673,000	3,537,000	14,437,000
1943	5,665,000	3,740,000	14,806,000
1944	5,756,000	3,636,000	14,897,000

DECLINE IN MALE EMPLOYMENT IN CONSUMER SECTOR, PRE-WAR VS 1940

Economic Sector	Pre-war	1 June 1940
Brewing	71,742	56,720
Ceramic Industry	57,013	44,202
Clothing	54,302	40,598
Foodstuffs	169,478	151,015
Glass Industry	70,909	58,492
Leather Industry	126,515	87,437
Metal Goods	116,371	94,991
Paper	43,987	35,047
Printing	149,300	125,019
Spirits Industry	17,571	21,891
Sugar Industry	24,926	24,432
Textile Industry	424,795	294,819
Woodworking	217,833	167,351

Data source: Richard Overy, War and Economy in the Third Reich

EMPLOYMENT OF WOMEN BY SECTOR, 1939–SEPTEMBER 1944

Sector	1939	1940	1941	1942	1943	1944
Agriculture/Forestry	4,880,000	5,689,000	5,369,000	5,673,000	5,665,000	5,756,000
Industry	3,310,000	3,650,000	3,677,000	3,537,000	3,740,000	3,636,000
Trade/Commerce/Transport	2,227,000	2,183,000	2,167,000	2,225,000	2,320,000	2,219,000
Service Industries/Admin	954,000	1,157,000	1,284,000	1,471,000	1,719,000	1,748,000
Domestic Service	1,560,000	1,511,000	1,473,000	1,410,000	1,362,000	1,287,000

Data source: Tim Kirk, Longman Companion to Nazi Germany

PERCENTAGE OF GERMAN WOMEN IN THE WORKFORCE, 1939–44

Year	Percentage
1939	37.3%
1940	41.4%
1941	42.6%
1942	46%
1943	48.8%
1944	51%

or metal ores?') It was clear that militaristic imperatives rather than rational fiscal decisions were now running the German economy.

New economy

With Göring's Four-Year Plan in place, Schacht, a man who had done considerable service to the growth of the Third Reich, resigned in 1937 and Göring became the Minister of the Economy. Schacht's predictions about the future state of the German economy were in the process of being fulfilled. Between 1933 and 1939, for example, German state revenue was 62 billion Reichsmarks, yet its expenditure during the same period was some 101.5 billion Reichsmarks. Germany was heading for bankruptcy, which was probably an additional reason behind going to war in 1939 – conquering foreign territories was one way of tackling the balance-of-payments deficit. Yet in the short term, buoyed by hefty public spending, Germany's employment situation seemed set on inexorable improvement. By January 1937, unemployment had dropped to 1.8 million, and to 1 million by January 1938. A year later, with the German workforce heavily employed in public works schemes and recruitment to the military services rocketing, unemployment stood at a record 302,000, practically full-employment conditions.

Labour effects

The transformation of the German economy had some interesting side-effects in terms of employment. One particular phenomenon was the accelerated growth of white-collar professional employment. In its visual propaganda, the Nazi Party was fond of showing the Führer rubbing shoulders with manual labourers rather than with business leaders, emphasizing that Hitler was a man of the common worker, not of the affluent classes. Something of the 'socialism' within National Socialism comes through in the following passage from Robert Ley, written for the laudatory photo-collection book Adolf Hitler (1936):

When you work, you work for the people. Consequently work is an honour. There is no partiality or distinction in work. The work of a General Manager has no more inner worth and is no better than the work of a street sweeper. It does not depend on what kind of work, but rather on how that work is done. Whoever does not work loses honour in the people's community. Work does not defile. It ennobles, regardless of whether the work is done with the mind or the fist.

(Translated from Quinn, 1978)

Ley makes it clear that all work is of equal status, regardless of its output. Implicit in this is a defence of the worth of blue-collar labour, which was indeed critical to Germany's war economy. Yet interestingly Germany's blue-collar workforce grew by only 10 per cent between 1928 and 1939, whereas the white-collar workforce increased in size by 25 per cent during the same period.

A fundamental reason behind the growth of the professional classes was the sprawling civil service created by the Nazis, with new Party and governmental apparatuses springing up at national and local levels, fuelling the need for

UNEMPLOYMENT DATA, 1932–39

Month	1932	1933	1934	1935	1936	1937	1938	1939
January	6,041,900	6,013,600	3,300,000	2,973,500	2,520,400	1,853,700	1,051,700	301,800
February	6,128,400	6,000,900	3,372,600	2,764,100	2,514,800	1,610,900	946,300	196,300
March	6,034,100	5,598,800	2,798,300	2,401,800	1,937,100	1,245,300	507,600	134,000
April	5,739,000	5,331,200	2,608,600	2,233,200	1,762,700	960,700	422,500	93,900
May	5,582,600	5,038,600	2,528,900	2,019,200	1,491,200	776,300	338,300	69,500
June	5,475,700	4,856,900	2,480,800	1,876,500	1,314,700	648,400	292,000	48,800
July	5,392,200	4,463,800	2,426,000	1,754,100	1,169,800	562,800	218,300	38,300
August	5,223,800	4,124,200	2,397,500	1,706,200	1,098,400	509,200	178,700	33,900
September	5,102,700	3,849,200	2,281,800	1,713,900	1,035,200	469,000	155,900	77,500
October	5,109,100	3,744,800	2,226,600	1,828,700	1,177,400	501,800	163,900	79,400
November	5,355,400	3,714,600	2,352,600	1,984,400	1,197,100	572,600	152,400	72,500
December	5,772,900	4,059,000	2,604,700	2,507,900	1,478,800	994,700	455,600	104,400
Average	5,575,400	4,804,400	2,718,300	2,151,000	1,592,600	912,300	429,400	104,200

Data source: Richard Overy, The Penguin Historical Atlas of the Third Reich

managers, accountants, lawyers, administrators and similar positions. Furthermore, the major public works spending promoted businesses, and their growth in turn led to increases in layers of management. It is also worth noting that in 1936 the average white-collar worker earned 50-plus per cent more than the average blue-collar worker, although wage disparities did close up a little over time, particularly during the war when emergency conditions flattened out most people's salaries.

When war came, conscription naturally fell hardest on the manual classes. As the table to the right illustrates, in June 1941 a total of 3,617,762 blue-collar workers were conscripted for military service, compared with 907,974 workers in white-collar jobs.

Women in work

Another significant labour effect of the Nazi era was the increased importance of women in the Reich labour force. The *Führer* was no advocate of equality. During an address in 1934 at a Nuremberg Rally, Hitler stated:

If a man's world is said to be the state, his struggle, his eagerness to dedicate his powers to the service of the community, then we can say that the woman's is a smaller world. Her world is her husband, her children, her home. These two worlds are not in opposition. They complement each other; they belong together in the same way that man and woman belong together.

Such a world view, however, ran up against hard realities, particularly during the war years when millions of young men were conscripted and shipped off to war, leaving the labour force with some serious shortages. A significant element of these shortages, as we have seen, was filled by forced labour, but other gaps were handled by increasing the proportion of women in the labour market. In 1939, just over 37 per cent of women were in the workforce; by 1944 the figure was 51 per cent.

Women were employed heavily in service industries and in administration roles, but the largest proportion went to agricultural work, which had been stripped of its men by military conscription. Hitler had overseen a transformation both economic and social.

CONSCRIPTS BY OCCUPATIONAL SECTOR, JUNE 1941

Sector	Conscripts
Agriculture	1,114,986
Building workers	584,588
Labourers and general workers	604,928
Metal workers	827,363
Transport workers	485,897
White-collar workers	907,974
All others (e.g. school leavers)	2,121,944

Data source: Richard Overy, War and Economy in the Third Reich

Industry and Business, 1933–45

The Nazi relationship with industry and business was frequently ambiguous. On the one hand, it seemed to encourage private initiative, while on the other such initiative had to be constrained by the limited horizons of economic policy.

In the early years of the Third Reich, the Nazi Party's relationship to business was ostensibly focused on promoting the local, middle-class, artisan businesses, rather than major industry. This emphasis was opportunistic, as Hitler was eager to attract the politically powerful middle classes to his fold, and be seen as a safe pair of hands for the 'respectable' masses. Protectionism for some businesses expressed itself in several forms, not least in prohibiting the expansion or new-build of chain department stores, and restricting the levels of service they could provide. The large department

stores, for example, were disallowed from providing barbering or baking services, these being delivered by small local companies instead. (This policy was given ideological backing by the fact that many department stores were Jewish-owned.) Nazi Party organizations were also instructed to purchase essential

items of uniform and kit from local producers. Trade union antagonism was also obviated by Hitler's removal of the unions from the economy.

In balance, the regime also tightened up the restrictions on who could deliver small business services. The owners of new artisan businesses were first vetted to see if

INCOME, BUSINESS AND SALES TAXES COLLECTED BY THE STATE, 1938–43 (MILLION RM)						
Date	1938	1939	1940	1941	1942	1943
Income/Business Taxes	8186	12,227	14,490	19,185	21,808	21,954
Sales Taxes	3356	3734	3929	4148	4160	4177

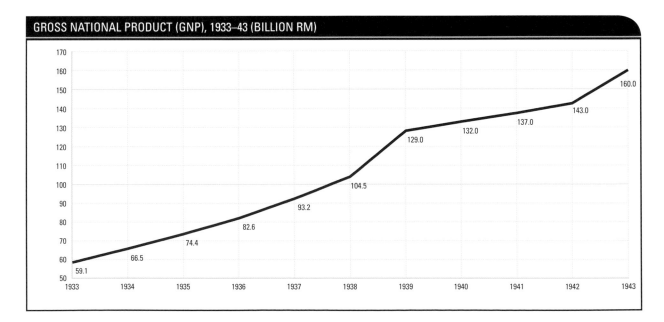

GROSS NATIONAL PRODUCT (GNP), 1933–43 (BILLION RM)

59.1 — 1933
66.5 — 1934
74.4 — 1935
82.6 — 1936
93.2 — 1937
104.5 — 1938
129.0 — 1939
132.0 — 1940
137.0 — 1941
143.0 — 1942
160.0 — 1943

they were professionally qualified, and relevant Master's Examination qualifications became complusory for such owners from 1935.

Big business

Yet as with so much about the Third Reich, there was a distinct gulf between image and reality when it came to Nazi business interest. The fact is that it was big business which was integral to Germany's development of a true war economy, not artisan enterprises, and such became more apparent once Göring had launched his Four-Year Plan. As Richard Grunberger has pointed out in his *A Social History of the Third Reich* (Phoenix, 2005): 'The number of artisan enterprises had increased by nearly a fifth between 1931 and 1936 to 1,650,000, but the last pre-war years were to see a decrease of 11 per cent.'

What we see under Göring is a steady concentration of industrial power in the hands of a few major concerns, such as Krupp, I.G. Farben, Thyssen and Mannesmann. By 1936, some 70 per cent of industrial production was controlled by monopolies, up from 40 per cent just four years earlier. The most

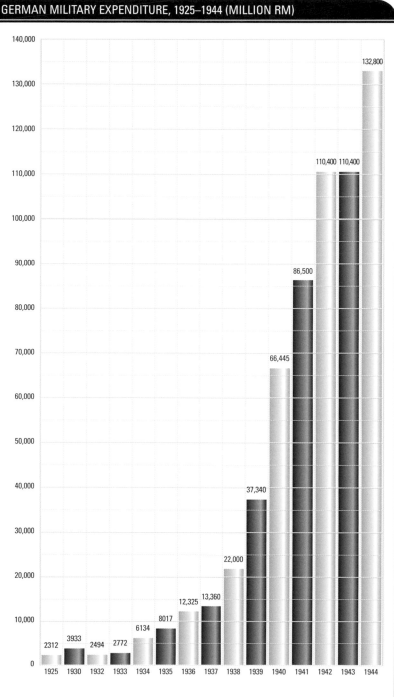

GERMAN MILITARY EXPENDITURE, 1925–1944 (MILLION RM)

Year	Value
1925	2312
1930	3933
1932	2494
1933	2772
1934	6134
1935	8017
1936	12,325
1937	13,360
1938	22,000
1939	37,340
1940	66,445
1941	86,500
1942	110,400
1943	110,400
1944	132,800

GERMAN MILITARY EXPENDITURE BETWEEN MAIN SERVICES, 1934–39 (MILLION RM)

Fiscal Year	Heer	Luftwaffe	Kriegs-marine
1934/5	815	642	496
1935/6	1041	1035	695
1936/7	2435	2225	1161
1937/8	3537	3258	1478
1938/9	9465	6026	1756

egregious example of a monopoly has to be Reichswerke 'Hermann Göring', a monstrous steelworks controlled by Göring himself, which spread out from Germany into Austria, Poland and France, while also acquiring controlling stakes in major banks to ensure its financial flow.

Note, however, that having a monopoly in Nazi Germany was not necessarily financially beneficial. Although the German economy was not 'planned' in the Soviet sense, levels of state intervention were high, and many companies were forced into investments or lines of production they might otherwise have avoided, particularly in inefficient projects focused on synthetic raw material production. In fact, as time went on, German industry became subservient to the demands of autarky, and combined with the accelerating demands for war

COMPARATIVE MOTOR-VEHICLE PRODUCTION, 1925–1938 (000s)							
Country	1925	1926	1927	1928	1929	1930	1931
France	177	192	191	224	248	222	197
Germany	56	42	106	133	140	85	70
Italy	40	55	65	55	60	48	30
UK	153	180	212	212	239	237	225
USA	4266	4301	3401	4359	5358	3356	2390
Country	1933	1934	1935	1936	1937	1938	
France	189	181	165	204	201	227	
Germany	118	186	248	303	331	340	
Italy	40	45	48	45	71	67	
UK	286	342	404	461	507	447	
USA	1920	2753	3946	4454	4808	2489	

Data Sources: Society of Motor Manufacturers and Traders, The Motor Industry of Great Britain: 1938 *(London, 1939);* League of Nations, Review of World Production, 1925–31 *(Geneva, 1932).*

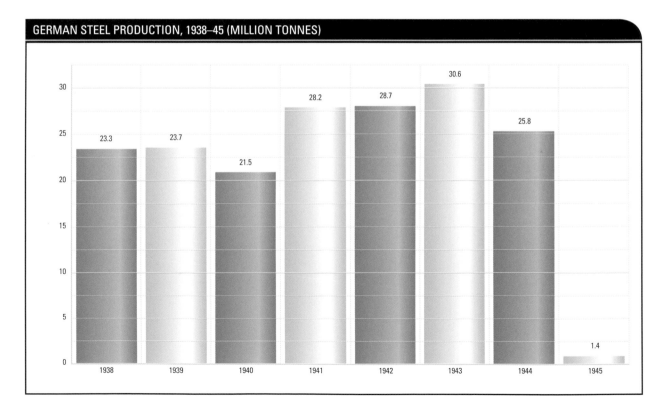

GERMAN STEEL PRODUCTION, 1938–45 (MILLION TONNES)

Year	Production
1938	23.3
1939	23.7
1940	21.5
1941	28.2
1942	28.7
1943	30.6
1944	25.8
1945	1.4

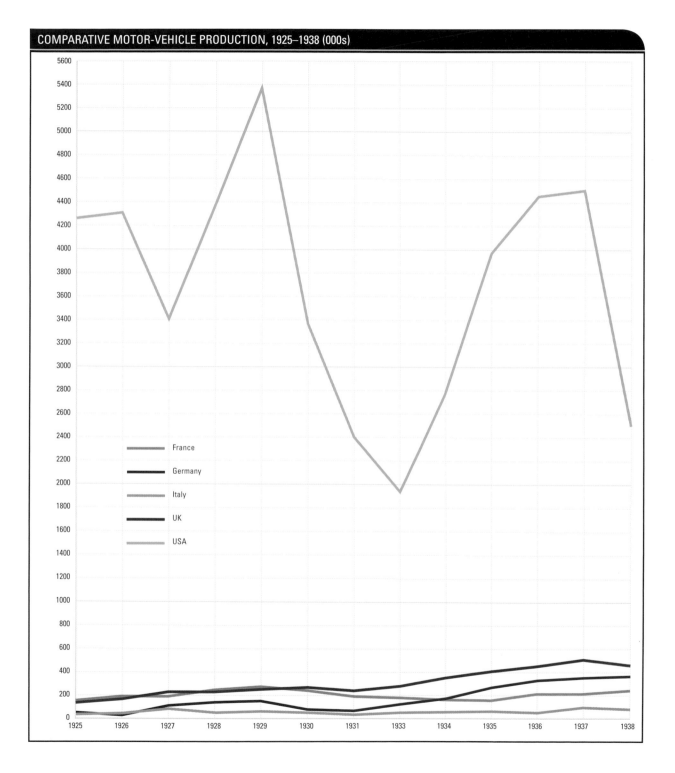

COMPARATIVE MOTOR-VEHICLE PRODUCTION, 1925–1938 (000s)

Legend:
- France
- Germany
- Italy
- UK
- USA

TOTAL PRODUCTION/IMPORTS OF PETROLEUM PRODUCTS, 1940–45 (000s TONNES)						
Heading	1940	1941	1942	1943	1944	1945
Aviation Fuel	966	910	1472	1917	1105	12
Motor Fuel	2130	2284	2023	1937	1477	139
Diesel	1482	1726	1493	1793	1260	180

ALUMINIUM PRODUCTION, 1939–44 (000s TONNES)		
Date	1939	1940	1941
Production	199.4	211.2	233.6
Date	1942	1943	1944
Production	245.3	250	245.3

CRUDE OIL AND SYNTHETIC OIL PRODUCTION, 1939–45 (MILLION TONNES)							
Type	1939	1940	1941	1942	1943	1944	1945
Crude Oil	3.1	4.8	5.7	6.6	7.6	5.6	negligible
Synthetic Oil	2.2	3.2	3.9	4.6	5.6	3.9	negligible
Imported Oil	5.2	2.1	2.8	2.4	2.7	0.9	negligible

production, we cannot view German industry as the product of enterprise.

Achieving autarky?

While we have introduced the concept of autarky, we need to ask how close Germany came to achieving its goal. First, as the tables in this chapter show, there was an increase in production across almost every type of raw material, and productivity generally kept climbing until the meltdown of late 1944 and 1945. Some of the statistics are impressive. Aluminium production, for example, climbed from 199,400 tonnes (196,210 UK tons) in 1939 to 245,300 tonnes (241,375 tons) in 1942, and crude oil production went from 3.1 million tonnes (3 million tons) to 6.6 million tonnes (6.5 million tons) in the same period. Iron ore production was 2.21 million tonnes (2.17 million tons) in 1939 but 5.4 million tonnes (5.5 million tons) in 1942.

Overall, industrial capital production rose by nearly 100 per cent between 1928 and 1944, and yet ironically these huge increases are not enough to say that autarky had succeeded. Across the board, German industry never achieved the raw materials targets set by the regime, and by the outbreak of war Germany was still importing about 30 per cent of these materials. Furthermore, during the war Allied bombing did not stop the Nazi economy from increasing production figures until the last year of fighting, but it certainly prevented Germany from achieving its full potential.

War economy

Once war began in 1939, the conflict produced an insatiable appetite for industrial resources and labour efforts. The table on p. 66 clearly shows how the percentage of the German industrial labour force working on military contracts tripled between 1939 and 1943, from 21.9 per cent at the beginning of the period to 61 per cent at the end.

Yet despite the apparent effort, much productivity was lost through a lack of coherent central leadership in planning a war economy. Göring did not have the acumen for his role, and industrial coordination was made problematic through multiple agencies and influential personalities all vying for resources and finance.

By 1942, with the war taking a critical turn, Hitler finally recognized that the efforts of total war required new levels of industrial efficiency. In February 1942, Hitler appointed Albert Speer, previously the *Führer*'s personal architect, to the position of Minister of Armaments and War Production. As we shall explore in the next chapter, Speer had a profound impact upon the productivity of the German war industry, pushing the output of everything from small arms to aircraft to new heights of success.

And yet even Speer's achievements were not enough to balance out the escalating losses of war machines as the conflict turned against Germany. Although he carried much greater centralized authority than Göring possessed, Speer still found some of his ambitions thwarted by competing interests. Heinrich Himmler, the head of the SS, for example, protectively ran his own economic agenda, particularly in occupied territories. Even local Nazi

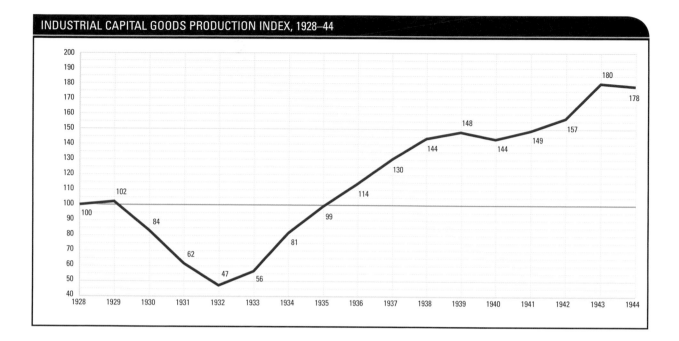

INDUSTRIAL CAPITAL GOODS PRODUCTION INDEX, 1928–44

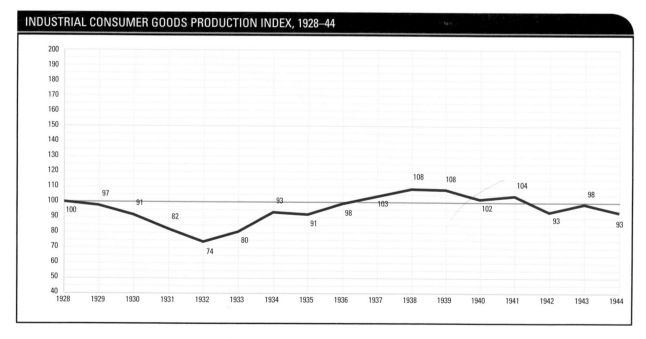

INDUSTRIAL CONSUMER GOODS PRODUCTION INDEX, 1928–44

Gauleiter could be awkward about industrial cooperation. Although Nazi Germany had made epic efforts to achieve autarky and *Wehrwirtschaft*, it never achieved the former and never realized the full potential of the latter. History is left to wonder what would have happened if it had been successful in these projects.

Military Output

Germany's war outputs rose steadily from 1933 to 1941, then dramatically from 1942 to 1944. Yet the story of its armament production is one of confused chains of command and energies frittered between too many projects.

German rearmament had secretly been taking place since the 1920s, despite the restrictions of the Versailles Treaty. Using civilian front companies, or companies established abroad, Germany managed to rebuild something of its air force and army, but when Hitler came to power in 1933 the days of furtive rearming were over.

Between 1932 and 1934 the world's powers were engaged in the Geneva Disarmament Conference, which sought to control the emerging global arms race. In 1933, Hitler withdrew from the conference, and took Germany out of the League of Nations, not only hobbling the relevance of the conference but also sending a clear signal that Germany was no longer going to hide its military aspirations.

Production figures

Although Germany certainly redeveloped itself significantly in the run-up to World War II, we shouldn't overstate any apparent superiority in arms when compared with the Allies. Germany was a single nation that chose to match itself against several powerful countries, including France and Britain. Furthermore, some of its early armament production figures were not too spectacular.

In 1939, for example, 247 tanks and self-propelled guns rolled off German assembly lines, compared with 969 in Britain. War did, admittedly, galvanize industry to greater heights, and during 1940 German factories produced 1643 armoured fighting vehicles (AFVs) compared with Britain's 1399, but thereafter Britain and Germany jockeyed for position in terms of production figures. (It is worth noting that by 1941 British military aircraft production was almost double that of Germany. Only in 1944 did German aircraft production overtake Britain's, but that fact was irrelevant on account of aircraft production figures in the

PRODUCTION OF TANKS AND SELF-PROPELLED GUNS, 1939–45 (INDIVIDUAL UNITS)			
Date	1939	1940	1941	1942
Units	247	1643	3790	6180
Date	1943	1944	1945	
Units	12,063	19,002	3932	

United States and Soviet Union.)

Britain was only one of Germany's opponents, and a small one compared with the industrial might of the Soviet Union and United States. To put things into perspective, between 1939 and 1945 Germany manufactured 46,857 AFVs, 159,144 artillery pieces and 189,307 military aircraft. The Soviet Union, by contrast, ultimately produced 105,251 AFVs, 516,648 artillery pieces and 157,261 military aircraft. Figures for the United States are 88,410 AFVs, 257,390 artillery pieces and 324,750 military aircraft.

Similar disparities are reflected in Germany's maritime production. In 1938, the *Kriegsmarine* drew up its 'Z-Plan', a list of the ship types it planned to build between 1939 and 1947, to provide it with the capability to take on the Royal Navy at sea. The plan included six new battleships, three battlecruisers, eight heavy cruisers, six light cruisers

PERCENTAGE OF GERMAN INDUSTRIAL LABOUR FORCE WORKING ON MILITARY CONTRACTS, 1939–43

1939	21.9%
1940	50.2%
1941	54.5%
1942	56.7%
1943	61%

PRODUCTION OF KEY TANK/SP GUN TYPES, 1939–45

Panzer I Type	1939	1940	1941	1942	1943	1944	1945
Panzer I	1839 (pre-war)	–	–	–	–	–	–

Panzer II Type	1939	1940	1941	1942	1943	1944	1945
Panzer II		15	9	223	302	77	7 –
Panzer II (f)	–	90	42	23	–	–	–
Marder II	–	–	–	511	212	–	–
Wespe	–	–	–	–	514	144	–
Bison	–	–	–	12	–	–	–

Panzer 38 (t) Type	1939	1940	1941	1942	1943	1944	1945
Panzer 38 (t)	153	367	678	198	–	–	–
Marder 138	–	–	–	110	783	323	–
Marder 139	–	–	–	344	–	–	–
Grille	–	–	–	–	225	346	–
Hetzer	–	–	–	–	1687	1335	–

Panzer III Type	1939	1940	1941	1942	1943	1944	1945
Panzer III A–F	157	396	–	–	–	–	–
Panzer III G–J	–	466	1673	251	–	–	–
Panzer III J/I–M	–	–	–	1907	64	–	–
Panzer III N	–	–	–	449	213	–	–
Panzer III (f)	–	–	–	–	100	–	–
Sturmgeschütz III A–E	–	192	540	93	–	–	–
Sturmgeschütz III F–G	–	–	–	695	3011	3849	1038
Sturmgeschütz 42	–	–	–	12	204	903	98

Panzer IV Type	1939	1940	1941	1942	1943	1944	1945
Panzer IV A–F1	45	268	467	124	–	–	–
Panzer IV F2–J	–	–	–	870	3013	3126	385
Sturmgeschütz IV	–	–	–	–	30	1006	105
Jagdpanzer IV	–	–	–	–	–	769	–
Jagdpanzer IV/70	–	–	–	–	–	767	441
Sturmpanzer IV	–	–	–	–	66	215	17
Hornisse	–	–	–	–	345	133	16
Hummel	–	–	–	–	368	289	57
Möbelwagen	–	–	–	–	–	205	35
Wirbelwind	–	–	–	–	–	100	6
Ostwind	–	–	–	–	–	15	28

Panzer V (Panther) Type	1939	1940	1941	1942	1943	1944	1945
Panther	–	–	–	–	1848	3777	507
Jagdpanther	–	–	–	–	1	226	198

Panzer VI (Tiger) Type	1939	1940	1941	1942	1943	1944	1945
Tiger I	–	–	–	78	649	623	–
Sturmtiger	–	–	–	–	–	18	–
Tiger II	–	–	–	–	1	377	112
Jagdtiger	–	–	–	–	–	51	28

and 12 aircraft carriers (including cruiser carriers). In the end, production and commissioning fell well short of those targets – although several new battleships and cruisers were commissioned during the war, all were laid down prior to the Z-Plan, and no aircraft carriers were operationally realized.

Germany did, however, produce 1141 U-boats during the war, but these figures were way below what was required for these potentially war-winning weapons. At the beginning of the war, despite urging from *Großadmiral* Karl Dönitz, the head of the *Kriegsmarine*, submarine production remained sluggish, with only 58 submarines produced in 1939. Production of U-boats peaked at 282 in 1942, but by that time the increase in output was necessary simply to counter the losses inflicted by the Allies, who were mastering anti-submarine warfare. In 1943, for example, the German Navy lost 237 U-boats, and 242 the following year.

Funding conflicts

We have already seen something of the scale of pre-war spending on rearmament. The naval Z-Plan was only one major rearmament project that demanded Göring's cash at this time, which together from the late 1930s demanded an increase in armaments production of about 300 per cent. The total military expenditure went from 1.95 billion Reichsmarks in the fiscal year (FY) 1934/35, to 17.25 billion Reichsmarks in FY 1938/39.

Although money was flowing, this did not mean that spending it was a coordinated process. Until Speer took over armaments production in 1942 (although problems to an extent continued after then), military spending was divided between several agencies, all competing against each other. Richard Overy has explained the conflictual process in rearmament requisitions:

The armed forces saw the militarized economy as their affair, and through a system of armaments inspectorate both in Germany and in the conquered areas, they tried to organize the production of armaments and the diversion of resources. They were in direct competition with Göring's Four Year Plan organization, the Economics and Labour ministries, and the local party Gaue, all of which had some claim on economic policy.

(Overy, 1996)

The result of this Byzantine approach to rearmament was that money was dispersed between multiple interests, rather than unified in a coherent strategy, with the consequent restrictions on armaments production. It would take the appointment of Albert Speer as Minister of Armaments and War Production to rectify the situation.

Enter Speer

The effect Albert Speer had on the German war economy was profound. Some figures will clarify his value. When he took office as Armaments Minister in February 1942, following the death of his predecessor, Fritz Todt, in an air crash, German industry had produced a total of 4500 tanks. Two years later, Speer had overseen

a production leap to 17,300 vehicles. In terms of military aircraft production, Germany produced 11,772 aircraft of all types in 1941, but 15,556 in 1942, 25,257 in 1943 and 39,807 in 1944. Artillery production rose from 11,200 weapons in 1941 to 70,700 in 1944. In only the first six months of his tenure, total arms production jumped by 59 per cent. By the second half of 1944, when production in all areas peaked, Speer's industry was

producing almost more weapons than there were divisions to use them, and he undoubtedly made life far more difficult for the Allies.

Planning military production

So how did he achieve such impressive results? First, Speer wrested much of rearmament policy away from the competing interests of Party and military control, establishing a Central Planning Board

PRODUCTION OF KEY AIRCRAFT TYPES, 1939–45

Bomber	1939	1940	1941	1942	1943	1944	1945	Total
Arado Ar 234	–	–	–	–	150	64	–	214
Dornier Do 17	215	260	–	–	–	–	–	475
Dornier Do 217	1	20	277	564	504	–	–	1366
Heinkel He 111	452	756	950	1337	1405	756	–	5656
Heinkel He 177	–	–	–	166	415	565	–	1146
Junkers Ju 88	69	1816	2146	2270	2160	661	–	9122
Junkers Ju 188	–	–	–	–	165	301	–	466
Junkers Ju 388	–	–	–	–	–	4	–	4

Fighter	1939	1940	1941	1942	1943	1944	1945	Total
Dornier Do 17	9	–	–	–	–	–	–	9
Dornier Do 217	–	–	–	–	157	207	–	364
Dornier Do 335	–	–	–	–	–	7	4	11
Focke-Wulf Fw 190	–	–	228	1850	2171	7488	1630	13367
Focke-Wulf Ta 152	–	–	–	–	–	34	?	?
Focke-Wulf Ta 154	–	–	–	–	–	8	–	8
Heinkel He 162	–	–	–	–	–	–	116	116
Heinkel He 219	–	–	–	–	11	195	62	268
Junkers Ju 88	–	62	66	257	706	2513	355	3959
Messerschmitt Me 109	449	1667	2764	2657	6013	12807	2798	29155
Messerschmitt Me 110	156	1006	594	501	641	128	–	3026
Messerschmitt Me 163	–	–	–	–	–	327	37	364
Messerschmitt Me 210	–	–	92	93	89	74	–	348
Messerschmitt Me 262	–	–	–	–	–	564	730	1294
Messerschmitt Me 410	–	–	–	–	271	629	–	900

Ground Attack	1939	1940	1941	1942	1943	1944	1945	Total
Focke-Wulf Fw 190	–	–	–	68	1183	4279	1104	6634
Henschel Hs 129	–	–	7	221	411	302	–	941
Junkers Ju 87	134	603	500	960	1672	1012	–	4881
Junkers Ju 88	–	–	–	–	–	3	–	3

in April 1942 that concentrated much decision-making in the hands of industrial committees. Further, Speer surrounded himself with industrial leaders and engineers, people who had both the knowledge required and vested interests for achieving maximum productivity.

Speer also focused his attentions on improving labour productivity, and on streamlining the logistical infrastructure that surrounded the arms industry. He rearranged freight and transport systems so that the flow of raw materials and finished goods was far more efficient.

Limitations

While all historians acknowledge the incredible results of Speer's efforts, many also point out that while the increased outputs were impressive, they still fell short of what Germany was capable of achieving. Partisan interests still held sway over much of German politics. The rich resources of the occupied territories, for example, were generally controlled by local SS or Party officials, who jealously guarded their interests, and there were often similar problems with local *Gauleiter*.

Another fundamental problem within German war production stemmed from Germany's technological sophistication and inventiveness. These qualities led to a critical over-diversification in the types of weapons fielded as the war progressed, particularly in terms of tanks and artillery. For example, Soviet anti-tank artillery consisted of a handful of mass-produced types, while the *Wehrmacht* fielded 21 different types in total, each with its own ammunition, spare parts and transportation requirements. In the field of tank production, by 1945 the Soviets had produced more than 57,000 T-34 or T-34-85 tanks, the bulk of its armoured force; in 1943, there were 20 different tanks or self-propelled guns in German production.

Admittedly, the investment in technical excellence produced some of the finest weapons of the war, but the emphasis on quality over quantity was largely a mistake – a German Tiger may have been able to take out two or three Shermans before it was destroyed, but the Allied armour would eventually prevail through weight of numbers alone.

As the war progressed, and steadily turned against Hitler, the *Führer* became more interested in encouraging experimental and research projects to develop what he felt might be war-winning

Reconnaissance	1939	1940	1941	1942	1943	1944	1945	Total
Dornier Do 17	16	–	–	–	–	–	–	16
Dornier Do 215	3	92	6	–	–	–	–	101
Focke-Wulf Fw 189	6	38	250	327	208	17	–	846
Focke-Wulf Fw 200	1	36	58	84	76	8	–	263
Henschel Hs 126	137	368	5	–	–	–	–	510
Junkers Ju 88	–	330	568	567	394	52	–	1911
Junkers Ju 188	–	–	–	–	105	432	33	570
Junkers Ju 290	–	–	–	–	23	18	–	41
Junkers Ju 388	–	–	–	–	–	87	12	99
Messerschmitt Me 109	–	–	26	8	141	979	171	1325
Messerschmitt Me 110	–	75	190	79	150	–	–	494
Messerschmitt Me 210	–	–	2	2	–	–	–	4
Messerschmitt Me 410	–	–	–	–	20	93	–	113

Amphibious	1939	1940	1941	1942	1943	1944	1945	Total
Arado Ar 196	22	104	94	107	104	–	–	431
Blohm & Voss BV 138	39	82	85	70	–	–	–	276
Blohm & Voss BV 222	–	–	–	–	4	–	–	4
Dornier Do 18	22	49	–	–	–	–	–	71
Dornier Do 24	–	1	7	46	81	–	–	135
Heinkel He 115	52	76	–	–	141	–	–	269

Transport	1939	1940	1941	1942	1943	1944	1945	Total
Gotha Go 244	–	–	–	43	–	–	–	43
Junkers Ju 52	145	388	507	503	887	379	–	2809
Junkers Ju 252	–	–	–	15	–	–	–	15
Junkers Ju 352	–	–	–	–	1	49	–	50
Messerschmitt Me 323	–	–	–	27	140	34	–	201

weapons. In reality, what these projects achieved was largely the diversion of technical and financial resources away from more important war production.

The V2 rocket programme, for example, had a negligible impact on the outcome of the war, yet each of the 3225 rockets built cost in the region of 100,000 Reichsmarks. A series of experimental jet fighters produced in 1944/45 was another source of financial drain.

The results of interference

For Armaments Minister Speer, Hitler's interference in war production was infuriating. In his book *Inside the Third Reich* (1970), he explained more about Hitler's skewed sense of priority when it came to manufacturing:

Hitler's decisions led to a multiplicity of parallel projects. They also led to more and more complicated problems of supply. One of his worst

GERMAN TOTAL PRODUCTION OF ARTILLERY UNITS, 1939–45

Field and Siege Artillery	Number
75mm leFK 18	104
75mm leFK 38	80
75mm FK 7M 59	10
75mm FK 7M 85	10
105mm K. 18	1515
105mm leFH 18	6986
105mm leFH 18/40	10,265
105mm leFH Sfl.	1181
150mm sFH 18	5403
150mm sFH Sfl.	1215
150mm K. 18	101
150mm K. 39	64
150mm in Mrs.-Laf.	8
170mm in Mrs.-Laf.	338
210mm Mörser 18	711
210mm K. 38	15
210mm K. 39/40/41	59
210mm K. 52	12
240mm K. 3	10
240mm H. 39/40	18
355mm M 1	7
420mm Gamma	1

Infantry Guns	Number
75mm leIG 18	8266
75mm IG 37	2279
75mm IG 42	527
150mm sIG 33	4155

Mountain Guns	Number
75mm Geb.Gesch. 36	1193
105mm Geb.H. 40	420

Recoilless Rifles	Number
75mm L.G.	653
105mm L.G.	528

Anti-Tank Guns	Number
37mm Pak 35/36	5339
37mm Pak M 37 (t)	513
37mm Pak 39/40	34
42mm Pak 41	313
47mm Pak 46 (t)	273
47mm Pak (t)	214
47mm Pak 35/36 (ö)	150
50mm Pak 38	9568
75mm Pak 37	358
75mm Pak 97/38	3712
75mm Pak 39	3166
75mm Pak 40	23,303
75mm Pak 41	150
75mm Pak 42	1462
76.2mm Pak 36 (r)	560
88mm Pak 43/41	1403
88mm Pak 434	2098
128mm Pak 80	150
7.5mm Rf.K 43	922
88mm R.Wfr. 43	3150
PWK 8 H 63	260

Railroad Guns	Number
203mm K.(E)	8
210mm K. 12N.(E)	1
280mm Kz.Br.K.(E)	2
280mm Br.KN.(E)	3
310mm K.5 Glatt(E)	2
380mm Siegfried(E)	3
800mm Dora(E)	2

Rocket Launchers	Number
150mm Nb.W. 41	5769
150mm Pz.W. 42	240
210mm Nb.W. 42	1487
280/320mm Nb.W. 41	345
300mm Nb.W. 42	380
30mm R.Wfr. 56	694
sW.G. 40	9552
sW.G. 41	4003
sWu.R. 40	1980

Army Flak Guns (to March 1945)	Number
20mm Flak 30 and 38	13,845
20mm Flakvierling 38	2140
20mm Flak Scotti and Breda	361
20mm MG 151/20 Drilling	4114
30mm Flak 103/38 Jaboschrek	149
30mm MK. 303	222
37mm Flak 18 and 36	1178
37mm Flak 43	928
37mm Flakzwilling 43	185
88mm Flak 18 and 36	1170

Luftwaffe Flak Guns (to March 1945)	Number
20mm Flak 30 and 38	121,677
37mm Flak 18 and 36	12,034
37mm Flak 43	5918
88mm Flak 18, 36 and 38	13,125
105mm Flak 38 and 39	3981
128mm Flak 40	1129

failings was that he simply did not understand the necessity for supplying armies with sufficient spare parts. General Guderian, the Inspector General of Tank Ordnance, frequently pointed out to me that if we could repair our tanks quickly, thanks to sufficient spare parts, we could have more available for battle, at a fraction of the cost, than by producing new ones. But Hitler insisted on the priority of new production, which would have had to be reduced by 20 percent if we made provision for such repairs.

On top of Speer's problems, the industrial effects of Allied bombing raids became more pronounced from 1943. It is incredible that German industry managed to increase armaments production right up until the summer of 1944, despite the strategic bombing campaign. Nevertheless, in 1944 some 20 per cent of German war production facilities were destroyed by bombing. In addition, the increasingly accurate bombing of the transport network caused enormous disruptions for industry. In the industrially vital Ruhr region, for example, air attacks cut 113 bridges and destroyed 4000 locomotives and 28,000 rail cars. By the end of 1944, the Allies had complete air superiority over Germany, so road freight traffic was subject to strafing and rocket attacks,

Area	1939	1940	1941
Aircraft	1040	4141	4452
Armour	8.4	171.6	384
Explosives	17.6	223.2	338.4
Ships	41.2	474.0	1293.6
Weapons	180.0	676.8	903.6

WEAPONS EXPENDITURE, 1939–41 (MILLION RM)

Data source: Richard Overy, War and Economy in the Third Reich

further hampering movement. In 1945, German industry finally went into meltdown, both from bombing and from Allied occupation of German territory. Speer had worked wonders, but not miracles.

Home Front Living

The employment boom in Germany between 1933 and 1939 must not mask the fact that during the lifespan of the Third Reich, the civilian population had to work longer hours for decreasing wages in real terms, while enduring increasingly tough food rationing.

During the first six years of Hitler's reign, the standard of living of a German citizen was not always as rosy as the German propaganda painted. From 1933 to c.1943, it was true that wages generally rose across society, but the levels of increase depended very much on the profession. Skilled engineers, white-collar professionals, or those working in important industries such as building, saw wage rises of up to 30 per cent, while others in consumer industries or textiles saw the contents of their pay packets grow by only single-digit percentages.

Yet the wage increases were compromised by various other factors. First, under the Third Reich workers had up to four per cent more tax deductions made from their wage packets. Moreover, working hours were progressively extended. In 1933, the average working week in Germany was 43 hours, but by 1937 that week had increased to 47 hours. Such changes could be made abruptly – in 1938, for example, lead and zinc miners had one-and-a-half hours added to their working day. Nor was it advisable to complain – an act that the much-feared local

Gestapo might see as tantamount to social rebellion.

Workers' control over their own destinies could also be affected by Nazi industrial conscription policies. Known as *Dienstverpflichtung*, 'civil conscription' was used to recruit workers forcibly for key industrial projects. Some 450,000 workers, for example, were drafted before 1939 to work on the West Wall defences, and there were more than 500,000 civil conscription orders given out in September 1939 alone. By January 1941, there were 1.4 million civilian conscripts in service, but sensing the

RATIONING, 1939

Item	Allowance per Person*
Meat	500g (18oz) per week
Butter	125g (4.4oz) per week
Margarine	100g (3.5oz) per week
Sugar	250g (9oz) per week
Cheese	62.5g (2.2oz) per week
Eggs	1 per week
Clothing	100 points per year

(Examples of clothing 'costs' – Dress: 40 points; Woman's Suit: 45 points; Man's Suit: 60 points)

* Food allowance could be increased for those in heavy manual work, and special increases were implemented during Christmas week.

PRICES OF KEY FOODSTUFFS, 1932–38 (PRICES IN *PFENNIGE*)

Foodstuff	1932	1933	1934	1935	1936	1937	1938
Eggs (each)	9.5	10.2	10.7	11	11	11.3	12
Milk (litre)	15.9	15.4	16.9	16.5	16.9	17.1	17.1
Chicken (kg)	197	190	198	219	263	253	250
Beef (kg)	147	143	146	158	165	167	167

unpopularity of the policy, the Nazis thereafter reduced conscription levels, no doubt helped by the influx of foreign labour.

War conditions

War brought huge changes in the living experience of German workers. For one thing, between 1939 and 1945 the total native German civilian workforce declined by more than 10 million, the effect of millions of Germany's men being siphoned off to uncertain futures in military service. The gap was plugged in some measure by foreign forced labour, which also had the effect of depressing German wages and giving indigenous workers less influence in the work marketplace.

What forced labour couldn't prevent, however, was the slow, inexorable rise in working hours as fewer German workers attempted to achieve more productivity. By the later months of World War II, the typical working week in Germany was anywhere between 60 and

80 hours as standard. Furthermore, many workers were attempting to meet this demand under the horrors of Allied bombing.

In major industrial areas, workers' housing often clustered around the very factories and plants that were the targets for the Allied bombers, with predictable results. In total, more than one million Germans were either killed or wounded by the air raids. In addition, some 1.9 million homes were destroyed and 4.9 million people were evacuated from vulnerable target areas.

Naturally, the effects of bombing impacted on workplace attendance, either through the direct killing or wounding of the workers, or through the sheer disruption to travel and home life. During 1944, the average German factory could expect around 23 per cent absenteeism every day, a situation that stretched out the working week of those who could

make it. Richard Overy points out that 'In Mainz alarms were in force for a total of 540 hours in 1944, the equivalent of five or six weeks work' (Overy, 1996).

Rationing and consumption

For much of the 1930s and many of the war years, Germany was better provisioned than many of the other European nations. Partly this was because of efficient agriculture but also because of food acquisitions from the conquered territories. The stripping of the Netherlands' cattle in late 1944, for example, helped stem a meat crisis back at home, while leaving the Dutch in appalling starvation conditions.

The pre-war years were largely a time of plenty in Germany, at least when compared to the terrible austerity of the Great Depression era. Richard Grunberger points out that 'Between 1932, the last year of the

GERMAN CIVILIAN WORKFORCE, 1939–45 (MILLIONS)

May 1939	39.1
May 1940	34.8
May 1941	33.1
May 1942	31.3
May 1943	30.3
May 1944	28.9
May 1945	28.4

Weimar Republic, and 1938 – Nazism's last full peacetime year – the turnover of food in Germany increased by one sixth, that of clothing and textiles by over a quarter, and that of furniture and household goods by a good half' (Grunberger, 2005). This picture of increasing abundance requires some qualification. In 1938, rationing was introduced, but the German people continued to do fairly well in terms of provisions, even into the war years. Between 1939 and 1941, for example, the daily calorific value of rationed foods actually went up from 2435 to 2445 calories. Yet not all foodstuffs were equally accessible. Meat supplies were volatile, with the 1939 allowance of 500g (18oz) per week cut to 300g (10.5oz) in 1942, then 250g (8.7oz) in 1943. Potato rationing varied between 2 and 5kg (4.4 and 11lb) per week, making potatoes a vital food resource for an increasingly hungry population. Of course, a citizen could supplement the official rations with foods acquired from the black market.

Austerity and starvation

In the final months of the war, the full hardships of defeat began to inflict themselves on the German people. The calorific value of the total ration dropped to around 1500 calories by December 1944, below the recommended minimum for an adult. Bombing also destroyed food stores, making the hunt for something to eat a daily act of survival. The depths to which the Reich had plunged were revealed in the Allied occupation, as Michael Burleigh describes: 'Children lacked food, and were below their normal height and weight, while even

in later 1946 one hundred thousand people in Hamburg exhibited the physical effects of malnutrition…'

(Michael Burleigh, 2000). Ultimately, Hitler's people paid a hard price for the policies of their leader.

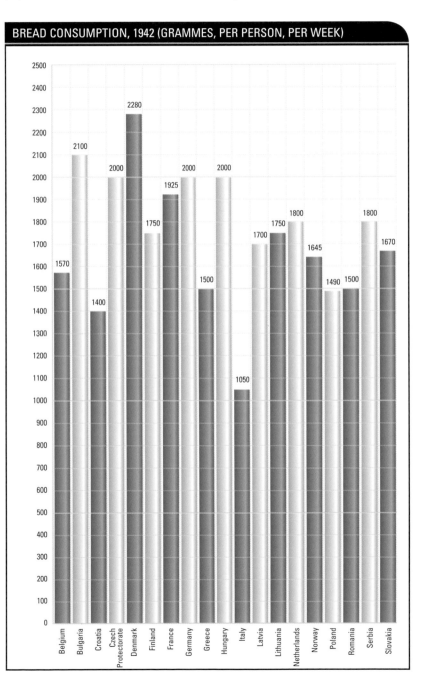

BREAD CONSUMPTION, 1942 (GRAMMES, PER PERSON, PER WEEK)

CHAPTER 4

Politics and Leadership

The government of the Third Reich is not an easily accessible entity to study, and historical debate over the exact nature of the Nazi state remains lively. On the one hand, there are historians who see the Third Reich as centrally controlled by Hitler's territorial, racial and political programme. On the other, some historians argue that while Hitler's manipulation was of course vital, the arcane nature of German government between 1933 and 1945 meant that policy was more chaotic, dispersed amongst multiple agencies.

What is certain is that Hitler did not create a unified hierarchical government. Instead he formed state and Party organizations in which competition between rival, overlapping ministries and personalities was dominant. The result was a Byzantine system of decision-making that ultimately did not help Germany in sustaining its expansion then defence of the Reich.

Hitler gathers with *Wehrmacht* generals in an operations room. As the war progressed, Hitler became increasingly involved in the day-to-day management of German forces, often undermining the authority of his most competent generals.

The Party and the State

The government of the Third Reich is confusing because it essentially existed on two parallel levels – Party government and state government. The tensions between these two strata were never fully reconciled.

As we have seen, one of the seminal changes Hitler brought to German government was to concentrate all political power in the hands of one party, the NSDAP. The cabinets of the Weimar Republic were distinctly coalition affairs, the various ministries being divided between contrasting party and non-political groupings. In the Papen cabinet of 1932, for example, nine of the ministries (Foreign, Finance, Economics, Defence, Posts, Transport, Labour and two without portfolio) were under non-party politicians, while the remainder belonged to the *Deutschnationale Volkspartei* (DNVP). (Papen himself was non-party from 3 June 1932.) The subsequent Schleicher cabinet was similar in composition, although the *Osthilfe* post (*Osthilfe* means 'Help for the East', and referred to German subsidies for areas east of the Elbe River) moved into the hands of a *Christliches Landvolk* (Christian Agrarian Party) member.

Hitler's ministers

The first Hitler cabinet, assembled in 1933, remained a politically composite affair. Of the cabinet members, only Göring, Wilhelm Frick and Hitler were NSDAP members, the remainder being mostly continuity members from the previous Schleicher cabinet. Yet in the Reich government of 1 January 1936, there were 18 ministers (Hitler significantly expanded the number of ministries and minsters without portfolio – see below), and of these eight were NSDAP members; by September 1939, of 21 ministers, all but four were Party members. Combined with the fact that opposition parties no longer existed, and that elections were no

PAPEN CABINET, 1932	
Official	*Position*
Franz von Papen (non-party)	Chancellor
Franz Gürtner (DNVP)	Justice Minister
Hermann Warmbold (non-party)	Economics Minister
Hugo Schäffer (non-party)	Labour Minister
Johann Ludwig von Krosigk (non-party)	Finance Minister
Johannes Popitz + Franz Bracht (non-party)	Ministers Without Portfolio
Constantin Freiherr von Neurath (non-party)	Foreign Minister
Kurt von Schleicher (non-party)	Defence Minister
Magnus Freiherr von Braun (DNVP)	Food Minister
Magnus Freiherr von Braun (DNVP)	*Osthilfe*
Paul Freiherr Eltz von Rübenbach (non-party)	Posts Minister, Transport Minister
Wilhelm Freiherr von Gayl (DNVP)	Interior Minister

SCHLEICHER CABINET, 1932–33	
Official	*Position*
Kurt von Schleicher (non-party)	Chancellor
Franz Bracht (non-party)	Interior Minister
Franz Gürtner (DNVP)	Justice Minister
Friedrich Syrup (non-party)	Labour Minister
Hermann Warmbold (non-party)	Economics Minister
Johann Ludwig von Krosigk (non-party)	Finance Minister
Johannes Popitz (non-party)	Minister Without Portfolio
Constantin Freiherr von Neurath (non-party)	Foreign Minister
Kurt von Schleicher (non-party)	Defence Minister
Magnus Freiherr von Braun (DNVP)	Food Minister
Günther Gereke (*Christliches Landvolk*)	*Osthilfe*
Paul Freiherr Eltz von Rübenbach (non-party)	Posts and Transport Minister

longer held, it was clear by this time that Germany was living under a political dictatorship.

The Nazi membership

During the Third Reich, the Nazi Party was the only permitted political entity. Culturally, its leanings were pro-youth (its membership was heavily concentrated in the 18–40 age bracket) and pro-worker, although its pragmatism also allowed it to cooperate with the older ruling classes where necessary.

Membership of the Nazi Party grew fairly steadily from the 1920s to the mid-1930s, then accelerated distinctly from 1935 right until the very end of the war. In 1923, for example, NSDAP membership sat at a respectable 55,287 people, but by 1933 that figure had climbed to 849,000. Two years later, and membership was 2,493,000, and in the opening year of the war it grew to 5,339,567. In the last year of the war, by which time we would expect the population to be thoroughly disillusioned with Nazi politics, the membership stood at eight million plus.

Rapid growth

The growth of Nazi membership is, of course, not explained purely by the people's enthusiasm for National Socialism, although that certainly accounts for much of the membership before 1941. Nor, once unpacked, are the figures quite as impressive as they might initially seem, bearing in mind that the 1939 German population was around 80 million people. For a start, the figures are cumulative – once you were a Party member, it was

HITLER'S CABINET, 30 JANUARY 1933	
Official	*Position*
Adolf Hitler (NSDAP)	Chancellor
Alfred Hugenberg (DNVP)	Economics, Food and Agriculture Minister
Franz Gürtner (DNVP)	Justice Minister
Günther Gereke (*Christliches Landvolk*)	Employment Minister
Hermann Göring (NSDAP)	Minister Without Portfolio
Johann Ludwig von Krosigk (non-party)	Finance Minister
Constantin Freiherr von Neurath (non-party)	Foreign Minister
Paul Freiherr Eltz von Rübenbach (non-party)	Posts and Transport Minister
Franz Seldte (non-party)	Labour Minister
Franz von Papen (non-party)	Vice-Chancellor and Reich Commissioner for Prussia
Werner von Blomberg (non-party)	Defence Minister
Wilhelm Frick (NSDAP)	Interior Minister

GOVERNMENT OFFICIALS IN THE NAZI PARTY, 1936	
Individual	*Position/Office*
Hitler, Adolf	*Führer* and Reich Chancellor
Hess, Rudolf	Deputy *Führer*
Bormann, Martin	Staff of *Führer*'s Deputy
Schwarz, Franz	Treasurer
Buch, Walter	Supreme Party Court
Grimm, W.	Supreme Party Court
Frick, Wilhelm	Leader of *Reichstag* Delegation
Ley, Robert	German Labour Front; Political Organizations (Cadres)
Goebbels, Joseph	Head of Propaganda
Dietrich, Otto	Press Chief
Amann, Max	*Reichsleiter*, Press
Bouhler, Philipp	Nazi Literature
Darré, Walther	Agrarian Policy; Reich Agriculture Minister; Reich Peasant Leader
Frank, Hans	Reich Law Officer
Rosenberg, Alfred	Foreign Policy Office
von Epp, Franz	Head of Colonial Office
von Schirach, Baldur	Youth Leader
Lutz, Victor	SA
Hierl, Konstantin	Reich Labour Service
Hühnlein, A.	National Socialist Motor Corps
Himmler, Heinrich	Reich Leader SS and Head of German Police

inadvisable to revoke membership. Second, membership became compulsory for many vocations, such as the civil service (see below), so there were certainly a large number of opportunistic members simply looking to advance their careers. Several other paramilitary military organizations also stipulated or encouraged Nazi credentials.

STRUCTURE OF THE NSDAP LEADERSHIP CORPS, FROM 1933

Section	Translation
Führer	Leader
Reichsleiter and Main Office	Reich Leaders
Landesinspekteure	Regional Inspectors
Gauleiter and Staff Officers	District Leaders
Kreisleiter and Staff Officers	County Leaders
Ortsgruppenleiter and Staff Officers	Local Group Leaders
Zellenleiter and Staff Officers	Cell Leaders
Blockwarte and Staff Officers	Block Wardens

The *Wehrmacht*, by contrast, actually declared itself a non-party organization, and during the 1930s soldiers technically had to resign their Party membership if they joined the non-SS armed forces. This restriction fell out of use by the war years, however, leaving serving soldiers, sailors and airmen free to join the NSDAP.

Controlling government
The government of the Third Reich was a truly Byzantine affair, and one not open to ready understanding. In essence, all the previous state structures of government remained in place, working alongside, or often competing against, new layers of Party officials imposed across the country. Hitler clearly did not want the state authorities operating independently of his wishes – at a Party Congress in September 1934, Hitler told Party officials that 'the state does not control us, we control the state'. For this reason, civil service appointments and promotions came under Nazi control. Jewish civil servants were purged in the Restoration of the Professional Civil Service law in April 1933, and in 1935, Rudolf Hess, Deputy *Führer* and Reich

Minister Without Portfolio, was given authority to vet all civil service appointments and promotions. By 1939, Nazi Party membership was a compulsory element for all civil service offices.

A further layer of Party influence came in the form of Martin Bormann, chief of staff and secretary to Rudolf Hess from 1933. Bormann oversaw the creation of two new Party agencies – the Department for Internal Party Affairs, and the Department for Affairs of State. While the former was concerned with ideological discipline and coordination within the Nazi Party, the latter was focused on extending Party doctrine over state administration. Increasingly, the state, at least at the level of significant policy, was under deeper Nazi control, particularly in areas such as race relations and foreign relations. Note that the NSDAP per se, in William Carr's words, 'exercised no specific governmental function in the Third Reich' (Carr, 1978, p. 44). Rather, Nazi influence came from the appointment of NSDAP members to specific state positions, in which they could exert their influence.

Party structure
Although there was, as we shall see, a certain degree of chaos in Nazi government, the NSDAP did have a fairly clear administrative structure that extended from the *Führer* at the top of the tree right down to the ordinary members at the roots. Hitler held the supreme position of undisputed dictator, below which came the *Reichsleitung der NSDAP* (Reich Leadership of the NSDAP). This second level of authority was composed essentially of *Reichsleiter* (Reich Leaders) – executive ministers and departmental chiefs. From here authority devolved down to the *Landesinspekteur* (Regional Inspector), an official with Party responsibility for several *Gaue* (Districts). (Initially there were nine *Landesinspekteure*, each overseeing four *Gaue*.) Each *Gau* was governed by a *Gauleiter* (District Leader), a position that remained influential throughout the Third Reich.

Below the *Gaue* and *Gauleiter* were the various strata of local government. The *Kreis* was the next

MEMBERSHIP OF THE NSDAP, 1923–45

Date	Number
1923	55,287
1928	96,918
1930	129,563
1933	849,000
1935	2,493,890
1937	2,793,890
1938	4,985,400
1939	5,339,567
1942	7,100,000
1943	7,600,000
1945	8,000,000+

administrative unit down, akin to a local council, and this was controlled by a *Kreisleiter* (County Leader). Next came the *Ortsgruppenleiter* (Local Group Leader), overseer of an *Ortsgruppe* (Local Group) town section, then the *Zellenleiter* (Cell Leader), responsible for a specific area of housing. Finally, the *Blockwart* (Block Warden) took charge of a specific facility or building, while below him were the ordinary Party members filling out the rank and file.

Decline of Party influence

In balance to this picture of order, we also have to acknowledge that the Nazi Party was, increasingly, itself an organization fractured by the competing interests and partisan agendas. The NSDAP was divided between several distinct and powerful agencies, such as the Hitler Youth and the SS, and they did not always sing from the same hymn sheet.

Also, once Hitler was in power he largely lost interest in the minutiae of NSDAP politics (note that there were no more cabinet meetings from 1938), being far more committed to prosecuting his military and racial agendas (see 'The *Führer* as Leader' below), the former fulfilled by the *Wehrmacht* and the latter by the SS, which eventually made Himmler the second most powerful individual in the Third Reich.

Bormann's influence within the Nazi Party increased dramatically in 1941, when Hess shocked the German establishment with his baffling flight to Britain, apparently to propose a peace plan for the two

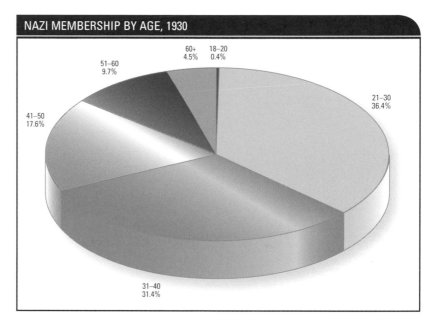

NAZI MEMBERSHIP BY AGE, 1930

- 60+ 4.5%
- 18–20 0.4%
- 51–60 9.7%
- 21–30 36.4%
- 41–50 17.6%
- 31–40 31.4%

countries. Hitler abolished the post of Deputy *Führer* and instead created the *Parteikanzlei* (Party Chancellery). Directed by Bormann, the office was responsible for overseeing all Party affairs. The position was one of genuine power, as Bormann in effect began to control access to Hitler, who had the final say over all important legislation.

While it is true that the Third Reich was a Nazi state – Hitler would have been unable to achieve his racial policies or many of his military ambitions without some ideological bedrock – the fact remains that the Nazi Party was just one element, albeit an important one, of an arcane governmental structure, which we shall now explore.

NAZI PARTY MANUAL STATEMENT CONCERNING THE AUTHORITY OF HITLER

'By the authority of the law concerning the Chief of State of the German Reich, dated 1 August 1934, the office of the Reich President has been combined with that of the Reich Chancellery. Consequently, the powers previously possessed by the Reich President were transferred to the Führer, Adolf Hitler. Through this law, the government of Party and State has been combined in one hand. By desire of the Führer, a plebiscite was conducted on this law on 19 August 1934. On this day, the German people chose Adolf Hitler to be their sole leader. He is responsible only to his conscience and to the German nation.'

Ministries and Command Structure

The various ministries of the Third Reich existed in a combative political environment, each trying to gain access to the Führer's *authority, often in direct competition with overlapping agencies and envoys.*

The historian W. Petwaidic published in 1946 a study of the German catastrophe in World War II. The title was *Die autoritäre Anarchie: Streiflichter des deutschen Zusammenbruchs* ('The Authoritarian Anarchy: Highlights of the German Collapse'). The main title of the book is an apt description of the government of the Third Reich, upon which historian William Carr has elaborated:

The popular picture of the Third Reich as a monolithic unit with all parts of the well-oiled machine responsive to the Führer's will has long been discredited by historians. A more exact parallel would be with feudal society, where vassals great and small struggled endlessly with each other and with their overlords to establish themselves as the king's chief adviser.

(Carr, 1978)

Carr's description is indeed an accurate one, and sums up the experience of the Nazi Party ministries and command structure. What we have in the Third Reich is not a coherent dictatorship unifying government from the top, but large competing blocs of special interests – the SS, SD, *Gestapo*, the Army, industry, the civil service, state legislatures, big business, occupation forces – all fighting for the their own interests and the ear of the *Führer*. Hitler's personal handling of government is explored in greater depth in the next section, but here we shall look at the critical sub-units of Nazi government, and some of the issues they faced in having their voices heard.

Decision-making

Taking a top-down perspective on the Nazi government in 1941, at the summit we had, as already noted, Hitler in his role as *Führer*. Surrounding Hitler, and largely controlling access to him, was the *Führerkanzlei* (*Führer* Chancellery), his private Berlin offices controlled by Philipp Bouhler, and the *Parteikanzlei* under Bormann. Note also that relations between Hitler's personal offices could be less than cordial, introducing an additional friction to the policy-making process at the highest level. Beneath Hitler's primary offices were the various ministries and departments concerned with running the Reich, such as Propaganda, Foreign Policy, Law, Finance, Health and Race.

The impression we have of policy-making under Hitler is something akin to the grains of sand running through an hourglass, each vying to push through a narrow funnel of decision-making. Generally, the ministries, departments and civil service offices

NAZI GOVERNMENT AND KEY MINISTRIES, 1 SEPTEMBER 1936	
Position/Ministry	*Official*
Führer & Chancellor	Adolf Hitler
Agriculture	Walther Darré
Aviation	Hermann Göring
Defence	Werner von Blomberg
Economics	Walther Funk
Finance	Johann Ludwig von Krosigk
Foreign Affairs	Constantin Freiherr von Neurath
Interior	Wilhelm Frick
Justice	Franz Gürtner
Labour	Franz Seldte
Post and Communication	Paul Freiherr Eltz von Rübenbach
Public Enlightenment and Propaganda	Joseph Goebbels
Religion	Hans Kerrl
Science, Education and Culture	Bernhard Rust

NAZI GOVERNMENT AND KEY MINISTRIES, SEPTEMBER 1943–MAY 1945

Position/Ministry	Sep 1943	Apr 1945	May 1945
Führer & Chancellor	Adolf Hitler	Adolf Hitler	Karl Dönitz
Agriculture	Herbert Backe	Herbert Backe	Herbert Backe
Armaments and Munitions	Albert Speer	Albert Speer	Karl Saur
Aviation	Hermann Göring	Hermann Göring	–
Defence	–	–	Karl Dönitz
Eastern Occupied Territories	Alfred Rosenberg	Alfred Rosenberg	–
Economics	Walther Funk	Walther Funk	Walther Funk
Finance	Johann Ludwig von Krosigk	Johann Ludwig von Krosigk	Johann Ludwig von Krosigk
Foreign Affairs	Joachim von Ribbentrop	Joachim von Ribbentrop	Arthur Seyss-Inquart
Interior	Heinrich Himmler	Heinrich Himmler	Paul Giesler
Justice	Otto Thierack	Otto Thierack	Otto Thierack
Labour	Franz Seldte	Franz Seldte	Theodor Hupfauer
Post and Communication	Wilhelm Ohnesorge	Wilhelm Ohnesorge	Wilhelm Ohnesorge
Public Enlightenment and Propaganda	Joseph Goebbels	Werner Naumann	Werner Naumann
Religion	Hermann Muhs	Hermann Muhs	Hermann Muhs
Science, Education and Culture	Bernhard Rust	Bernhard Rust	Bernhard Rust

responded to general directives, often vaguely formulated, from Hitler, and went away and created specific policies, or often multiple policies from different agencies. The policies were then funnelled back through to Hitler for final approval.

Competition

This description of Nazi government sounds relatively predictable, but it doesn't quite do justice to the convoluted threads of German governance. The biggest confusion by far was the way that multiple agencies had overlapping agendas and responsibilities, yet still worked largely independently of one another. For example, as we saw in earlier chapters, Göring became responsible for the Four-Year Plan in 1936, supplanting Hjalmar Schacht as the most influential figure in the Reich's fiscal policy. Yet as the war progressed, new agencies arose that

had control over similar portions of the economic pie. While Göring's Four-Year Plan and Schacht's former Economic Office continued, alongside them arose the Army Economics and Armaments Office (General Georg Thomas), then the Ministry of Armaments and War Production (Fritz Todt/Albert Speer). In March 1942, furthermore, Fritz Sauckel was appointed *Generalbevollmächtigter für den Arbeitseinsatz* (General Plenipotentiary for Labour Deployment), with a theoretical control over the applications of German labour. Ultimately, there were five different agencies attempting to design armaments policy, with no clear leadership from above to determine who had jurisdiction in common issues.

Personalities and ministries

Similar problems existed in many other areas of the Nazi government.

Hitler would sometimes appoint a special envoy with policy responsibilites without telling a rival agency about the new position. At the more regional level, local *Gauleiter* sought to control state resources and functions, attempting to create their own fiefdoms, using their Nazi affiliations to overrule competing state bodies. Furthermore, the Third Reich was replete with powerful, vain, complicated and charismatic leaders, and they added their own personal agendas to the mix. It is worth looking more closely at some of the key ministries of the Third Reich, and their leaders, to gain deeper insight into the priorities and workings of the Nazi government.

The Propaganda Ministry under Joseph Goebbels (Minister for Public Enlightenment and Propaganda) had one of the clearest and most self-sufficient remits of all the Third Reich offices. Its primary objectives were promoting National Socialist values, defining and eulogizing the Aryan race, attacking Judaism in all its cultural and social forms and, above all, promoting allegiance to the *Führer*. During the war, Goebbels also set his mind to controlling the flow of public information through the press, cinema, posters, leaflets and radio, emphasizing victories and heroic defences and downplaying defeats and setbacks. Goebbels was also a talented writer of both political pamphlets and speeches.

His ministry grew in power on the back of superb stage management during the 1920s and 1930s, being particularly remembered for the great rallies held at Nuremberg. By the early days of World War II, Goebbels headed a staff including more than 800 employees, all striving to manage the public's perception of events.

Göring and Ribbentrop

Hermann Göring was another individual central to German policy-making, at least during the 1930s and early 1940s. As well as being Plenipotentiary for the Four-Year

GLOSSARY OF GOVERNMENT TERMS

Abbreviation	German	Translation
Abt.	Abteilung	Unit, battery, battalion, section, branch, work group, detachment
Abt. Chef	Abteilung chef	Section chief
AGF	Arbeitsgauführer	Provincial Labour Leader
AkDR	Akademie für Deutsches Recht	Academy for German Law
ANST	Arbeitsgemeinschaft Nationalsozialistischer Studentinnen	Work Organization of National Socialist Students
AO	Auslandsorganisation (der NSDAP)	Foreign Organization (of the NSDAP)
A.W.A.	Allgemeines Wehrmachtamt	General Armed Forces Office
bayer.	Bayerische	From or pertaining to the German state of Bavaria; Bavarian
Bev.	Bevollmächtigter	Plenipotentiary
Bevollm.	Bevollmächtigter	Plenipotentiary
Bez.	Bezirk	District
BL.	Bereitschaftsleiter	Political Leader of the NSDAP
Bz.	Bezirk	District
CdZ	Chef der Zivilverwaltung	Head of the Civilian Administration – occupied territory
dant.	deutschnational	German national
DRB	Deutsche Reichsbahn	German National Railway
D.R.P.u.A.P.	Deutsches Reichs-Patent und Ausländische Patente	German Patent and Foreign Patents
E	Entwicklung	Development
EL	Einsatzleiter	Action Leader
f.	für	for
F. Oa.	Führer Oberabschnitt	Commander of an SS or SA region
Fü. Lehrg.	Führer Lehrgang	Leadership Training
FuR	Führer und Reichskanzler	Leader and Reich Chancellor

Abbreviation	German	Translation
Gaul.	Gauleiter	NSDAP District Leader
Gaultr.	Gauleiter	NSDAP District Leader
Gauleit.	Gauleitung	NSDAP District Leadership
GauOVwR.	Gauoberverwaltungsrat	District Senior Administrative Official
Gauprop.Leit.	Gaupropagandaleitung	District Propaganda Leadership
Gauramt.	Gaurechtsamt	District Legal Department
GauVwAmtm.	Gau-Verwaltungsamtmann	District Administrative Employee
GAF	Generalarbeitsführer	General Work Leader
GBA	Generalbevollmächtigter für den Arbeitseinsatz	General Plenipotentiary for Labour Deployment
Ge.Ka.Do.S.	Geheime Kommandosach	Top Secret
GG	Generalgouvernement	The General Government of occupied Poland
g.K.	Geheime Kommandosach	Top Secret
g.Kdos.	Geheime Kommandosach	Top Secret
GKS	Geheime Kommandosach	Top Secret
GL	Gauleiter	District Leader
HAL	Hauptarbeitsleiter	Senior Labour Leader
HBefl.	Hauptbefehlsleiter	Senior Command Leader
HBL	Hauptbereitschaftsleiter	Senior Political Leader
HEL	Haupteinsatzleiter	Senior Action Leader
HGL	Hauptgemeinschaftsleiter	Senior Association Leader
I.	Inspektor; Inspekteur	Inspector
In.	Inspektionen	Inspectorate
KL	Kreisleiter	County Leader
KLtr.	Kreisleiter	County Leader
Krsltr.	Kreisleiter	County Leader
Kr.Walt.	Kreiswaltung	County Administration
Landw.	Landwirtschaft	Agriculture
Mil. Bef.	Militär Befehlshaber	Military Commander
Mil. Verw.	Militär Verwaltung	Military administration

Plan, he was also Aviation Minister, responsible for the *Luftwaffe* and civil aviation. Göring had numerous powerful business interests, and was also an approving authority behind Hitler's racial policies, but his failure to make good on his boast that he would defeat the Royal Air Force in 1940 led to a loss of both personal vitality and authority.

The conduct of foreign policy provides a classic example of the convoluted Third Reich politics. Foreign policy was an issue central to Hitler's thinking, and on taking power he quickly became irritated by what he saw as the conservatism of the existing Foreign Office, headed by Constantin Freiherr von Neurath. In response, later in 1933 he created the

Dienststelle Ribbentrop (Ribbentrop Bureau), headed by the largely unliked but fiercely loyal Joachim von Ribbentrop. Ribbentrop's office gained in power, and in 1938 the bureau was abolished and Ribbentrop became Reich Minister for Foreign Affairs, Neurath having been sacked. Ribbentrop was central to Germany's pre-war diplomacy,

Abbreviation	German	Translation
Min.Dir.	Ministerialdirektor	Ministerial Director; a senior civil service official; Department head in a ministry
Min. Dir.	Ministerial Dirigent	Ministerial Director
Min.Präs.	Ministerpräsident	Minister-President
Min.Rat	Ministerialrat	Head of a ministry section
NS	Nationalsozialistische	National Socialist
NSDAP	Nationalsozialistische Deutsche Arbeiterpartei	NS German Workers' Party – Nazi Party
OAL	Oberarbeitsleiter	Senior Labour Leader
OGL	Obergemeinschaftsleiter	Municipal Group Leader
Promi.	Propagandaministerium	Propaganda Ministry
RA	Reichsamt	Reich Department
RAD	Reichsarbeitsdienst	Reich Labour Service
RAM	Reichsaußenminister	Reich Foreign Minister
RDFDV	Reichskommissar für die Festigung deutschen Volkstums	Reich Commissioner for the Strengthening of the German Nation
RdL	Reichsminister der Luftfahrt	Reich Minister of Air Traffic
RFM	Reichsfinanzministerium	Reich Finance Ministry
RG	Reichsgau	NSDAP administrative region, usually in annexed areas
RKF	Reichskommissar für die Festigung deutschen Volkstums	Reich Commissioner for the Strengthening of the German Nation
RKFDV	Reichskommissar für die Festigung deutschen Volkstums	Reich Commissioner for the Strengthening of the German Nation
RL	Reichsleitung	Reich leadership
RL	Reichsleiter	Reich Leader
R.L.	Reichsleiter	Reich Leader
Rl.	Reichsleitung	Reich Leadership
RLM	Reichsluftfahrtministerium	Ministry of Aviation

Abbreviation	German	Translation
RLP	Reichsleiter für die Presse	Reich Leader for the Press
RM	Reichsmarschall	Marshal of the Reich
R. Mi.	Reichsminister	Cabinet Minister
Rm.f.Rü.u.Kr.Prod.	Reichministerium für Rüstung und Kriegsproduktion	Reich Ministry for Armaments and War Production
RMfVuP.	Reichsminister(ium) für Volksaufklärung und Propaganda	Reich Minister [Ministry] for Public Enlightenment and Propaganda
RMVP	Reichsministerium für Volksaufklärung und Propaganda	Reich Ministry for Public Enlightenment and Propaganda
RPA	Rassenpolitisches Amt der NSDAP	Racial Politics Department of the NSDAP
RPC	Reichspressechef	Reich Press Chief
RPL	Reichspropagandaleitung	Reich Propaganda Leadership
R.P.T.	Reichsparteitag	Reich Party Day
Rst.	Reichsstatthalter	Reich Governor
R. st.	Reichsstatthalter	Reich Governor
St. Sek.	Staatsekretär	Under-secretary in a department of provincial government
stv.	stellvertretend	deputy
V.	Verwaltung	Administration
VB	Völkischer Beobachter	*Popular Observer* newspaper
VDA	Volksbund für das Deutschtum im Ausland	People's Association, for Germans living in foreign countries
Verw.	Verwaltung	Administration
WE.	Weltanschauung	world view or outlook
WE-F.	weltanschaulicher Führer	Political Science Leader
Z.	Zivilbeauftragter	Civil Commissioner or Representative

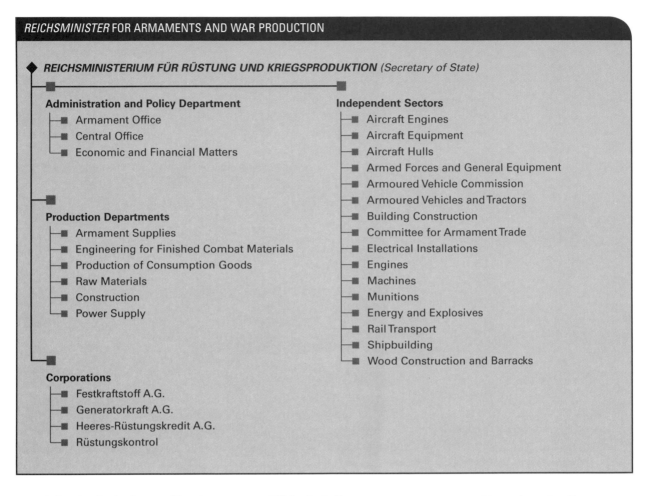

REICHSMINISTER FOR ARMAMENTS AND WAR PRODUCTION

◆ **REICHSMINISTERIUM FÜR RÜSTUNG UND KRIEGSPRODUKTION** (Secretary of State)

Administration and Policy Department
- Armament Office
- Central Office
- Economic and Financial Matters

Production Departments
- Armament Supplies
- Engineering for Finished Combat Materials
- Production of Consumption Goods
- Raw Materials
- Construction
- Power Supply

Corporations
- Festkraftstoff A.G.
- Generatorkraft A.G.
- Heeres-Rüstungskredit A.G.
- Rüstungskontrol

Independent Sectors
- Aircraft Engines
- Aircraft Equipment
- Aircraft Hulls
- Armed Forces and General Equipment
- Armoured Vehicle Commission
- Armoured Vehicles and Tractors
- Building Construction
- Committee for Armament Trade
- Electrical Installations
- Engines
- Machines
- Munitions
- Energy and Explosives
- Rail Transport
- Shipbuilding
- Wood Construction and Barracks

negotiating the Anglo-German Naval Agreement in June 1935, and signing the German-Soviet alliance in August and September 1939.

Ribbentrop retained his post as Foreign Minister for the rest of the war, but his influence declined as delicate foreign diplomacy became less relevant under the conditions of total war. Nor was he the only foreign policy presence in Hitler's government. Alfred Rosenberg, for example, was appointed the Reich Minister for the Eastern Occupied Territories in July 1941, with responsibilities including Germanization policies, deportations, the extermination of Jews and the acquisition of slave labour.

Add to this mix various Reich protectorates, commissars and plenipotentiaries, NSDAP foreign agencies, plus the jurisdictions of the SS in occupied lands, and we see that foreign policy was dispersed amongst a wide range of bodies. Yet such was Hitler's clarity on racial and foreign mattters, that even amongst such diverse organizations there appears to have been something approaching coherent policy, otherwise the Holocaust would scarcely have been possible.

Financial matters, as we have seen, under the Reich were similarly scattered, although the two primary ministerial figures were Walther Funk, the Minister of Economics, and Johann Ludwig von Krosigk, the Finance Minister. Krosigk was integral to financing German rearmament during the 1930s; Funk was Schacht's replacement after the latter's dismissal in 1938, and he went on to take additional economic roles as *Reichsbank* president and also as Plenipotentiary for the War Economy.

Power offices

In terms of sheer power, however, Heinrich Himmler, head of the SS and the Interior Minister from 1943, had no superiors. We shall explore Himmler's state and Party apparatuses more fully in the next chapter, but he not only had ultimate jurisdiction over the entire German security and police service, but he also was the primary figure behind the implementation of Hitler's racial policy (including the running of the concentration camps) and was the commander of his very own combat army, the *Waffen-SS*. If anything, Himmler's SS represents the purest continuity of Party identity, and its unilateral powers became so great that it almost formed an entire state apparatus within itself.

Although names such as Göring, Speer, Rosenberg, Ribbentrop and Funk would become well known to later history, there were other ministers in the Third Reich who achieved much less notoriety. The Third Reich expanded the number of ministerial posts significantly when compared with the Weimar government, particularly through establishing ministries with a cultural bias, such as Religion and Science,

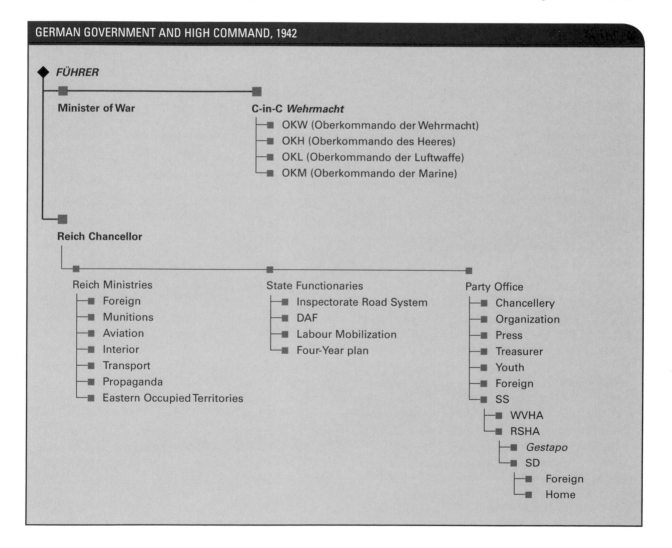

GERMAN GOVERNMENT AND HIGH COMMAND, 1942

- ◆ *FÜHRER*
  - **Minister of War**
  - **C-in-C** *Wehrmacht*
    - OKW (Oberkommando der Wehrmacht)
    - OKH (Oberkommando des Heeres)
    - OKL (Oberkommando der Luftwaffe)
    - OKM (Oberkommando der Marine)
  - **Reich Chancellor**
    - Reich Ministries
      - Foreign
      - Munitions
      - Aviation
      - Interior
      - Transport
      - Propaganda
      - Eastern Occupied Territories
    - State Functionaries
      - Inspectorate Road System
      - DAF
      - Labour Mobilization
      - Four-Year plan
    - Party Office
      - Chancellery
      - Organization
      - Press
      - Treasurer
      - Youth
      - Foreign
      - SS
        - WVHA
        - RSHA
          - *Gestapo*
          - SD
            - Foreign
            - Home

Education and Culture. The former belonged to Hermann Muhs, officially entitled the *Minister für Kirchenfragen* (Minister for Church Affairs), while the latter was run by Bernhard Rust, a former schoolteacher and NSDAP *Gauleiter* for Hannover-Braunschweig who governed Nazi education until 1945.

Nazi endgame
It is one of the ironies of Third Reich history that although the influence of the NSDAP in a sense waned throughout much of the war, it revived somewhat as Nazi Germany neared its end in 1944/45. The *Volkssturm*, Germany's last-ditch defence, was raised directly under

Party control by Martin Bormann, the local units commanded by *Gauleiter* and *Kreisleiter*. Furthermore, Hitler relied increasingly on Party diehards to sustain his futile defence of the Reich. The July Bomb Plot of 1944 had shown, after all, that loyalty within the wider German leadership was not universally unconditional.

The Führer as Leader

Hitler's leadership was the fulcrum of Nazi government. The territorial rewards it brought between 1938 and 1942 partially masked the fact that his style of personal rule was chaotic, preferential and militarily unsound.

Otto Dietrich was appointed Press Chief of the Reich and State Secretary to the Propaganda Ministry in 1938, and thereafter gained an intimate insight into the workings of Hitler's mind. After the war, during which he had had a nervous breakdown owing to the strain of war politics, Dietrich delivered a harsh judgment on Hitler's style of leadership:

In the twelve years of his rule in Germany, Hitler produced the biggest confusion in government that has ever existed in a civilized state. During his period of government, he removed from the organization of the state all clarity of leadership. It was not all laziness or an excessive degree of tolerance which led the otherwise so energetic and forceful Hitler to tolerate this real witch's cauldron of struggles for position and conflicts over competence. It was

intentional. With this technique he systematically disorganised the upper echelons of the Reich leadership in order to develop and further his own authority until it became a despotic tyranny.

(Quoted in J. Noakes and G. Pridham, 1983)

Although Dietrich doubtless writes as someone whose experience of the Third Reich ultimately did him no

REICHSTAG CONFIRMATION OF HITLER'S POWERS, 26 APRIL 1942

'There can be no doubt, that in the present conflict, with the German people faced with a struggle for its existence or complete destruction, the Führer must have all the rights given by him that serve to further or achieve victory. Therefore – without being bound by existing legal regulations – in his role as Leader of the Nation, Supreme Commander of the Armed Forces, Head of Government and Supreme Executive Chief, as Supreme Justice and Leader of the Party, the Führer must be in a position to force with all means at his disposal every German, if necessary, whether he be regular soldier or an officer, low or high official or judge, leading or minor official of the Party, worker or employee – to fulfill his duties. In case of violation of these duties, the Führer is entitled after due thought, regardless of so-called rights, to give out appropriate punishment and remove the offender from his post, rank and position without introducing prescribed procedures.'

TEXT OF THE ENABLING ACT, 23 MARCH 1933

Law to Remedy the Distress of the People and the Nation
The Reichstag has enacted the following law, which is hereby proclaimed with the assent of the Reichsrat, it having been established that the requirements for a constitutional amendment have been fulfilled:

Article 1
In addition to the procedure prescribed by the constitution, laws of the Reich may also be enacted by the government of the Reich. This includes the laws referred to by Articles 85 Paragraph 2 and Article 87 of the constitution.

Article 2
Laws enacted by the government of the Reich may deviate from the constitution as long as they do not affect the institutions of the Reichstag and the Reichsrat. The rights of the President remain undisturbed.

Article 3
Laws enacted by the Reich government shall be issued by the Chancellor and announced in the Reich Gazette. They shall take effect on the day following the announcement, unless they prescribe a different date. Articles 68 to 77 of the Constitution do not apply to laws enacted by the Reich government.

Article 4
Treaties of the Reich with foreign states which affect matters of Reich legislation shall not require the approval of the bodies of the legislature. The government of the Reich shall issue the regulations required for the execution of such treaties.

Article 5
This law takes effect with the day of its proclamation. It loses force on 1 April 1937 or if the present Reich government is replaced by another.

favours, his perspective cuts to the heart of the Hitler paradox. On the one hand, he achieved absolute power in Germany and maintained it to the very last days of the Third Reich. On the other hand, his abilities as a practical leader appear limited, and his sense of administrative responsibility was woefully lacking at times. How did the two elements of his leadership sit side by side?

Leadership style
Hitler's style of leadership is a curious mix of quirks and abilities. His hours of work were notoriously out of sync with many of his subordinates' – he would generally rise about midday and pass a sedate few hours watching films or eating before attending to guests and meetings in the early hours of the evening. He could be extremely unpunctual, although he visited this vice mainly on Party and civilian officials, and was more scrupulous about time-keeping with military personnel.

Hitler had no love of bureaucracy and administration, although his genuinely quick intelligence still allowed him to gain expertise in a wide range of subjects, enough to keep his subordinates on their toes. Nor does it appear that Hitler was particularly decisive. Officials might emerge from a meeting with Hitler with no clear decision, just hints from the *Führer* about possible directions, leaving the official to divine Hitler's desired course of action. Yet there were times when Hitler was decisive and argumentative, particularly in his principal fields of interest – military strategy, race and foreign policy.

Military commander
As commander-in-chief of the *Oberkommando der Wehrmacht* (OKW), Hitler was the ultimate military authority in World War II. Unlike Stalin, who eventually seemed to realize his limitations and gave more strategic authority to his field commanders, Hitler's military will intruded until the very end of the war.

What we must not do is reject Hitler as a pure military novice. In fact, he had a tremendously detailed grasp of military tactics and technology, and frequently impressed his generals with his comprehension of military realities (Hitler had an extremely retentive memory). Yet

MAJOR GERMAN INTERNATIONAL TREATIES, 1922–39

Treaty	Date	Outline of Key Policies
Rapallo Treaty	April–July 1922	Mutual trade/military training assistance agreement between Germany and the USSR
Locarno Treaties	5–16 October 1925	Multiple agreements achieved by major European powers. Included: guarantee of inviolability of Germany's western border; treaties of arbitration between Germany and Belgium, France, Poland and Czechoslovakia; Germany's agreement not to attempt restructuring of its eastern boundaries
Berlin Treaty	24 April 1926	Agreement between USSR and Germany that each would maintain neutrality if attacked by a third party
German-Polish Non-Aggression Pact	26 January 1934	Agreement between Germany and Poland to refrain from armed conflict with each other for a period of 10 years
Anglo-German Naval Agreement	18 June 1935	Agreement that Germany was permitted to develop naval surface fleet 35 per cent the size of the Royal Navy, plus an equivalent submarine force
Anti-Comintern Pact	25 November 1936	Cooperative agreement between Japan and Germany to work together against the influence of the Communist International
German-Soviet Non-Aggression Pact	23 August 1939	Ten-year treaty in which Germany and USSR agreed not to engage in conflict with each other, plus maintain the commitments of the Berlin Treaty

once the war expanded to multiple fronts, it is likely that such a grasp of facts became a burden for the *Führer*. From 1942 the German prosecution of the war increasingly revolved around issues of logistics, war economy and deployment, as well as strategy and tactics, and the conflict likely became simply too complex for Hitler to handle, especially as age, ill-health and work stress took their toll.

If we were to ascribe one central failing to Hitler's capability as a military commander it would be his intensifying insistence that willpower was *the* decisive factor in a military campaign. In one evening discussion in August 1942, Hitler stated:

If one enters a military operation with the mental reservation: 'Caution! this may fail,' then you may be quite certain that it will *fail. To force a decision one must enter battle with a conviction of victory and the determination to achieve it, regardless of the hazards. Just*

imagine what would have happened if we had undertaken the Crete operations with the idea: 'We'll have a crack at it; if it succeeds, so much the better; if it fails, we'll pull out!'

(Trans in Trevor Roper, 2002)

Hitler's reference to the battle for Crete in May and June 1941 is a good example of his perception of military events. The invasion was eventually a strategic success – the island was captured from the Allies – but it was largely a tactical disaster. Losses were so heavy amongst the German airborne forces that they were never used in large-scale airborne deployments again.

Between 1939 and 1942, Hitler's insistence on willpower paid off in operations of daring victory that even stunned experienced generals. From 1942, however, the emphasis on will, admittedly combined with some poor intelligence information, led him to disastrous decisions. Hitler's commitment to the no-retreat defence

of Stalingrad doomed the Sixth Army to destruction; his Ardennes offensive was almost suicidal in its objective, Antwerp (although an offensive with more limited goals may have been profitable); he continued to command a defence even as Soviet forces wrapped themselves around Berlin itself. Overall, Hitler's greatest errors were a failure to appreciate the tactical reality of war in the Soviet Union – a war of attrition and logistics rather than *Blitzkrieg* – and his declaration of war on the United States, the most industrially powerful nation on the planet. Hitler undoubtedly had a military acumen that cannot be dismissed easily, but he steadily lost a grip on tactical realities, which in turn consigned Germany to strategic defeat.

Foreign policy

Foreign policy is another interesting area of Hitler's psyche. Historians have broadly divided themselves into two camps: those who see Hitler's foreign policy developing in a clear and programmatic fashion, and those who feel that foreign policy evolved more haphazardly, and was influenced by agencies other than Hitler. Both positions have their merits, but here it is worth remembering that while Hitler might not have had a specific endgame in sight, expansionism was integral to his outlook from the very beginning, expressed in his ideas of *Lebensraum* and in his strident development of a war economy.

It was this general instinct, rather than specific long-term policies, that probably guided Hitler's foreign policy decisions, as well as his reaction to events abroad, the opinions of those around him, and new opportunities. For example, Hitler originally appears to have favoured an alliance with Britain, thus preventing a two-front war in his long-term ambition of conquering the Soviet Union. This alliance, of course, did not transpire;

instead Britain declared war following the invasion of Poland. Furthermore, Hitler's invasion of Poland was made possible by the German-Soviet Non-Aggression Pact, and by Hitler's reassurance that Britain and France would not physically intervene. However, with war declared, Hitler had to neutralize the threat to the west before he could turn east. Hitler's foreign policy, therefore, appears as a blend between a long-term general desire for territorial expansion (with specific ambitions towards the Soviet Union), and reactions to unfolding events. In the mid-1930s it is unlikely that Hitler would have envisaged a war in Western Europe, Italy, the Balkans, North Africa, Eastern Europe and the Soviet Union as in any way desirable.

Race
Hitler was vehemently interested in issues of racial purity and racial

destiny. A passionate anti-Semite, his overall antipathy towards the Jews led directly to the Holocaust – of that there can be little doubt. Yet, much like his military and foreign policy, Hitler's racial policy seems to have unfolded opportunistically over time, aided by agencies such as the SS, which sought to translate his general will into specific actions. As such, there is a strong argument that although Hitler was ultimately responsible for the Holocaust – he knew of it and had the power to stop it – the broader German population and armed forces share in the guilt to varying degrees (see 'Racial Policy' chapter for deeper analysis).

Leading to defeat
As the Allies themselves recognized by 1944, Hitler was taking Germany on the path to utter defeat. His leadership, and a chaotic form of government, ensured this destiny.

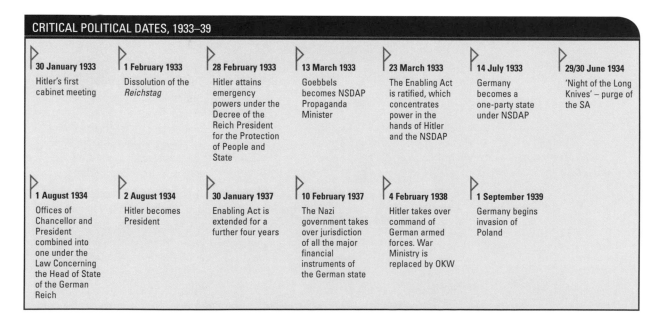

CRITICAL POLITICAL DATES, 1933–39

30 January 1933
Hitler's first cabinet meeting

1 February 1933
Dissolution of the *Reichstag*

28 February 1933
Hitler attains emergency powers under the Decree of the Reich President for the Protection of People and State

13 March 1933
Goebbels becomes NSDAP Propaganda Minister

23 March 1933
The Enabling Act is ratified, which concentrates power in the hands of Hitler and the NSDAP

14 July 1933
Germany becomes a one-party state under NSDAP

29/30 June 1934
'Night of the Long Knives' – purge of the SA

1 August 1934
Offices of Chancellor and President combined into one under the Law Concerning the Head of State of the German Reich

2 August 1934
Hitler becomes President

30 January 1937
Enabling Act is extended for a further four years

10 February 1937
The Nazi government takes over jurisdiction of all the major financial instruments of the German state

4 February 1938
Hitler takes over command of German armed forces. War Ministry is replaced by OKW

1 September 1939
Germany begins invasion of Poland

CHAPTER 5

The Law and Internal Security

In the early days of the Nazy Party, it was the blunt muscle of the Sturmabteilung *that was largely responsible for maintaining order and ideology amongst Party members, separate from the regular state police forces. Once Hitler was in power, however, he created several new layers of law enforcement, eventually all under the auspices of the SS.*

The Nazi system of policing was not only dedicated to the traditional practices of combating crime and punishing miscreants. It also included the powerful Reichssicherheitshauptamt (RSHA), a sprawling organization that included the Gestapo, foreign and domestic intelligence services, and counter-espionage.

Combined with a politically directed or influenced judiciary, the Nazi system of law and order was as much concerned with policing ideology as it was with countering crime, and it became an immensely influential tool of coercion for Hitler's government.

■ A soldier from the 1st SS Panzer Division *Leibstandarte Adolf Hitler* stands guard on a street corner in Ostrova, in the Czech region of Silesia.

Controlling the Reich

Policing in the Third Reich was intimately bound up with the SS, and the SS leader, Heinrich Himmler. Eventually all German police organizations were brought under SS control, making them directly subservient to Party political and racial ideology.

The SS was born from a small element of the SA, initially chosen as a personal bodyguard for Hitler. This bodyguard, which was labelled the *Schutzstaffel* (SS) in 1925, grew steadily in jurisdiction and influence, particularly under the command of Heinrich Himmler, who took control of the SS in 1929.

SS dominance

In 1934, Hitler deployed the fanatically loyal SS to destroy the SA leadership, after which the SS became the chief paramilitary wing of the Third Reich. Even as Himmler came to power, he had already developed tools for policing, including the civilian security service known as the *Sicherheitsdienst* (SD). He also became the police chief in Munich in 1933, and acting chief of the *Gestapo* a year later, making him the overlord of political policing in Nazi Germany. In April 1934, Himmler extended his control over local, regional and state police forces, including the uniformed and criminal branches (see below), making him all-powerful in terms of manipulating law and order. His final extension of power came in August 1943, when he was promoted to Minister of the Interior – a position that enabled him to interfere more directly in the judicial processes.

The SD

The original SS security agency (as opposed to the regular police force) was the SD, formed in 1931 by Himmler as a security offshoot of his burgeoning SS organization. In terms of its role, Himmler himself described its activities thus: 'The SD will

---

GRÜNDSÄTZE FÜR DIE POLIZIE (FUNDAMENTAL PRINCIPLES FOR THE POLICE)

Issued on 18 January 1935 by the Secretary for the Interior for Prussia and the Reich:

1. Keep your oath with full loyalty and complete dedication to the Führer, People and Fatherland.

2. The great authority that has been given to you as the most visible holder of the power of the nation is not a privilege, but a duty. Complete your duties as a servant of the people.

3. Be diligent and discrete in official duties, brave and confident but also just, and fervent in the fight against all enemies of the people and of the state.

4. Act against others as you would want to be acted against if you were in their position.

5. Be honest, humble and controlled. Lies are mean, gifts put you in obligation, and lack of control is undignified.

6. Help all those who need your help.

7. Do not neglect your outer appearance, as it is a mirror of your inner self.

8. Obey your superiors, be an example to your subordinates, maintain discipline and keep a sense of camaraderie.

9. As holder of a weapon, you have the greatest honour of a German man. Remember this.

THIRD REICH POLICE UNITS, 1934–39

◆ **POLICE FORCE**

Sonderpolizei (Special Police)
- Eisenbahnpolizei (Railway Police) Ministry of Transport
- Bahnschutzpolizei (Railway Protection Police) SS
- Bergpolizei (Mines Police) Ministry of Economic Affairs
- Reichsbahnfahndungsdienst (Railway Criminal Investigation Service) Ministry of Transport
- Postschutz (Post Office Protection) Ministry of Post & Telegraph
- Zollbeamten (Customs Officials) Ministry of Finance
- Forstschutzpolizei (Forestry Police) Forestry Office
- Werkschutz (Factory Protection) Air Ministry
- Deichpolizei (Dyke & Dam Police) Ministry of Economic Affairs
- Flurschutzpolizei (Agricultural Police) Ministry of Agriculture
- Jagdpolizei (Game Conservation Police) Forestry Office
- Hafenpolizei (Harbour Police) Ministry of Transport
- Hilfspolizei (Auxiliary Police)

Sicherheitspolizei, Sipo (Security Police)
- Kriminalpolizei, Kripo (Criminal Police)
- Geheime Staatspolizei, Gestapo (Secret State Police)
- Grenzpolizei (Border Police)
- Weibliche Kriminalpolizei (Women's Branch of the Criminal Police)

Sicherheitsdienst, SD (Security Service)
- Inland SD (Domestic SD)
- Ausland SD (Foreign SD)

Ordnungspolizei, Orpo (Order Police)
- Schutzpolizei, Schupo (Protection Police)
- Schutzpolizei des Reichs
- Verkehrsbereitschaften (Traffic Police)
- Kasernierte Polizei (Barrack Police)
- Schutzpolizei der Gemeinden (Municipal Police)
- Polizei Fliegerstaffeln (Police Flying Units)
- Polizei Nachrichtenstaffeln (Police Signal Units)
- Gendarmerie (Rural Police)
- Polizei Reiterstaffeln (Mounted Police Units)
- Verkehrskompanien (mot) zbV (Motorized Special Duty Traffic Police)
- Wasserschutzpolizei (Waterways Protection Police)
- Motorisierte Gendarmerie (Motorized Traffic Gendarmerie)
- Feldjägerkorps, FJK (Auxiliary Police)
- Verwaltungspolizei (Administrative Police)
- Gesundheitspolizei (Health Police)
- Hochgebirgs Gendarmerie (Mountain Gendarmerie)
- Gewerbepolizei (Factory & Shops Police)
- Baupolizei (Buildings Police)
- Feuerschutzpolizei (Fire Protection Police)
- Feuerwehren (Fire Brigades)
- Luftschutzpolizei (Air Raid Police)
- Technische Nothilfe, TeNo (Technical Emergency Service)
- Landespolizei (Barracked Territorial Police)
- Landwacht (Rural Guards)
- Stadtwacht (City Guards)

STRUCTURE OF THE *GESTAPO*, 1939

Division	Commander	Responsibility
Division I	Werner Best	Organization, administration, legal affairs
Division II	Reinhard Heydrich	Aggressive actions against opponents of the Nazi regime
Division III	Guenther Palten	Counter-intelligence

GESTAPO PRISONS, 1939–45

▲ *GESTAPO* PRISONS: The prisons of the *Gestapo*, which formed a network throughout Germany, Austria, Poland and Czechoslovakia, were insidious tools of social control. They not only served as places of incarceration and interrogation, they also acted as visible reminders of Nazi power amongst local communities, and enforced the need for compliance to Nazi ideology.

discover the enemies of the National Socialist concept and it will initiate countermeasures through the official police authorities.' In short, it was to spy on the people, watching out for any individuals or activities considered subversive to the Nazi regime. To this end, it built up a major network of agents and informants throughout Germany and later into the occupied territories, filling out

thousands of confidential reports that were filtered through to the central office of the SD, headed by Reinhard Heydrich. (Heydrich was also the chief of the *Gestapo* from 1936 until his assassination in 1942.)

Enemies of the state

The SD definition of a subversive became extremely broad, especially once the full spectrum of Nazi racial policy came into play. Historian Louis L. Snyder here reflects on the varied hues of those targeted by the Reich security services:

Few could escape this monolithic organ of the Hitler terror. Its victims included Jews, Communists, pacifists, Seventh day Adventists, political criminals, professional criminals, beggars, antisocials, 'the work shy,' beggars, homosexuals, prostitutes, drunkards, swindlers and psychopaths. SD men were called on for such major tasks as arresting 67,000 'enemies of the state' in Vienna during the occupation of Austria in 1938.
(Snyder, 1998)

Once a person had been arrested by the SD, a fast-track judicial system could process the prisoner and, with little respect for any human rights, have him or her tortured, imprisoned or executed. By the time the SD were rounding up unfortunate people in Austria in the late 1930s, they had been joined in their efforts by another agency, the infamous *Gestapo*.

The *Gestapo*

The *Gestapo* (short for *Geheime Staatspolizei* – Secret State Police) had different origins to the SD. Its precedent was the Prussian political police of the Weimar Republic, a part of the Prussian Interior Ministry although with Germany-wide authority. By 1933, the Prussian Interior Minister was none other than Göring, and in April he established the *Gestapo* as a state security force that, like the SD, was dedicated to protecting National Socialism against 'enemies of the state'. During 1934, the *Gestapo* also came under the spreading control of the SS.

The *Gestapo* was truly a law unto itself, and from its formation until the end of the war it terrorized the German people and the citizens of

occupied lands. There was a definite overlap in SD and *Gestapo* responsibilities that was never entirely resolved, and relations between the two organizations could be frosty and competitive.

The situation was made more complicated by the fact that from June 1936 Heydrich was chief of both the SD and the *Sicherheitspolizei* (Security Police; *Sipo*), the SS intelligence organization that included the *Gestapo* and the *Kriminalpolizei* (Criminal Police; *Kripo*). The *Sipo* and SD were combined in a single command (*Sipo und SD*), which from 1939 was under the authority of the

Reichssicherheitshauptamt (Reich Main Security Office; RSHA), the governing security organization of the Third Reich, with power over all state and SS security services.

Yet the *Gestapo* undoubtedly emerged as the more powerful of the two agencies. For example, by 1939 the SD had 3000 operatives and 50,000 informers. The *Gestapo*, by contrast, had 20,000 members and 100,000 informers. The *Gestapo* also seemed to take the ear of the authorities more readily.

Yet although the *Gestapo* was certainly a large and influential organization, it was still spread thinly once the Third Reich expanded through war. In fact, recent research has indicated that many major German cities were monitored by only a few dozen *Gestapo* agents, meaning that its reach was not universal, unlike the fear it instilled.

POLICE HANDGUNS

Weapon	Calibre	Manufacturer	Notes
Dreyse	7.65mm (0.32in)	Dreyse	Designed by Louis Schmeisser
Model 1912	9mm (0.35in)	Steyr	Used a more powerful 9mm cartridge than the Parabellum
Model 1934	7.65mm (0.32in)	Mauser	Also produced for military service
Model HSc	7.65mm (0.32in)	Mauser	Hammerless, double-action pistol
P.08	9mm (0.35in)	Mauser	Police version initially had a sear safety above the side plate
P.38	9mm (0.35in)	Mauser and Walther	Acquired directly from military stocks
PP	7.65mm (0.32in)	Walther	Also went to *Luftwaffe* and Nazi Party officials
PPK	7.65mm (0.32in)	Walther	PPK stood for *Polizeipistole Kriminalmodell* (Police Pistol Detective Model)

GERMAN POLICE RANKS

Rank	Equivalent
Generaloberst	Colonel-General
General	General
Generalleutnant	Lieutenant-General
Generalmajor	Major-General
Oberst	Colonel
Oberstleutnant	Lieutenant-Colonel
Major	Major
Hauptmann	Captain
Oberleutnant	First lieutenant
Leutnant	Second lieutenant
Meister	Sergeant-Major
Hauptwachtmeister	Master Sergeant
Zugwachtmeister	Sergeant 1st Class
Oberwachtmeister	Staff Sergeant
Wachtmeister	Sergeant
Rottwachtmeister	Senior Police Officer
Unterwachtmeister	Police Officer
Anwärter	Officer Candidate

Crime and Punishment

Although existing state courts were in place when Hitler came to power in 1933, the Nazi Party had little problem influencing and controlling the judiciary, resulting in a court process in which many defendants faced almost certain verdicts from the outset.

There were three principal reasons why the judicial system was so easily controlled by the Nazis during the Third Reich, despite the fact that many judges had appointments that pre-dated the regime. First, Germany's courts were under no higher constitutional standard against which their policies could be judged, or which could form the basis of appeal. For this reason, once the Nazis were in power the dictates of National Socialist ideology became the only benchmark governing legal standards. Second, the executive, focused on Hitler, was not legally separated from the judiciary, meaning that Hitler and his authorities could interfere directly in the judicial process, altering sentences or effectively predetermining the outcome of cases. This power was critical, and was made clear by Hitler himself in an address to the *Reichstag* on 26 April 1942:

I expect one thing: that the state gives me the right to intervene immediately and to take action whenever a person has failed to give unqualified obedience... I therefore ask the German Reichstag to confirm without reservation that I have the legal right to ensure everyone keeps his duty and to cashier or remove from office or position, without regard for his

person or his established rights, whoever, in my view and according to my considered opinion, has failed to do his duty... From this time on, I shall intervene in these cases and remove from office those judges who plainly do not understand the urgency of the hour.

The *Reichstag*, of course, rubber-stamped Hitler's demand, and the

judiciary was subsequently looking over its shoulder for approval in all its major decisions.

Judicial bias

The third major factor in Nazi judicial bias was that although the judges in place were not necessarily Nazis, they did share a broadly authoritarian frame of mind that did not require much of a shift to become favourable

SIGNIFICANT INDIVIDUALS EXECUTED FOLLOWING TRIAL BY THE *VOLKSGERICHTSHOF* (PEOPLE'S COURT), 1942–45	
1942	**Notes**
Hübener, Helmuth	Youngest person to be executed as a result of a trial by the *Volksgerichtshof*; conspiracy to commit high treason
1943	**Notes**
Fucík, Julius	Czech journalist; high treason
Graf, Willi	Member of the White Rose Movement
Huber, Kurt	Member of the White Rose Movement
Kreiten, Karlrobert	German pianist; made negative remarks about Adolf Hitler and the war effort
Probst, Christoph	Member of the White Rose Movement
Schmorell, Alex	Member of the White Rose Movement
Scholl, Hans	Member of the White Rose Movement
Scholl, Sophie	Member of the White Rose Movement
1944	**Notes**
Metzger, Max Josef	German Catholic priest; guilty of anti-Nazi political views
von Witzleben, Erwin	German field marshal; conspirator in the 20 July Bomb Plot
Kirchner, Johanna 'Hanna'	member of the Social Democratic Party of Germany; treason
1945	**Notes**
Planck, Erwin	Politician and businessman; alleged conspirator in the 20 July Bomb Plot
Nebe, Artur	SS general; conspirator in the 20 July Bomb Plot

KEY ASSASSINATION ATTEMPTS AGAINST ADOLF HITLER, 1933–45*

Date	Location	Details
3 March 1933	Königsberg	Kurt Luttner arrested while planning to kill Hitler the following day at a rally
21 December 1936	Nuremberg	Jewish student Helmut Hirsch arrested, and confesses his intent to kill Hitler using bombs at Hitler's Nuremberg HQ
October 1938	Munich	Swiss citizen Maurice Bavaud makes several unsuccessful attempts to kill Hitler, but is finally arrested, tried and executed
8 November 1939	Munich	George Else plants bomb in the *Bürgerbräukeller*, which detonates after Hitler had left, killing eight people
March 1943	Smolensk	Three German officers place a bomb aboard Hitler's Focke-Wulf 200 Condor, but the bomb fails to detonate
11 March 1944	Obersalzberg	*Hauptmann* Eberhard von Breitenbuch plans to shoot Hitler, but cannot get access to him
20 July 1944	Wolfschanze	*Oberst* Claus Schenk Graf von Stauffenberg injures Hitler in a bomb attack

Note: There were many other plans to assassinate Hitler; the ones listed here are those that went beyond intention to meaningful action, or that had a significant chance of success.

to Nazi doctrine. As Richard Grunberger comments:

...the majority of the legal profession did not hold clearly formulated Nazi beliefs, and nor did they necessarily adopt them after the seizure of power. (The basic faith of older jurists – as of academics, officers and civil servants – was authoritarian rather than totalitarian.) But although authoritarianism and totalitarianism diverged, they also shaded into one another, and it was temptingly easy to cross the boundary while pretending not to notice it.
(Grunberger, 2005)

This tendency, plus other tactics we shall now explore, made the judiciary a significant tool of Nazi policy.

Ideological courts
Few institutions represent more perfectly the excesses of the Nazi legal system than the *Volksgerichtshof* (People's Court). A year after Hitler became Chancellor, he sought to establish a specialized high court that would deal exclusively with those charged with high treason or classified as traitors to the state. The *Volksgerichtshof* was the result, at first presided over by Fritz Rehn (July–September 1934) and then by Otto Thierack (1934–42), Roland Freisler (1942–February 1945) and Harry Haffner (March–April 1945).

In its appearance alone the *Volksgerichtshof* stated its credentials, heavily adorned with swastikas and images of Hitler. Most of the court officials, including the panel of judges, were Party members or SS men. The trials conducted therein worked largely on the basis of foregone conclusions – to appear before the court almost guaranteed a long prison sentence or death. Furthermore, the judges worked outside of independent scrutiny, and

once the verdict was delivered there was no further avenue of appeal. Many cases, however, were recorded for posterity on film, the films being a record for Hitler and his officials or for selective use in newsreels. The evidential process in the trials was highly skewed, and the proceedings placed a high emphasis on humiliation and verbal abuse, particularly under the rule of Freisler.

Freisler himself was a perfect example of a Nazi judge. He had joined the Nazi Party back in 1925, and went on to become a Nazi delegate to the Prussian *Landtag* before taking up a *Reichstag* position as representative for Hesse-Nassau. In May 1934, he was appointed to a special state position with responsibility for combating sabotage. Note that he was also one of the people present at the Wannsee Conference in January 1942, at which the 'final solution' for European Jewry was officially set down. In something approaching genuine justice, Freisler, who had been responsible for sending dozens of people to their deaths, was killed when an Allied bomb hit the courtroom in 1945.

The *Volksgerichtshof* was the venue for some of the most important treason trials of the Third Reich. In 1943, for example, it quickly processed the defendants of the 'White Rose Group', a small body of student activists from Munich University who attempted to alert German citizens to the barbarity of occupation policies. (Some of the group had served as German soldiers, and had witnessed *Einsatzgruppen* operations.)

The *Volksgerichtshof*, however, achieved even greater prominence in the aftermath of the 'July Bomb Plot' against Hitler in 1944, attempted by *Oberst* Claus Schenk Graf von Stauffenberg but with support from numerous others. The violent aftermath of the failed assassination attempt resulted in 200 individuals being hunted down and either murdered or tried and executed. The *Volksgerichtshof* handled 24 of the key plotters, these individuals heading off to their death sentences within hours of the inevitable verdicts. To add to the humiliation of the procedings – and therefore to emphasize the low status of the defendants – the accused *Generalfeldmarschall* Erwin von Witzleben was made to stand before the court with no belt and braces, and therefore had to hold up his trousers throughout his cross-examination. After his sentence of death was passed, Witzleben threw a verbal shot at court president Freisler: 'You can hand us over to the hangman. In three months, the disgusted and harried people will bring you to book and drag you alive through the dirt in the streets!'

Direct influence

The *Volksgerichtshof* was the most extreme form of the Nazi judicial process, but that process was also expressed in many other far less visible ways. The Ministry of Justice, for example, took over responsibility for the appointment of judges, and the state prosecutor could direct the verdict and sentencing of local court judges. Furthermore, the *NS Rechtswahrerbund* (Nazi Lawyers Association) could discipline or debar any lawyer who failed to deliver National Socialist principles. Lawyers undergoing their legal training were directly imbued with Nazi legal principles from the outset. All told, those who found themselves under legal scrutiny in the Third Reich were in a precarious position.

Policing at Home and Abroad

Of course, not all policing in the Third Reich was about ideological crimes. The regular police forces of Nazi Germany continued in their familiar roles, although even they became swept into the less palatable aspects of Nazi policy.

The police forces of the Third Reich were, as we have seen, steadily aligned with the controlling influence of the SS, although in many localities the regular police services would have continued in familiar style. A landmark structural change came in April 1934 with the creation of the post of *Chef der Deutschen Polizei im Reichsministerium des Innern* (Chief of the German Police in the Reich Ministry of the Interior). When taken by Himmler, this position extended SS control across all aspects of policing.

Another major organizational change in policing came with the formation of the *Reichssicherheits-hauptamt*, which was established in September 1939 as the supreme security office in the Third Reich. Headed by Reinhard Heydrich until his assassination in 1942, the RSHA became a searching instrument for suppressing so-called 'enemies of the state'.

Structured law enforcement

The RSHA was divided into seven major departments, including two SD departments (*Amt* III and *Amt* VI) responsible for domestic and foreign intelligence respectively, and *Amt* IV – the *Gestapo*. It also included the *Kriminalpolizei* in *Amt* V (see below).

In terms of their regional and local arrangements, the police forces within Germany were administratively divided as follows. At the regional level was the *Landspolizeibehörde* (Regional Police Authority), controlled by the *Länder* authorities or, in the case of Prussia and Bavaria, by the *Regierungspräsident* (Government President).

Beneath the regional level of command were the *Kreispolizeibehörde* (City/County Police Authority), headed by various civic officials depending on the nature of the territory, and finally the *Ortspolizeibehörde* (Local Police

Authority), controlled typically by a local mayor.

While the security services (see above) were the most feared elements of Third Reich policing, the main interface of law and order was the regular police forces, uniformed and detective.

Ordnungspolizei

The two major regular police forces in the Third Reich were the *Kriminalpolizei*, better known as the *Kripo*, and the *Ordnungspolizei* (Order Police; *Orpo*). The *Orpo* was commanded from 1936 to 1945 by the thuggish SS officer Kurt Daluege, and his leadership sat somewhat ill at ease with the civilan career policemen who made up the ranks. Daluege set about stripping out *Orpo* officials who were not 'on message' with Nazi ideology, an act that deprived the force of hundreds of excellent officers and consequently reduced its efficiency. He also encouraged members of the *Allgemeine-SS* to join the police ranks, breeding tensions and suspicions amongst the older officers and the new intake.

The command structure of the *Orpo*, below the regional SS levels (see below), was principally ordered around *Hauptamt Ordungspolizei* (Order Police Headquarters), and then the *Befehlshaber der Ordnungspolizei* (Chiefs of the Order Police), which were district command positions. The more local sub-divisions were the responsibility of the *Kommandeure der Orpo* (Commanders of the Order Police). The police officers themselves were broadly split into two categories: the

HÖHERE SS- UND POLIZEIFÜHRER (HSSPF)

- Höhere SS- und Polizeiführer Adriatisches Küstenland – HQ: Trieste
- Höhere SS- und Polizeiführer Albanien – HQ: Tirana
- Höhere SS- und Polizeiführer Alpenland – HQ: Salzburg
- Höhere SS- und Polizeiführer Belgien-Nordfrankreich – HQ: Brussels
- Höhere SS- und Polizeiführer Böhmen und Mähren – HQ: Prague
- Höhere SS- und Polizeiführer Danmark – HQ: Copenhagen
- Höhere SS- und Polizeiführer Donau – HQ: Vienna
- Höhere SS- und Polizeiführer Elbe – HQ: Dresden
- Höhere SS- und Polizeiführer Frankreich – HQ: Paris
- Höhere SS- und Polizeiführer Fulda-Werra – HQ: Arolsen
- Höhere SS- und Polizeiführer Griechenland – HQ: Athens
- Höhere SS- und Polizeiführer Kroatien – HQ: Zagreb
- Höhere SS- und Polizeiführer Main – HQ: Nuremberg
- Höhere SS- und Polizeiführer Mitte – HQ: Braunschweig
- Höhere SS- und Polizeiführer Nord – HQ: Oslo
- Höhere SS- und Polizeiführer Nordost – HQ: Königsberg
- Höhere SS- und Polizeiführer Nordsee – HQ: Hamburg
- Höhere SS- und Polizeiführer Nordwest – HQ: Den Haag
- Höhere SS- und Polizeiführer Ost – HQ: Cracow
- Höhere SS- und Polizeiführer Ostland und Rußland-Nord – HQ: Riga
- Höhere SS- und Polizeiführer Ostsee – HQ: Stettin
- Höhere SS- und Polizeiführer Rhein-Westmark – HQ: Wiesbaden
- Höhere SS- und Polizeiführer Rußland-Mitte – HQ: Mogilev, then Minsk
- Höhere SS- und Polizeiführer Rußland-Süd – HQ: Kiev
- Höhere SS- und Polizeiführer Schwarzes-Meer – HQ: Nikolayev
- Höhere SS- und Polizeiführer Serbien, Sandschack und Montenegro – HQ: Belgrade
- Höhere SS- und Polizeiführer Slowakien – HQ: Pressburg
- Höhere SS- und Polizeiführer Spree – HQ: Berlin
- Höhere SS- und Polizeiführer Süd – HQ: Munich
- Höhere SS- und Polizeiführer Südost – HQ: Breslau
- Höhere SS- und Polizeiführer Südwest – HQ: Stuttgart
- Höhere SS- und Polizeiführer Ungarn – HQ: Budapest
- Höhere SS- und Polizeiführer Warthe – HQ: Posen
- Höhere SS- und Polizeiführer Weichsel – HQ: Danzig
- Höhere SS- und Polizeiführer West – HQ: Düsseldorf

RSHA ORGANIZATION

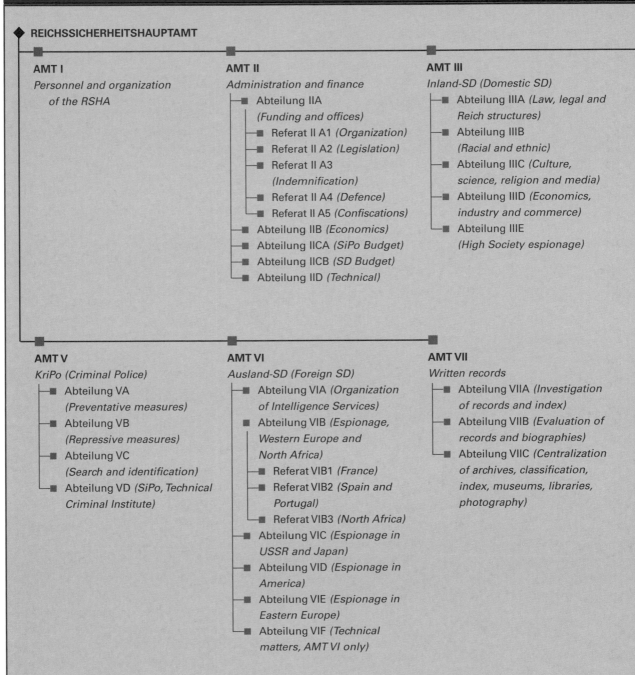

REICHSSICHERHEITSHAUPTAMT

AMT I
Personnel and organization
of the RSHA

AMT II
Administration and finance
- Abteilung IIA
  (Funding and offices)
  - Referat II A1 (Organization)
  - Referat II A2 (Legislation)
  - Referat II A3
    (Indemnification)
  - Referat II A4 (Defence)
  - Referat II A5 (Confiscations)
- Abteilung IIB (Economics)
- Abteilung IICA (SiPo Budget)
- Abteilung IICB (SD Budget)
- Abteilung IID (Technical)

AMT III
Inland-SD (Domestic SD)
- Abteilung IIIA (Law, legal and
  Reich structures)
- Abteilung IIIB
  (Racial and ethnic)
- Abteilung IIIC (Culture,
  science, religion and media)
- Abteilung IIID (Economics,
  industry and commerce)
- Abteilung IIIE
  (High Society espionage)

AMT V
KriPo (Criminal Police)
- Abteilung VA
  (Preventative measures)
- Abteilung VB
  (Repressive measures)
- Abteilung VC
  (Search and identification)
- Abteilung VD (SiPo, Technical
  Criminal Institute)

AMT VI
Ausland-SD (Foreign SD)
- Abteilung VIA (Organization
  of Intelligence Services)
- Abteilung VIB (Espionage,
  Western Europe and
  North Africa)
  - Referat VIB1 (France)
  - Referat VIB2 (Spain and
    Portugal)
  - Referat VIB3 (North Africa)
- Abteilung VIC (Espionage in
  USSR and Japan)
- Abteilung VID (Espionage in
  America)
- Abteilung VIE (Espionage in
  Eastern Europe)
- Abteilung VIF (Technical
  matters, AMT VI only)

AMT VII
Written records
- Abteilung VIIA (Investigation
  of records and index)
- Abteilung VIIB (Evaluation of
  records and biographies)
- Abteilung VIIC (Centralization
  of archives, classification,
  index, museums, libraries,
  photography)

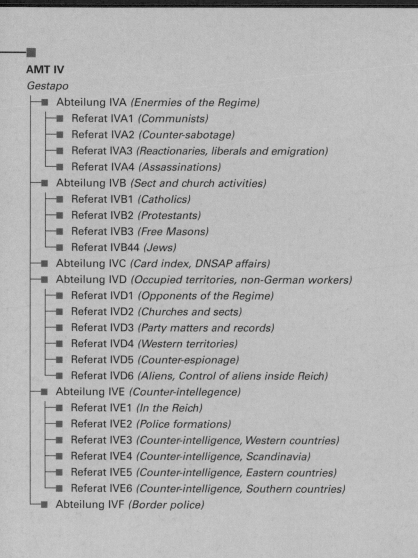

AMT IV
Gestapo
- Abteilung IVA *(Enermies of the Regime)*
  - Referat IVA1 *(Communists)*
  - Referat IVA2 *(Counter-sabotage)*
  - Referat IVA3 *(Reactionaries, liberals and emigration)*
  - Referat IVA4 *(Assassinations)*
- Abteilung IVB *(Sect and church activities)*
  - Referat IVB1 *(Catholics)*
  - Referat IVB2 *(Protestants)*
  - Referat IVB3 *(Free Masons)*
  - Referat IVB44 *(Jews)*
- Abteilung IVC *(Card index, DNSAP affairs)*
- Abteilung IVD *(Occupied territories, non-German workers)*
  - Referat IVD1 *(Opponents of the Regime)*
  - Referat IVD2 *(Churches and sects)*
  - Referat IVD3 *(Party matters and records)*
  - Referat IVD4 *(Western territories)*
  - Referat IVD5 *(Counter-espionage)*
  - Referat IVD6 *(Aliens, Control of aliens inside Reich)*
- Abteilung IVE *(Counter-intelligence)*
  - Referat IVE1 *(In the Reich)*
  - Referat IVE2 *(Police formations)*
  - Referat IVE3 *(Counter-intelligence, Western countries)*
  - Referat IVE4 *(Counter-intelligence, Scandinavia)*
  - Referat IVE5 *(Counter-intelligence, Eastern countries)*
  - Referat IVE6 *(Counter-intelligence, Southern countries)*
- Abteilung IVF *(Border police)*

Polizeivollzugsbeamten (Uniformed Police) and the non-uniformed *Polizeiverwaltungsbeamten* (Administrative Police).

The *Orpo*'s duties were those of any regular police force, from policing towns, cities and rural areas to managing traffic and monitoring waterways. The *Schutzpolizei*, for example, functioned as the standard municipal police force. It was divided into *Reviere Polizei* (Precinct Police) – units of about 40 officers that patrolled a designated locality; five or more of these would form a *Polizei Abschnitte* (Police Sector). In turn, large and heavily populated cities or districts might then arrange several police sectors into a *Polizei Gruppe* (Police Group). Yet there were several more specialist sections. The *Kasernierte Polizei* (Barrack Police), for example, was a trained civic emergency unit, heavily armed with automatic weapons and armoured cars to handle riots and similar breakdowns in social order. The *Technische Nothilfe* (Technical Emergency Service) was another emergency response unit, but it was dedicated to restoring public services should they be disrupted.

Foreign auxiliaries
One notable aspect of the *Orpo*'s wartime existence was that it provided the manpower to form around 80 military-style police formations, organized into battalions and equipped with light infantry weapons rather than standard police-issue firearms. These formations were increasingly open to sympathetic volunteers from the occupied territories, and were used

SS- UND POLIZEIFÜHRER (SSPF), 1942

- Polizeigebietsführer Agram
- Polizeigebietsführer Banja-Luca
- Polizeigebietsführer Copenhagen
- Polizeigebietsführer Essegg
- Polizeigebietsführer Knin
- Polizeigebietsführer Sarajewo
- SS- und Polizeiführer Aserbeidschan
- SS- und Polizeiführer Awdejewka
- SS- und Polizeiführer Bergvolker-Ordshonikidseo
- SS- und Polizeiführer Bialystok
- SS- und Polizeiführer Bozen
- SS- und Polizeiführer Charkow
- SS- und Polizeiführer Dnjepropetrowsk-Krivoi-Rog
- SS- und Polizeiführer Estland
- SS- und Polizeiführer Friaul
- SS- und Polizeiführer Görz
- SS- und Polizeiführer Istrien
- SS- und Polizeiführer Kattowitz
- SS- und Polizeiführer Kaukasien-Kuban
- SS- und Polizeiführer Kertsch-Tamanhalbinsel
- SS- und Polizeiführer Kiew
- SS- und Polizeiführer Krakau
- SS- und Polizeiführer Lemberg
- SS- und Polizeiführer Lettland
- SS- und Polizeiführer Litauen
- SS- und Polizeiführer Lublin
- SS- und Polizeiführer Metz
- SS- und Polizeiführer Minsk – see Weißruthenien
- SS- und Polizeiführer Mitteitalien-Verona
- SS- und Polizeiführer Mitte-Norwegen
- SS- und Polizeiführer Mogilew
- SS- und Polizeiführer Montenegro
- SS- und Polizeiführer Nikolajew
- SS- und Polizeiführer Nord-Kaukasien
- SS- und Polizeiführer Nord-Norwegen
- SS- und Polizeiführer Ober-Elsaß
- SS- und Polizeiführer Oberitalien-Mitte
- SS- und Polizeiführer Oberitalien-West
- SS- und Polizeiführer Pripet
- SS- und Polizeiführer Quarnero
- SS- und Polizeiführer Radom
- SS- und Polizeiführer Rowno
- SS- und Polizeiführer Rostow-Awdejewka – see Stanislav-Rostow
- SS- und Polizeiführer Salzburg
- SS- und Polizeiführer Sandschak
- SS- und Polizeiführer Saratow
- SS- und Polizeiführer Shitomir
- SS- und Polizeiführer Stalino-Donezgebiet
- SS- und Polizeiführer Stanislav-Rostow
- SS- und Polizeiführer Süd-Norwegen
- SS- und Polizeiführer Taurien-Krim-Simferopol
- SS- und Polizeiführer Triest
- SS- und Polizeiführer Tschernigow
- SS- und Polizeiführer Warsaw
- SS- und Polizeiführer Weißruthenien
- SS- und Polizeiführer Wolhynien-Brest-Litovsk

heavily in the policing of these occupied lands.

The creation of German-controlled foreign police stemmed from the fact that any local police forces in an occupied country automatically came under the control of the local SS formations. Himmler realized in 1941 that the extent of the occupation zones meant that policing could not be provided purely by German units, despite the fact that Hitler had shown a passionate opposition to allowing foreigners to bear arms and police the Reich. Yet Himmler got his way, and on 25 July 1941 ordered that occupation SS forces organize 'additional protective units from the ethnic groups suitable to us in the conquered area as soon as possible.' In November of that year, Himmler also ordered that these auxiliary police be formed into units called the *Schutzmannschaften der Ordnungspolizei* (Detachments of Order Police). They were also known as *Hilfspolizei* (Auxiliary Police; *Hipo*) or, in the occupied Soviet territories, as *Hilfswillige* (Voluntary Assistants; 'Hiwis'). The enthusiasm for joining the police military units was impressive, as Gordon Williamson illustrates in his book *The SS: Hitler's Instrument of Terror*.

From among the Volksdeutche elements in Poland, some 12 polizei regiments were formed; in Estonia 26 regiments. Latvia and Lithuania between them raised 64 battalions totalling around 28,000 men, and in the Ukraine an astonishing 70,000 volunteers came forward, sufficient to form 71 battalions. In the Balkans the Croats produced some 15,000 volunteers, the Serbs some 10,000, and even Albania was able to produce sufficient volunteers to form two police battalions.

(Williamson, 1994)

The *SS-Polizei* Regiments, as they became known from 1943, and the various foreign auxiliary police units were generally used in anti-Partisan, ghetto policing, Jewish deportation and general order roles in the East. The battalions were typically about 500 men strong, divided into one command and four regular companies, each with its own machine-gun support group.

Some of the foreign auxiliary police units were also deployed in assisting the *Einsatzgruppen* during extermination and deportation

---

BEFEHLSHABER DER ORDNUNGSPOLIZEI (BDO)

Befehlshaber der Ordnungspolizei Salzburg
- Oberst der Polizei Hellmut Mascus (June 1939–Feb 1942)
- Generalmajor der Polizei Karl Brenner (Feb 1942–July 1942)
- Generalmajor der Polizei Oskar Knofe (July 1942–Mar 1943)
- Generalmajor der Polizei Karl Brenner (Mar 1943–Oct 1943)
- Oberst der Polizei Hans Griep (Oct 1943–Oct 1944)
- Oberst der Polizei Kurt Wolter (Oct 1944–May 1945)

Befehlshaber der Ordnungspolizei Stettin
- Generalmajor der Polizei Erik von Heimburg (Sep 1939–May 1940)
- Generalmajor der Polizei Konrad Ritzer (May 1940–Feb 1942)

Befehlshaber der Ordnungspolizei Stuttgart
- Generalmajor der Polizei Gerhard Winkler (Sep 1939–Aug 1941)
- Oberst der Polizei Wieder (Aug 1941–Feb 1942)
- Generalmajor der Polizei Hellmut Mascus (Feb 1942–May 1942)
- Generalmajor der Polizei Gerhard Winkler (May 1942–Jan 1944)
- Generalmajor der Polizei Petersdorff (Jan 1944–Apr 1945)

Befehlshaber der Ordnungspolizei Wien
- Generalmajor der Polizei Herbert Becker (Jan 1939–Nov 1939)
- Generalmajor der Polizei Dr Carl Retzlaff (Nov 1939–Sep 1943)
- Generalmajor der Polizei Dr Kurt Bader (Sep 1943–Feb 1944)
- Generalleutnant der Polizei Otto Schumann (Feb 1944–Oct 1944)
- Generalmajor der Polizei Dr Kurt Bader (Oct 1944–Apr 1945)

Befehlshaber der Ordnungspolizei Wiesbaden
- Generalmajor der Polizei Georg Jedicke (Sep 1939–May 1941)
- Generalmajor der Polizei Paul Scheer (May 1941–Mar 1942)
- Generalmajor der Polizei Karl Franz (Mar 1942–July 1942)
- Oberst der Gendarmerie Fritz Schuberth (July 1942–Aug 1942)
- Generalmajor der Polizei Hellmut Mascus (Aug 1942–Dec 1943)
- Generalmajor der Polizei Walther Hille (Dec 1943–Oct 1944)
- Oberst der Gendarmerie Niemann (Oct 1944–Apr 1945)

operations. In fact, their behaviour in support of *Wehrmacht* and SS units could shock even racially hardened German sensibilities. In Poland in 1939, for example, *Volksdeutche* serving with the *Orpo* behaved with such violent prejudice against Jews and other elements of the Polish community that the local *Gauleiter* recommended they be disbanded.

Regarding the command relationship between foreign police formations and German police operating abroad, the principal regional command authority was the *Höherer SS- und Polizeiführer* (High SS and Police Leader; HSSPF). The HSSPF posts had been created in 1937 as an evolutionary development of the *SS-Oberabschnitt Führer* (Leaders of the Main Districts), and the HSSPFs became, in the words of Mark Yerger, 'the most powerful (and feared) SS posts created by Himmler' (Yerger, 1997). These positions were not only related to the occupied territories – German HSSPFs were in control of *Oberabschnitt* districts within Germany, and as such controlled all the related *Allgemeine-SS* units. Indeed HSSPFs' control extended over most of the policing and security apparatuses in their given area, although in occupied areas the power was a little more dispersed depending upon the occupation arrangements between civil and military authorities.

The next level of subordinate command after the HSSPF was the *SS- und Polizeiführer* (SSPF). SSPFs were powerful leaders in themselves, with immediate control over a substantial locality. Note too that there was an appointment that was

BEFEHLSHABER DER ORDNUNGSPOLIZEI (BDO)

Befehlshaber der Ordnungspolizei Berlin
- Generalmajor der Polizei Georg Schreyer (Sep 1939–Apr 1940)
- Generalmajor der Polizei Ernst Hitzegrad (Apr 1940–Feb 1942)
- Oberst der Gendarmerie Kowalski (Feb 1942–Oct 1942)
- Oberst der Polizei Wolfsteig (Oct 1942–Mar 1945)
- Oberst der Polizei von Schweinichen (Mar 1945–May 1945)

Befehlshaber der Ordnungspolizei Breslau
- Generalmajor der Polizei Paul Riege (Sep 1939–Apr 1940)
- Oberst der Polizei Oskar Grussendorf (Apr 1940–Sep 1943)
- Generalmajor der Polizei Reiner Liessem (Sep 1943–Aug 1944)
- Oberst der Polizei H. Müller (Aug 1944–Apr 1945)

Befehlshaber der Ordnungspolizei Brüssel
- Oberst der Polizei Wolter (Aug 1944–Sep 1944)

Befehlshaber der Ordnungspolizei Danzig
- Generalmajor der Polizei Leo von Falkowski (Sep 1939–Nov 1943)
- Generalmajor der Polizei Anton Diermann (Nov 1943–Mar 1944)
- Oberst der Polizei Strehlow (Mar 1944–June 1944)
- Generalmajor der Polizei Dr Hachtel (June 1944–Mar 1945)

Befehlshaber der Ordnungspolizei Den Haag
- Generalmajor der Polizei Otto Schumann (June 1940–Dec 1942)
- Generalmajor der Polizei Dr Heinrich Lankenau (Dec 1942–Jan 1944)
- Generalmajor der Polizei Hellmut Mascus (Jan 1944–Oct 1944)
- Oberst der Polizei Griep (Oct 1944–Feb 1945)
- Generalmajor der Polizei Hellmut Mascus (Feb 1945–May 1945)

Befehlshaber der Ordnungspolizei Hamburg
- Generalmajor der Polizei Rudolf Querner (Sep 1939–Oct 1940)
- Generalmajor der Polizei Herbert Becker (Oct 1940–Apr 1942)
- Generalmajor der Polizei Reiner Liessem (Apr 1942–Sep 1943)
- Generalleutnant der Polizei Dr Carl Retzlaff (Sep 1943–Jan 1945)
- Generalmajor der Polizei Walter Abraham (Jan 1945–May 1945)

Befehlshaber der Ordnungspolizei Hannover

- Oberst der Gendarmerie Dr Oscar Lossen (Sep 1939–Feb 1941)
- Generalmajor der Polizei Walter Basset (Feb 1941–May 1943)
- Generalmajor der Polizei Walter Keuck (May 1943–Apr 1945)

Befehlshaber der Ordnungspolizei Kassel

- Generalmajor der Polizei August Meyszner (Sep 1939–Sep 1940)
- Generalmajor der Polizei Karl Hoffmann (Sep 1940–Jan 1944)
- Oberst der Gendarmerie Matt (Jan 1944–Aug 1944)
- Generalmajor der Polizei Rudolf Mueller (Aug 1944–Apr 1945)

Befehlshaber der Ordnungspolizei Kattowitz

- No data

Befehlshaber der Ordnungspolizei Kiew

- Generalleutnant der Polizei Otto von Oelhafen (Sep 1941–Oct 1942)
- Generalleutnant der Polizei Adolf von Bomhard (Oct 1942–Oct 1943)
- Oberst der Gendarmerie Lorge (Oct 1943–Dec 1943)
- Generalleutnant der Polizei Karl Brenner (Dec 1943–June 1944)
- Oberst der Gendarmerie Lorge (June 1944)

Befehlshaber der Ordnungspolizei Königsberg

- Oberst der Schutzpolizei Curt Pohlmeyer (Sep 1939–Jan 1940)
- Generalmajor der Polizei Otto von Oelhafen (Jan 1940–May 1941)
- Generalmajor der Polizei Georg Jedicke (May 1941–July 1941)
- Generalmajor der Polizei Karl Franz (July 1941–Mar 1942)
- Generalmajor der Polizei Rudolf Mueller (Mar 1942–Aug 1944)
- Generalmajor der Polizei Fritz Schuberth (Aug 1944–Apr 1945)

Befehlshaber der Ordnungspolizei Kopenhagen

- Generalmajor der Polizei Erik von Heimburg (Oct 1943–Aug 1944)
- Oberst der Gendarmerie Lorge (Aug 1944–Apr 1945)
- Oberst der Polizei Englisch (Apr 1945–May 1945)

superior to the HSSPFs. This was the post of *Höchste SS- und Polizeiführer* (Supreme SS and Police Leader; HöSSPF), which combined multiple HSSPF and other command regions into a single major command. There were two HöSSPF posts created during the war: HöSSPF 'Italien', essentially responsible for Italy, and HöSSPF 'Ukraine', which made up one of the largest SS territorial commands in the occupied Soviet territories.

The SS police commanders had a variable relationship with the local Party authorities, typically either a *Gauleiter* in Germany proper or a *Reichskommissar* in the occupied territories. (Poland was an exception, controlled by a governor, Hans Frank.) On occasions, the relationship degenerated into a non-cooperative squabble over personnel and policing – like the higher echelons of the Third Reich leadership, authority was often combative rather than cooperative.

Kriminalpolizei

Falling under *Sipo* authority, the *Kripo* was essentially the plain-clothes detective force of the regular German police. As such, the *Kripo* was mainly concerned with high-end non-political crimes – murders, rapes, fraud etc. It was also heavily engaged in tackling Germany's thriving black market economy.

Yet the *Kripo*, like every other police service, had fallen under SS jurisdiction in 1936, and combined with the expanding emergencies of the war years there is a sense in which every police unit had political policing implications. Furthermore, there appears to have been a regular flow of personnel from the *Kripo* to the *Gestapo*, the civilian detectives having applicable investigative skills and local intelligence of great use to the security agency. Indeed, many *Kripo* members held a rank in the *Allgemeine-SS* that was equivalent to their *Kripo* rank, and some *Kripo* members even joined the ghastly *Einsatzgruppen* forces in their murder campaigns in the occupied territories. (The commander of one of the *Einsatzgruppen*, *Einsatzgruppe* B operating in the wake of Army Group Centre following Operation *Barbarossa*, was Artur Nebe, a former head of the *Kripo*.)

Specialist police

Although so far in this chapter we have covered the largest elements of German policing, there were many other forms of specialist policing in the Third Reich. Under the category of *Sonderpolizei* (Special Police), for example, there were a range of units dedicated to specific policing scenarios, and often run by distinct government offices rather than coming under the general police command structure. These units included the *Eisenbahnpolizei* (Railway Police), under the jurisdiction of the Ministry of Transport, the *Bergpolizei* (Mines Police – Ministry of Economic Affairs), *Jagdpolizei* (Game Conservation Police – Forestry Office) and the *Hafenpolizei* (Harbour Police – Ministry of Transport).

Another major strand of German policing was that delivered by the German Army. Military police duties were performed by the *Feldgendarmerie* (Field Police), which

Befehlshaber der Ordnungspolizei Krakau
- Oberst der Gendarmerie Emil Höring (Oct 1939–Nov 1939)
- Generalmajor der Polizei Herbert Becker (Nov 1939–Oct 1940)
- Generalleutnant der Polizei Paul Riege (Oct 1940–Aug 1941)
- Oberst der Gendarmerie Rudolf Mueller (Aug 1941–Dec 1941)
- Generalmajor der Polizei Gerhard Winkler (Dec 1941–May 1942)
- Generalleutnant der Polizei Herbert Becker (May 1942–Aug 1943)
- Generalmajor der Polizei Hans-Dietrich Grünwald (Aug 1943–Mar 1944)
- Generalmajor der Polizei Sendel (Mar 1944–Mar 1944)
- Generalleutnant der Polizei Emil Höring (Mar 1944–? 1944)

Befehlshaber der Ordnungspolizei München
- Oberst der Schutzpolizei Karl Hoffmann (Sep 1939–Sep 1940)
- Generalmajor der Polizei Otto von Oelhafen (Sep 1940–May 1941)
- Generalmajor der Polizei Walther Hille (May 1941–June 1942)
- Oberstleutnant der Polizei Kurt Wolter (June 1942–Oct 1942)
- Generalleutnant der Polizei Otto von Oelhafen (Oct 1942–Feb 1944)
- Generalmajor der Polizei Mühe (Feb 1944–Apr 1945)

Befehlshaber der Ordnungspolizei Münster
- Generalmajor der Polizei Dr Heinrich Lankenau (Sep 1939–Dec 1942)
- Generalmajor der Polizei Otto Schumann (Dec 1942–Sep 1943)
- Generalmajor der Polizei Kurt Goehrum (Sep 1943–Aug 1944)
- Oberst der Polizei Kruse (Aug 1944–Sep 1944)
- Generalleutnant der Polizei Reiner Liessem (Sep 1944–Apr 1945)

Befehlshaber der Ordnungspolizei Nürnberg
- Generalmajor der Polizei Paul Will (Sep 1939–Mar 1943)
- Generalmajor der Polizei Kurt Goehrum (Mar 1943–Sep 1943)
- Generalmajor der Polizei Walter Griphan (Sep 1943–Apr 1945)

Befehlshaber der Ordnungspolizei Oslo

- Generalmajor der Polizei Paul Riege (Apr 1940–Oct 1940)
- Generalmajor der Polizei August Meyszner (Oct 1940–Jan 1942)
- Generalmajor der Polizei Emil Höring (Jan 1942–June 1943)
- Generalleutnant der Polizei Jürgen von Kamptz (June 1943–Sep 1943)
- Generalmajor der Polizei Mackeldey (Sep 1943–Feb 1945)
- Generalmajor der Polizei Hermann Franz (Feb 1945–May 1945)

Befehlshaber der Ordnungspolizei Paris

- Oberst der Polizei von Schweinichen (May 1942–Mar 1943)
- Generalmajor der Polizei Walter Schimana (Mar 1943–May 1943)
- Generalmajor der Polizei Paul Scheer (May 1943–?)

Befehlshaber der Ordnungspolizei Posen

- Generalmajor der Polizei Oskar Knofe (Sep 1939–June 1942)
- Generalmajor der Polizei Walther Hille (June 1942–Dec 1943)
- Generalmajor der Polizei Podzun (Dec 1943–Mar 1944)
- Generalmajor der Polizei Dr Walter Gudewill (Mar 1944–Mar 1945)

Befehlshaber der Ordnungspolizei Prag

- Generalleutnant der Polizei Jürgen von Kamptz (Sep 1939–May 1941)
- Generalmajor der Polizei Otto von Oelhafen (May 1941–Aug 1941)
- Generalleutnant der Polizei Paul Riege (Aug 1941–Sep 1943)
- Generalleutnant der Polizei Ernst Hitzegrad (Sep 1943–Feb 1945)
- Generalmajor der Polizei Paul Otto Geibel (Feb 1945–May 1945)

Befehlshaber der Ordnungspolizei Riga

- Generalleutnant der Polizei Georg Jedicke (July 1941–Mar 1944)
- Generalmajor der Polizei Otto Gieseke (Mar 1944–?)

Befehlshaber der Ordnungspolizei Saarbrücken

- Oberst der Schutzpolizei Paul Scheer (? 1940–May 1941)
- Oberst der Polizei Hans Müller-Brunckhorst (May 1941–Dec 1941)
- Generalmajor der Polizei Ritter von Zottmann (Dec 1941–Dec 1943)

were sown throughout the structure of the *Wehrmacht*, from the *Wehrkreis* (Military District) downwards. The *Feldgendarmerie* performed a broad spectrum of duties that, in the occupied territories, included civil policing. Among these duties were traffic control, pursuing escaped POWs, handling POWs, checking transit and leave papers, enforcing curfews, controlling refugees, monitoring borders and also participating in combat operations. Towards the end of the war, the *Feldgendarmerie* became particularly feared for their role in capturing and executing deserters. In this capacity the police would work in tandem with the Court-Martial Department, or *Feldgerichtsabteilung*, which provided military courts for the rapid 'processing' of those accused of desertion or treason.

Another military police presence was provided by the *Feldjäger* (Sharpshooters), a police unit staffed entirely with combat veterans. The *Feldjäger* were often used as pure combat troops, sent by the OKW directly wherever they were needed – on these occasions the high command gave the *Feldjäger* authority even beyond the local military police commanders.

Both the Army and later the *Luftwaffe* also formed their own *Geheime Feldpolizei* (Secret Field Police; GFP). In essence, these bodies were internal military equivalents of the *Gestapo*, investigating crimes such as sabotage, treason, spying and black marketeering. Many GFP members were from the *Kripo*, and they often worked together with SD operatives.

CHAPTER 6

The Armed Forces

As Hitler came to power in 1933, his overarching priority was to reconstruct his armed forces, returning Germany to a position of military power and influence in Europe.

Back in 1919, the German Army, Navy and Air Force had been crippled by the arrangements of the Versailles Treaty, which placed severe limitations upon German military growth. Yet during the 1920s and 1930s, German militarism continued through various bullish paramilitary organizations, plus the covert development of regular forces through civilian front companies and foreign training centres.

Under Hitler's tenure, Germany finally shrugged off the shackles of Versailles and began the headlong acceleration of military development, making it one of the most powerful land armies and air forces in Europe by 1939, the year Germany committed itself to war.

◾ *Volkstürm* volunteers ready themselves in a trench to face the Allied advance somewhere in Germany, 1945.

Military Rebirth, 1919–39

The German armed forces were in a chaotic and humiliated state following World War I. Hitler not only oversaw the rebirth of Germany's material military strength, but the Third Reich brought new levels of tactical and organizational professionalism.

The armed forces of 1933, at the birth of the Third Reich, were the product of more than two decades of troubled evolution. Following the German defeat in 1918, hundreds of thousands of German soldiers returned home. Most were demobilized and went back to civilian lives, but large numbers retained their military connections by forming into paramilitary *Freikorps* (Free Corps) units, dedicated to fighting Communist revolutionaries.

New armies

The *Freikorps* formations could be of divisional strength in some instances, and were often heavily armed, so technically Germany was far from demilitarized in the aftermath of the war. Furthermore, on 6 March 1919, the newly created Weimar Republic also established its own official state armed forces, known as the *Vorläufige Reichswehr* (Provisional Defence Forces). This force was composed of two main elements, the *Vorläufige Reichsheer* (Provisional Army) and the *Vorläufige Reichsmarine* (Provisional Navy), the former attracting many *Freikorps* members into its ranks (although other groups of *Freikorps* went on to terrorize the Weimar state).

The *Vorläufige Reichsheer* constituted a reportable 400,000-strong force, divided between some

50 brigades, but in October 1919 it was scaled back to 30 brigades and renamed the *Übergangsheer* (Transitional Army). Yet more changes were to come.

Versailles restrictions

In 1920 the military clauses of the Versailles Treaty kicked in, and reduced the German armed forces to a shell of their former selves. In outline, the clauses: 1) limited the numbers of army personnel to 100,000 officers and men; 2) forbade the development of a combat air force; 3) restricted the naval force to six battleships, six cruisers, 12 destroyers and 12 torpedo boats (no submarines were permitted), manned by only 15,000 personnel; 4) ordered the disbandment of the air force.

The Versailles restrictions were aimed at effectively destroying any form of offensive military potential in Germany. The resultant army was called the *Reichswehr* (Reich Defence Forces), consisting of the *Reichsheer* and the *Reichsmarine*. It was this military force that Hitler would have to reshape from 1933.

Laying foundations

Although the greatest period of German military development was undoubtedly from 1933 to 1945, Germany began to bypass the conditions of the Versailles Treaty

well before Hitler attained the chancellorship. The chief organizer of the *Reichswehr* was *Generaloberst* Hans von Seeckt, and as well as the official on-paper armed forces, he promoted what became known as the *Schwarze Reichswehr* (Black *Reichswehr*), covert military formations and development concealed from the Versailles monitors. For example, although Germany was prohibited from having a General Staff, Seeckt simply created an equivalent disguised under the name *Truppenamt* (Troop Office). This office dedicated much of its energies to developing innovative military tactics, based on the experience of the recent war, and began laying many of the foundations for future *Blitzkrieg* warfare.

Germany also subverted the Versailles conditions by doing much of its military development abroad. The Soviet-German Treaty of Rapallo in 1922, for example, gave the Germans military basing rights on Soviet territory, allowing them to test and engineer prohibited weapons systems, and also to increase the size of their armed forces by keeping foreign-based personnel 'off the books'. Submarine design was conducted under a Dutch company established in The Hague in 1922. Civilian front companies also provided other opportunities. The

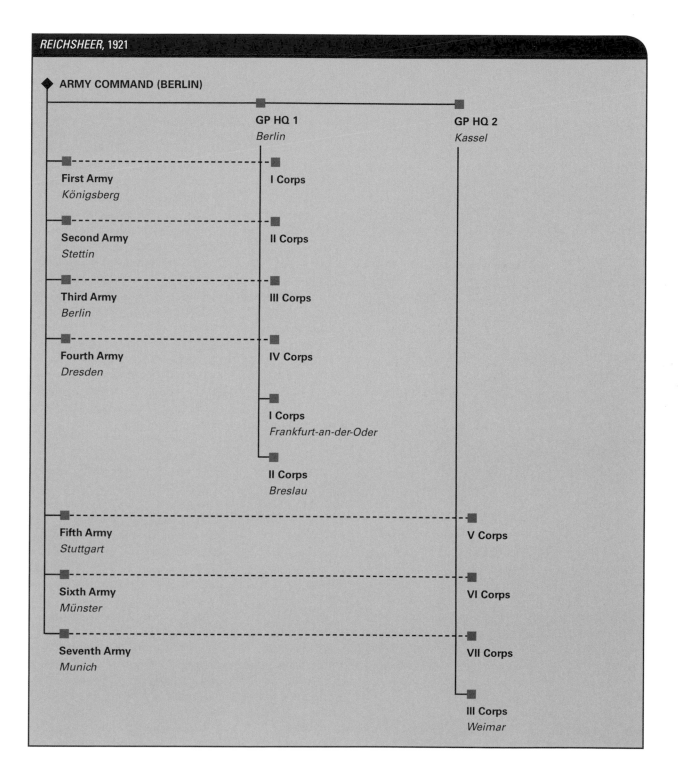

REICHSHEER, 1921

◆ **ARMY COMMAND (BERLIN)**

GP HQ 1
Berlin

GP HQ 2
Kassel

First Army
Königsberg

I Corps

Second Army
Stettin

II Corps

Third Army
Berlin

III Corps

Fourth Army
Dresden

IV Corps

I Corps
Frankfurt-an-der-Oder

II Corps
Breslau

Fifth Army
Stuttgart

V Corps

Sixth Army
Münster

VI Corps

Seventh Army
Munich

VII Corps

III Corps
Weimar

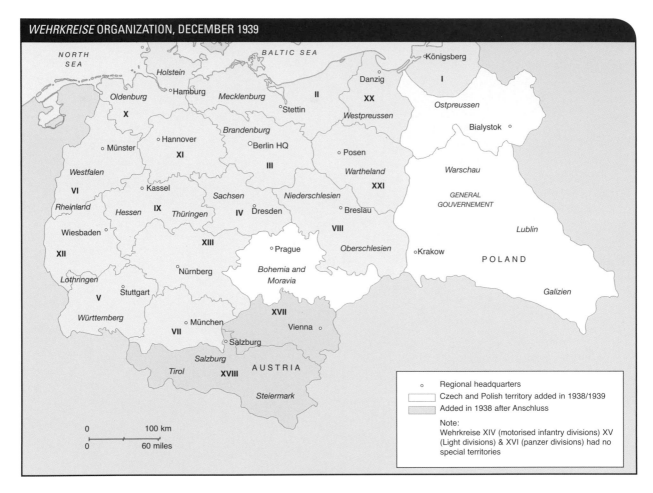

WEHRKREISE ORGANIZATION, DECEMBER 1939

NORTH SEA

BALTIC SEA

Holstein

Königsberg

Hamburg

Danzig

Oldenburg

Mecklenburg

II

X

Stettin

XX

I

Westpreussen

Ostpreussen

Brandenburg

Bialystok

Münster

Hannover

Berlin HQ

XI

Posen

Westfalen

III

Warschau

Warthexand

VI

Kassel

XXI

GENERAL
GOUVERNEMENT

Rheinland

Sachsen

Niederschlesien

Hessen

IX

Thüringen

IV

Dresden

Breslau

Lublin

Wiesbaden

VIII

Krakow

POLAND

XII

XIII

Oberschlesien

Prague

Nürnberg

Bohemia and
Moravia

Lothringen

V

Stuttgart

Galizien

Württemberg

XVII

Vienna

München

VII

Salzburg

Salzburg

AUSTRIA

Tirol

XVIII

Steiermark

o	Regional headquarters
☐	Czech and Polish territory added in 1938/1939
▨	Added in 1938 after Anschluss

Note:
Wehrkreise XIV (motorised infantry divisions) XV (Light divisions) & XVI (panzer divisions) had no special territories

0   100 km
0   60 miles

▲ **WEHRKREISE** The **Wehrkreis** system geographically streamlined the process of recruiting, training and assigning soldiers. By 1943 there were 19 **Wehrkreise**, and they corresponded with the peacetime corps areas, designated by Roman numerals. The headquarters of each **Wehrkreis** had an active field component and also a deputy component that remained in the home territory and was responsible for administering new intakes of soldiers and controlling the application of reserves.

civilian air transport firm Deutsche Luft Hansa Aktiengesellschaft – better known as Lufthansa – was used to train German combat pilots in flying aircraft such as the Junkers Ju 52 and Heinkel He 111, and youth pilot training was delivered though glider schools.

Paramilitaries and power
Even as the *Reichswehr* was furtively growing itself, the Nazi Party was emerging onto the political stage with its own paramilitary wing, the SA (although the SA actually pre-dated

the Nazi Party). The SA was organized into regional military-style formations throughout Germany, and by 1934 it numbered some three million members. The problem for Hitler, who was in personal command of the SA from 1930 to 1931, was that the organization under Ernst Röhm was striving effectively to supplant the *Reichswehr* (Röhm attempted to have himself made Minster of Defence). Partly in response to this ambition, Hitler purged the SA leadership, and thereby secured his relationship with the conventional

WEHRKREISE WITH ASSOCIATED DIVISIONS RAISED, SEPTEMBER 1939

District	Divisions
I	1st, 11th, 21st
II	12th, 32nd
III	3rd, 23rd
IV	4th, 14th, 24th
V	5th, 25th, 35th
VI	6th, 16th, 26th
VII	7th, 27th, 1st *Gebirgs*
VIII	8th, 18th, 28th
IX	9th, 15th
X	22nd, 30th
XI	19th, 31st
XII	33rd, 34th, 36th
XIII	10th, 17th, 46th
XVII	44th, 45th
XVIII	2nd and 3rd *Gebirgs*

GERMAN REARMAMENT, 1930–39

Year	Army (peacetime conscripts)	Military Aircraft	Major Warships	Military Expenditure
1932	100,000 soldiers	36	26	RM 0.61 billion
1939	730,000 soldiers	8295	88	RM 17.24 billion

armed forces hierarchy. Furthermore, the SS, which had grown out of a small SA personal bodyguard to Hitler, was by this time taking on a separate and salient identity as the Nazi Party's primary paramilitary force. In 1939, the armed elements of the SS were distilled into the *Waffen-SS* (Armed SS), a pure combat wing that became the most important land fighting arm of the German forces outside of the *Wehrmacht*.

Manpower
In March 1935, Hitler formally rejected the military conditions of the Versailles Treaty and set his country on the road to rearmament. The material results of this have been covered earlier, but the manpower deliveries were equally dramatic. In 1932, the *Reichswehr* had consisted of 100,000 troops, but by 1939 that number had escalated to 730,000

soldiers. The dramatic leap in numbers proceeded from Hitler's reintroduction of conscription within two years of coming to power – conscription had been banned under the terms of the Versailles Treaty, and the *Reichswehr* had consequently been composed purely of volunteers. To facilitate conscription, Hitler arranged the *Reich* into *Wehrkreise* (Military Districts), each *Wehrkreis* being responsible for the raising of divisions and corps of troops (see map opposite).

Oath of allegiance
In addition to bringing about manpower transformations, Hitler also ushered in a new era of command and control at the highest levels of the armed forces. His transparent objective, however, was to centralize military command, and military loyalty, on himself.

In August 1934, Hitler passed his 'Law Concerning the Head of State of the German Reich', which combined the offices of Chancellor and President into one. On 19 August, he proclaimed himself the *Führer* of Germany and the next day passed his 'Law On The Allegiance of Civil Servants and Soldiers of the Armed Forces'. This legislation changed the armed forces oath to one of direct allegiance to the *Führer*, rather than to 'the People and the Fatherland'

enshrined in the previous oath. From now on, Germany's soldiers would serve Hitler personally.

Command and control
The following year began a process of dramatic structural change in the armed forces command. On 15 October 1935, Germany officially announced the existence of the *Wehrmacht* (Armed Forces) as the replacement for the *Reichswehr*. The new military organization was a clear indication to the world that Germany had rejected the military restrictions of the Versailles Treaty. The *Wehrmacht* was under the command of the *Oberkommando der Wehrmacht* (Armed Forces High Command; OKW), under which came the *Oberkommando des Heeres* (OKH), *Oberkommando der Luftwaffe* (OKL) and *Oberkommando der Marine* (OKM) for the German Army, Air Force and Navy respectively. Note that the SS remained outside *Wehrmacht* authority, its command coming directly from Heinrich Himmler through consultation with Hitler.

The OKW was firmly under Hitler's control – on 4 February 1938 he took personal command of Germany's armed forces, prior to his invasion of Poland the following year. Hitler had, nonetheless, ensured that the *Wehrmacht* was ready for war.

OKW & OKH ORGANIZATION, 1940

◆ **SUPREME COMMANDER (HITLER)**

National Socialist Guidance of the Army

Führer's **Official Military Historian**
- Army Historical Branch
- Military History Research Institute
- Chief of Army Archive
- Chief of Army Library
- Captured Document Exploitation

Inspector-General of Panzer Troops
- Chief Anti-tank Officer for All Arms
- Inspector of Panzer Troops
- Field Army Branch
- Training Branch

C-in-C of the Army
- Chief Medical Inspector
- Chief Veterinary Inspector
- Army General Staff
  - Central Branch of General Staff
  - Supply and Administration
  - Operations
  - Field Army Training
  - Organization
  - Operational Intelligence
  - Military History
- Chiefs of Branches Attached to General Staff
  - Chief Infantry Officer
  - Chief of Armoured Trains
  - Chief Artillery Officer
  - Chief of Mapping and Survey
  - Chief Signal Officer
  - Chief Engineer and Fortress Engineer
  - Chief Chemical Warfare Officer
  - Chief of Volunteer Units
  - Chief Army Transportation Officer
  - General For Special Employment
- Army Personnel Office
  - Officers' Records, Transfer and Promotion
  - Officers' Education and Welfare
  - General Staff Officers
  - Officer Replacements
  - Decorations and Awards
  - Specialist Officers
  - Officers of *Volksgrenadier* Units
  - Ceremonial Occasions
  - Courses for Senior Personnel Officers

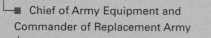

- Chief of Army Equipment and
  Commander of Replacement Army
  - General Army Office
    - Staff
    - Inspectorate of Arms and Services
    - General Troop Matters
    - Army Judge Advocate General
    - Unit Inactivation Staff
    - Demobilization Branch
    - Chief of Army Museums
  - Chief of Training in Replacement Army
    - Inspector of Infantry
    - Inspector of Riding and Driving
    - Inspector of Artillery
    - Inspector of Army AA Troops
    - Inspector of Engineers and
      Railway Engineers
    - Inspector of Construction Troops
    - Inspector of Signal Troops
    - Inspector of Supply Troops
    - Inspector of Chemical Troops
    - Training Film Branch
  - Army Ordnance Office
    - General Group
    - Development and Testing of
      Ordnance Equipment
    - Weapons and Equipment Manufacture
    - Ammunition Manufacture
    - Acceptance
    - Chief Ordnance Engineer
    - AA Artillery Development
    - Research Branch
  - Army Administration
    - Officials and Civilian Workers
    - Real Estate, Agriculture and Forests
    - Rations and Procurement Group
    - Construction Group
    - Budget Group
  - Inspector General for Potential Officers
    and NCOs
    - Procurement of Leaders
    - Cadet School Branch
    - NCO School Branch
    - Inspector of Army Officers
      Procurement Offices
  - Signal Communications
  - Army Raw Materials Branch
  - Army Map Service
  - Army Technical Bureau
  - Female Auxiliary Corps

The German Land Forces

When it swung into action in 1939, the German Army constituted the most professional land army in the world, although over time the mythologies that grew up about their capabilities have been unsettled.

The creation of the OKW brought with it fundamental implications for the leadership of the German Army, the primary force behind Hitler's territorial conquests. One of the most significant was the change in relationship between the state and the Army, as historian James Lucas here points out:

For the first time in German military history, a body stood between the Commander-in-Chief of the Army and the head of state, thus realizing the fears of many senior officers, who saw that with the setting up of the OKW, part of the prerogatives and the freedom of action of the

Army Commander-in-Chief would be diminished.

(Lucas, 2000)

Hitler handled resistance to his plans by massaging the appointments process in his own favour, placing compliant commanders in the key roles while muscling resistant leaders into retirement or resignation. *Generaloberst* Walther von Brauchitsch was head of the OKH at the start of the war, holding the post until December 1941, while the OKW chief was *Generaloberst* Wilhelm Keitel, who remarkably retained his position for the duration of the war, an indication of his diligent loyalty to

the *Führer*. Another key appointment was Alfred Jodl, who became the Chief of Operations Staff at OKW. He was responsible for briefing the *Führer* on the development of the military campaigns, and as such had a uniquely persuasive position in relation to Hitler's military thinking.

It should also be noted that in December 1941, Brauchitsch was replaced by none other than Hitler himself as head of the OKH. The German Army's failure to take Moscow, plus Brauchitsch's suffering

INDIVIDUALS PROHIBITED FROM MILITARY SERVICE

The following categories of men are described as 'unworthy to bear arms' and therefore 'excluded from military service':

- Those sentenced to penal servitude (Zuchthaus).
- Those who do not possess the honorary civil rights.
- Those subjected to 'security and improvement' measures (concentration camp for supposed habitual criminals).
- Those deprived of their 'worthiness to bear arms' by a court martial.
- Those sentenced for activities inimical to the state.
- Jews also are excluded from military service, but in wartime are required to do other types of service.

Information from US War Department Technical Manual, TM-E 30-451: Handbook on German Military Forces published in March 1945

CATEGORIZATION OF RESERVE MANPOWER

Information from US War Department Technical Manual, TM-E 30-451: Handbook on German Military Forces published in March 1945:

Reserve status. All men not doing their active military service are classified into the following categories:

Reserve Status	Description
Reserve I:	Those under 35 who have completed their regular period of active service and been discharged. There are only very few fit men in this group today.
Reserve II:	Those under 35 who have been through a period of short-term training. This applied before the war to some of the older classes.
Ersatzreserve I:	Fit men under 35 who have not been trained.
Ersatzreserve II:	Unfit and limited-service men under 35 who have not been trained.
Landwehr I:	Trained men between 35 and 45 (actually from 31 March of the year in which the 35th birthday occurs until the 31 March following the 45th birthday).
Landwehr II:	Untrained men between 35 and 45.
Landsturm I:	Trained men between 45 and 55 (actually from the 31 March following the 45th birthday until the 31 March following the 55th birthday).
Landsturm II:	Untrained men between 45 and 55. (The two categories of Landsturm applied in peacetime only to East Prussia; they now include men up to 61.)

a heart attack, motivated Hitler to tighten his control over his armed forces a little more.

Wartime structure

The wartime German Army was arranged according to two basic structures. Looking at the broadest levels of organization, the Army units and formations were sub-divided into the *Feldheer* (Field Army) and the *Ersatzheer* (Replacement Army). The *Feldheer*, as the name suggests, was the active combat and operational element of the Army. The *Ersatzheer*, by contrast, was a non-combat army used for sourcing and training recruits and resupplying manpower (such as handling soldiers returning to duty following convalescence), with *Ersatz* formations matched to those in the field. The *Ersatzheer* was itself sub-divided into *Ersatz* (Replacement) and *Ausbildungs* (Training) units, although changes in the second half of 1942 meant that the *Ersatz* units focused purely on taking in recruits and passing them on to the training units, which in turn became reserves for the field units.

For administrative purposes, the German Army also made distinctions between combat and non-combat zones. The combat zone was known as the *Operationsgebiet* (Operations Zone), separated into the *Gefechtsgebiet* (Combat Zone) and the *Rückwärtiges Gebiet* (Rear Area). Beyond the operational areas were the *Gebiet der Kriegsverwaltung* (Military Administrative Zone), which was essentially safe, occupied territory, and finally came the *Heimatsgebiet* (Home Zone). By dividing up a theatre in this way,

GERMAN PANZER ARMIES, 1940–45

Panzer Army	Date Formed	Notes
First Panzer Army	November 1940	From Nov 1940 to Oct 1941 known as Panzer Group I
Second Panzer Army	November 1940	From Nov 1940 to Oct 1941 known as Panzer Group II
Third Panzer Army	November 1940	From Nov 1940 to Dec 1941 known as Panzer Group III
Fourth Panzer Army	February 1941	From Feb 1941 to Dec 1941 known as Panzer Group IV
Fifth Panzer Army	December 1942	Destroyed May 1943, re-formed in July 1944
Sixth Panzer Army	September 1944	Created for the Ardennes offensive
Eleventh Panzer Army	January 1945	Renamed Army Detachment Steiner in March 1945
Panzer Army Afrika	August 1941	Initially known as Panzer Group Afrika, becoming Army in Jan 1942

GERMAN ARMIES, 1939–45

Army	Date Formed	Notes
First Army	August 1939	Stationed in Western Europe for duration of war
First Parachute Army	July 1944	Consolidated various *Luftwaffe* combat units in the West
Second Army	October 1939	Renamed Army Command East Prussia in April 1945
Third Army	August 1939	Became Sixteenth Army after Poland campaign
Fourth Army	August 1939	Destroyed in March 1945, and remnants used to form Twenty-First Army
Fifth Army	August 1939	Became Eighteenth Army in November 1940
Sixth Army	October 1939	Destroyed at Stalingrad in February 1943. Re-formed in March 1943
Seventh Army	August 1939	Served until its surrender in April 1945
Eighth Army	August 1939	Redesignated Second Army after Poland campaign
Ninth Army	May 1940	Surrendered April 1945
Tenth Army	August 1939	Redesignated Sixth Army after Poland campaign. Re-formed in August 1943
Eleventh Army	October 1940	Redesignated Army Group Don in November 1942. Re-formed in February 1945
Twelfth Army	October 1939	Redesignated Armed Force South East in June 1941, Army Group East in December 1942, then Twelfth Army in February 1945
Fourteenth Army	August 1939	Redesignated Twelfth Army after Poland campaign. Re-formed in November 1943
Fifteenth Army	January 1941	Served in West for duration of the war
Sixteenth Army	October 1939	Remained unchanged for duration of the war
Seventeenth Army	December 1940	Effectively destroyed in May 1944
Eighteenth Army	November 1940	Active to May 1945
Nineteenth Army	August 1943	Largely destroyed January/February 1945
Twentieth Mountain Army	June 1942	Formed from Army of Lapland
Twenty-First Army	April 1945	Created from Fourth Army
Twenty-Fourth Army	December 1944	Did not reach operational status until April 1945
Twenty-Fifth Army	January 1945	Deployed in West
Army of Norway	December 1940	Disbanded in December 1944
Army of Lapland	January 1942	Redesignated Twentieth Mountain Army in June 1942

German combat commanders had streamlined relationships to their major objectives and important command decisions, rather than being oppressed by too many non-relevant issues.

On a more fundamental level of operational command, the largest formation within the German Army was the *Heeresgruppe* (Army Forces Group), made up of several armies and, totalling hundreds of thousands of men, used for major theatre actions. Similar in principle was the

Armeegruppe (Army Group), also composed of a group of armies (although earlier in the war it could also mean an army-sized formation) but subordinate to the *Heeresgruppe*. Below the *Armeegruppe* came the formation and unit types familiar to most land armies: *Armee* (Army), *Korps* (Corps), *Division*, *Brigade*, *Regiment*, *Abteilung* or *Bataillon* (Battalion), *Kompanie* (Company) and *Zug* (Platoon).

One formation more particular to the German Army was the

Kampfgruppe (Battle Group), a mixed-arms formation that could range anywhere between battalion and corps size. *Kampfgruppen* were organized on an ad hoc basis to achieve specific tasks.

The heart of the German infantry was, however, the division. There were several different types of infantry division, based on composition and function (or sometimes just on honorary status). The *Jäger* ('Chasseur', or Light) divisions were equipped with limited

HEER RANK SYSTEM

German Rank	Translation	German Rank	Translation
Schütze	Rifleman	Gefreiter	Junior Cadet
Soldat	Soldier	Obergefreiter	Corporal
Grenadier	Infantryman	Stabsgefreiter	Staff Lance Corporal
Fusilier	Rifleman	Unteroffizier	Junior NCO
Musketier	Rifleman	Unterfeldwebel	Junior Sergeant
Jäger	Chasseur	Fähnrich	Officer Candidate
Reiter	Rider	Feldwebel	Sergeant
Kanonier	Gunner	Oberfeldwebel	First Sergeant
Panzerschütze	Tank Soldier	Hauptfeldwebel	Chief Sergeant
Panzergrenadier	Armour Infantryman	Stabsfeldwebel	Staff Sergeant
Pionier	Engineer	Leutnant	Second Lieutenant
Funker	Radio Operator	Oberleutnant	First Lieutenant
Fahrer	Horse Rider	Hauptmann	Captain
Kraftfahrer	Motor Driver	Major	Major
Musikerschütze	Musician	Oberstleutnant	Lieutenant-Colonel
Sanitätssoldat	Medical Orderly	Oberst	Colonel
Oberschütze	Chief Rifleman	Generalmajor	Major-General
Oberreiter	Chief Cavalryman	Generalleutnant	Lieutenant-General
Obergrenadier	Chief Infantryman	General der...	General of...
Oberjäger	Chief Chasseur	General der Infanterie	General of Infantry
Oberkanonier	Chief Gunner	General der Artillerie	General of Artillery
Panzerobeschütze	Chief Tank Soldier	General der Kavallerie	General of Cavalry
Oberpanzergrenadier	Chief Armour Infantryman	General der Panzertruppen	General of Armoured Troops
Oberpionier	Chief Engineer	General der Pioniere	General of Engineers
Oberfunker	Chief Radioman	General der Gebirgstruppen	General of Mountain Troops
Oberfahrer	Chief Rider	Generaloberst	Colonel-General
Oberkraftfahrer	Chief Motor Driver	Generalfeldmarschall	Field Marshal
Musikoberschütze	Chief Musician		
Sanitätsobersoldat	Chief Medical Orderly		

PERSONNEL IN ARMY *(HEER)* SERVICE, 1939–45 (MILLIONS, ESTIMATED)

Year	Value
1939	3.7
1940	4.6
1941	5
1942	5.8
1943	6.6
1944	6.5
1945	5.3

light transport and smaller artillery pieces, hence they were often applied as *Gebirgsjäger* (Mountain Light Infantry) for deployment into rugged or high-altitude terrain.

Grenadier divisions were essentially standard line infantry divisions but with an honorific title.

Panzergrenadier divisions, by contrast, were fully motorized formations, capable of transporting all troops and weapon systems by mechanized means. Note that the term was adopted only from 1943, and could refer to both mechanized divisions or the mechanized infantry

component of a Panzer division. As such, the *Panzergrenadier* divisions were mixed-arms formations, containing artillery, anti-aircraft, anti-tank, combat engineering, reconnaissance and other components. Prior to 1943, the motorized infantry divisions were known by the descriptive title *motorisierte Infanteriedivision*.

Festung (Fortress) and *bodenständige* (static) divisions, as their names suggest, were stationed in non-mobile positions and were often formations that were suffering from combat-depleted manpower. *Volksgrenadier* (People's Grenadier) divisions were essentially reconstituted formations from the

ORGANIZATION OF ARMY FORCES CORPS AREA ADMINISTRATION, 1939–45

Section A
Responsibilities: Fiscal matters; pay regulations; office equipment; travel, moving, and transportation allowances; welfare and pensions; vocational schools of the Army; libraries; regulations for cashiers, bookkeepers, and auditors; regulations for paymasters.

Section B
Also known as the auditing office (Abrechnungsintendantur). Responsibilities: Audited accounts of unit paymasters in the field and of ordnance installations in the corps area.

Section C
Responsibilities: Procurement, supply, administration, and issue of rations; procurement of forage for remount depots; bakeries; troop kitchens; field ration supply; auditing rations-related accounts; auditing of the accounts of the remount depots.

Section D
Responsibilities: Supervision/auditing of garrison administrations; billeting; administration of property.

Section E
Responsibilities: Administration of hospitals; auditing of hospital accounts; administration relating to civilian workers; relevant legal matters; clothing; supervision of clothing depots and auditing of their accounts.

Section F
Responsibilities: Construction matters; supervision of the construction offices; civilian contracts.

Section G
Responsibilities: Procurement of living quarters for members of the staff of the Corps Area Administration.

Section P
Responsibilities: (P I) personnel matters of the administrative officers; (P II) personnel matters of civilian workers.

remnants of embattled divisions, and were typically understrength.

Armour and artillery

The *Panzer* divisions were at the core of German *Blitzkrieg* tactics, providing the armoured spearheads for deep-penetration offensives, plus the mechanized muscle to take on enemy armoured formations. We should not think of the *Panzer* divisions as homogeneous armoured entities, however. Tanks were not self-sufficient fighting machines – as well as their thirsty logistical needs, they also required extensive infantry support to protect them from tank-hunting infantry. Taking a typical *Panzer* division of 1940, for example, it was composed of two regiments of tanks (some 240 machines), but in addition it contained a rifle regiment (later divisions had two *Panzergrenadier* regiments), an artillery regiment, an anti-tank regiment, a flak detachment, a reconnaissance group, a signals company, an engineering unit, a motorcycle battalion, plus a major

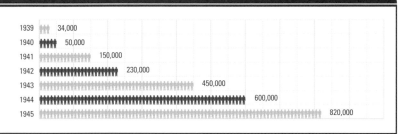

PERSONNEL IN *WAFFEN-SS* SERVICE, 1939–45 (ESTIMATED)

Year	Personnel
1939	34,000
1940	50,000
1941	150,000
1942	230,000
1943	450,000
1944	600,000
1945	820,000

GERMAN ARMED FORCES PERSONAL DOCUMENTATION

Service Record (Wehrpass)
The basic personal record of the members of the Armed Forces is their service record. This is a book of passport size issued to them at the time of their first physical examination for military service. It contains a complete record of their pre-military service in the German Labor Service (Reichsarbeitsdienst), their military status at all times, and all their military activities until the expiration of their liability to military service. This book is in their personal possession only while they are in inactive status, and is retained at their company headquarters as long as they are on active service. In exchange for it, as soldiers, they carry on their person a pay and identification book issued to them at the time of their first induction.

Paybook (Soldbuch)
The paybook of the German soldier is his official means of identification and contains, in addition to personal data, a record of all units in which he has served and their replacement affiliations; his clothing and equipment record, inoculations, hospitalization; his promotions, pay rate group, payments received from units other than his own, decorations, furloughs, and other data pertaining to his person or his active service. The paybook contains both the soldier's military registration number (Wehrnummer), under which his service record was issued to him before his actual induction, and the inscription and number on his identification disc (Beschriftung und Nummer der Erkennungsmarke).

Identification Disc (Erkennungsmarke)
The identification disc which the German soldier wears around his neck consists of two halves, both with identical inscriptions. It is issued to him by the unit (normally at company level) into which he is first inducted; both the name of that unit and the serial number under which the disc was issued to him are inscribed on it, as well as his blood type. Any unit, however, may issue a disc to a member who has lost his original one, with its own name and a new serial number.

Unit Roster Sheet (Kriegsstammrollenblatt)
Every Field Army unit and those units of the Replacement Army which are of Field Army or training type keep an individual roster sheet on every one of their members, containing the record of the individual's service in the

supply train. In total, the division had around 16,000 personnel in its ranks.

The German Army's artillery force was regimentally structured, the idea (and the ideal) being that each infantry division would have a similarly numbered artillery regiment attached as a support arm. In terms of divisional artillery, a typical field regiment would consist of regimental headquarters plus a signal section, three field batteries and one medium battery, as well as a three-troop ammunition column. In total, this type of regiment contained around 48 field guns, usually of 10cm (3.9in), 10.5cm

(4.1in) and 15cm (5.9in) types. An anti-aircraft section (typically two 2cm/0.78in guns and around 20 small-calibre guns) was attached to provide air cover. An armoured division, by contrast, usually had a two-battery regiment with around 24 guns but might also have a third battery of 15cm (5.9in) howitzers. Of course, under wartime conditions the strength and allocation of artilllery varied enormously, and the numbers of batteries and guns were adjusted accordingly as the war progressed.

James Lucas notes that 'The artillery was arranged regimentally because it was not foreseen that a

larger grouping than a regiment would be needed. That optimistic belief was soon shown to be false' (Lucas, 2000). Indeed, several infantry divisions and brigades were later created on both the Eastern and Western Fronts in an attempt to create more potent artillery arms.

Beyond the regular field artillery, the German Army also operated huge pieces of siege artillery, typically in the form of heavy-calibre mortars and howitzers or long-range railway guns. The largest of these specimens were up to 80cm (31.4in) in calibre – such as Krupp's *Gustav Gerät* – and were generally seen on the Eastern Front.

---

unit. This sheet is to be closed upon the termination of that service and then forwarded direct to the soldier's home recruiting station (Wehrersatzdienststelle), where his basic military records are kept. There are two different forms: one for officers and officials of all ranks, the other for enlisted men.

Basic Military Records
At the time of the first physical examination when the service record (Wehrpass) is issued to the soldier by his recruiting sub-area headquarters (Wehrbezirkskommando), the latter opens a corresponding basic military record book (Wehrstammbuch) for him, together with an accompanying health record book (Gesundheitsbuch) and a classification card (Verwendungskarte). His military registration card (Wehrstammkarte), which was made out by the police authorities as part of his military registration record (Wehrstammblatt), is pasted inside the front cover of the Wehrstammbuch. Actually, this card is an open envelope with the soldier's registration record on its face and containing a police report (Polizeibericht) on his conduct prior to registration.

Military Registration Number (Wehrnummer)
This is determined at the time the Wehrpass is issued to the soldier; in other words, while he is still a civilian. He retains it permanently, regardless of whether he is in active service or not, as his identifying number with the authorities which administer the conscription laws. It normally consists of the following five elements (although there are some variations):

■ *Name of the Wehrbezirkskommando.*
■ *Last two digits of the year of birth.*
■ *Number of military registration police precinct (in certain larger cities, number corresponding to first letter of family name).*
■ *Serial number of the conscription (or volunteer) roster sheet (Wehrstammrollenblatt).*
■ *Number indicating registrant's place on that sheet (from 1 to 10).*

From US War Department Technical Manual, TM-E 30-451: Handbook on German Military Forces published in March 1945

Strengths and Capabilities, 1939–45

The German Army, for all its eventual defeat, was a militarily talented organization that achieved great feats of arms. It limitations, however, were revealed in operations over large territories such as the Soviet Union.

A total of around 16 million men passed through the ranks of the German Field Army alone between 1939 and 1945, three million of them dying in the process. If we include the *Waffen-SS* in our calculations (see below), the figures for total numbers of fully operational fielded divisions are impressive:

Infantry divisions – 280
Panzer divisions – 38
Motorized and *Panzergrenadier* divisions – 29
Cavalry divisions – 5
Light, *Jäger* and *Gebirgsjäger* divisions – 30

Of course, a division on paper does not reveal the true condition of that formation, and particularly towards the end of the war a battle-worn division could plunge in manpower to little more than regimental or battalion strength, and lose its cohesion and relevance. Further German divisions were theoretically formed, but either did not achieve full establishment or were critically understrength from the outset and saw no active combat deployment.

Waffen-SS
The role of the *Waffen-SS* (as opposed to the *Allgemeine-SS*) in the

German land forces must not be underestimated, as in total it deployed some 39 divisions containing one million soldiers during World War II. The *Waffen-SS*, as a direct military expression of Nazi ideology and with unswerving loyalty to Hitler, is remembered by history for its frequently horrifying prosecution of the *Führer*'s racial war, yet as the war progressed its total manpower was increasingly reliant upon foreign contributions. Besides Germans, nationalities that served within the ranks of the *Waffen-SS* included Norwegians, Danes, Dutch, French, Yugoslavs, Belgians, Italians, Hungarians, Latvians, Estonians, Russians and even a handful of British.

Many of these foreign divisions were of questionable quality, however, particularly once they saw the writing on the wall later in the war. The purely German divisions – which included such famous formations as the 1.*SS-Panzerdivision* Leibstandarte Adolf Hitler, the 2.*SS-Panzerdivision* Das Reich and 3.*SS-Panzerdivision* Totenkopf – were, regardless of their war crimes, superb combat forces. They were often used in 'fire brigade' roles, sent to hold beleaguered sections of the line or used to spearhead attacks. Equipment standards in these divisions were generally high,

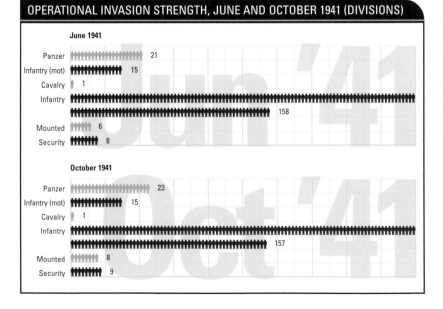

OPERATIONAL INVASION STRENGTH, JUNE AND OCTOBER 1941 (DIVISIONS)

June 1941

Panzer	21
Infantry (mot)	15
Cavalry	1
Infantry	158
Mounted	6
Security	8

October 1941

Panzer	23
Infantry (mot)	15
Cavalry	1
Infantry	157
Mounted	8
Security	9

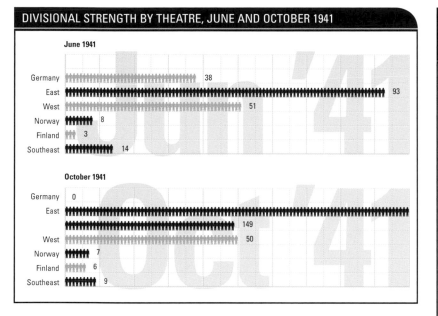

DIVISIONAL STRENGTH BY THEATRE, JUNE AND OCTOBER 1941

June 1941

Germany	38
East	93
West	51
Norway	8
Finland	3
Southeast	14

October 1941

Germany	0
East	149
West	50
Norway	7
Finland	6
Southeast	9

ARMOURED VEHICLE STRENGTHS ON EASTERN FRONT, 1941–45

Date	German AFVs	Soviet AFVs
June 1941	3671	28,800
March 1942	1503	4690
May 1942	3981	6190
Nov 1942	3133	4940
March 1943	2374	7200
August 1943	2555	6200
June 1944	4470	11,600
September 1944	4186	11,200
October 1944	4917	11,900
November 1944	5202	14,000
December 1944	4785	15,000
January 1945	4881	14,200

Source: John Ellis, The World War II Databook

although the notion that all *Waffen-SS* divisions boasted equipment superior to that of the *Heer* divisions is largely a myth.

Luftwaffe contributions

The *Luftwaffe*'s major contribution to World War II was obviously its aviation (see below), but it also formed significant elements of land defence. Its most illustrious combat formations were its *Fallschirmjäger* airborne troops, developed from the mid-1930s and arranged into an effective operational command under *Generalmajor* (later *Generaloberst*) Kurt Student in 1938. During the war years, a total of 11 airborne divisions were formed, and the German paratroops had a similar aura and reputation as elite troops as that enjoyed by *Waffen-SS* formations.

In airborne actions, the *Fallschirmjäger* were deployed either by low-altitude static-line parachute drop or by direct airlanding in DFS 230 gliders or Junkers Ju 52 transport aircraft. Their early operations during the campaigns of 1940 were a stunning success, particularly the assault on the Belgian fortress of Eben Emael, and they were lauded by both Hitler and the German public. Their greatest operation was by far the invasion of Crete on 20 May 1941, a feat conducted almost exclusively by the *Luftwaffe* soldiers. Against dramatic odds, Crete fell to the Germans, but the horrifying loss of some 25 per cent of the attacking force – 7000 dead – revealed the acute vulnerabilities of airborne deployments, and the *Fallschirmjäger* were never used again in large-scale airborne actions, being deployed instead as elite infantry.

As well as the *Fallschirmjäger*, the *Luftwaffe* also created a total of 21 field divisions, these being formed between 1942 and 1944. These were more about vanity projects for Göring, who wanted a significant land forces

VOLKSSTURM ORGANIZATION, 1945

Territorial Political Unit	Military Unit
Kreis (roughly equivalent to a US county; there are 920 kreise in Greater Germany)	*Bataillon* (battalion)
Ortsgruppe (roughly equivalent to a US Congressional district)	*Kompanie* (company)
Zelle (literally 'a cell'; roughly equivalent to a US precinct)	*Zug* (platoon)
Block (a city block)	*Gruppe* (squad)

From the US Intelligence Bulletin, published in February 1945

GERMAN SOLDIER'S TEN COMMANDMENTS (PRINTED IN PAY BOOK)

1. *While fighting for victory, the German soldier will observe the rules of chivalrous warfare. Cruelties and needless destruction are below his values.*

2. *Combatants will be wearing uniform or will wear specially introduced and clearly identifiable badges. Fighting in civilian clothes or without such badges is prohibited.*

3. *No enemy who has surrendered will be executed, including partisans and spies. They will be duly punished by courts.*

4. *POWs will not be ill-treated or mocked. Arms, maps and records will be taken away from them, but their personal belongings will not be touched.*

5. *Dum-Dum bullets are prohibited; also no other bullets may be transformed into Dum-Dums.*

6. *Red Cross institutions are sacrosanct. Injured enemies are to be treated humanely. Medical personnel and army chaplains should not be hindered in performing their medical or clerical activities.*

7. *The civilian population is sacrosanct. No looting nor egregious destruction is permitted by the soldier. Landmarks of historical value or buildings serving religious purposes, art, science, or charity are to be especially respected. Deliveries in kind made, as well as services rendered by the population, may be claimed only if ordered by superiors and only against compensation.*

8. *Neutral territory will never be entered nor passed over by aircraft, nor shot at; it will not be the focus of warmaking of any kind.*

9. *If a German soldier is made a POW he will give his name and rank if he is asked for them. Under no circumstances will he reveal the unit to which he belongs, nor will he give any information about German military, political and economic conditions. Neither promises nor threats may induce him to do so.*

10. *Offences against the a/m matters of duty will be punished. Enemy offences against the principles under 1 to 8 are to be reported. Reprisals are permissible only on order of higher commands.*

presence under his control, and they were of indifferent quality. Furthermore, in 1943 the *Heer* – which could make better use of additional land forces – took control of these divisions, changing the name from *Luftwaffe-Feld Division* to *Feld-Division (Luftwaffe)*.

Operational strengths

In many ways, the German Army laid the foundations for modern manoeuvre warfare, and its initial strengths in tactics and weaponry explain to a large extent the brilliance of German victories between 1939 and 1942.

Inspired by British experiments with armoured formations during the 1930s, which were refined by that pioneer of armoured warfare Heinz Guderian, the Germans put armour at centre stage of their *Blitzkrieg* tactics. Tanks and armoured vehicles would work in combined-arms formations with infantry, artillery, air support and reconnaissance forces, the whole package sewn together with radio communications. The effect was a fast-moving attack formation that could punch through enemy weak points and advance to take key positions before effective opposition could materialize. Accompanying the advance was a strong force of anti-tank artillery, whose purpose was to deplete enemy armour rather than waste German tanks in tank-on-tank engagements.

When properly executed under the right geographical conditions (see 'Operational weaknesses' below), *Blitzkrieg* was stunningly effective. Its effectiveness was aided by an extremely professional officer and NCO corps, the skills of which had been maintained even through the turbulence of the Weimar period. Forces worked on clear principles of *Auftragstaktik* (mission-oriented tactics), decision-making being devolved low down the ranks, encouraging each man to apply initiative and daring to solve tactical problems. Moreover, unlike centralized armies such as the Red Army, the *Heer* units did not become headless chickens with the loss of a key officer – his subordinates were usually capable of taking over and keeping the mission on track.

In addition to excellent manpower (diluted only in the last months of the war), the German Army also enjoyed advanced weaponry. Its small arms included some of the best machine guns in history, such as the MG42, and it had versatile artillery pieces such as the 8.8cm (3.5in) Flak 18, 36 or 37 (an anti-aircraft gun that proved itself a capable anti-tank weapon). In terms of armour, tanks like the Tiger and Panther were unsurpassed in terms of the complete package of armour protection and gunnery.

Operational weaknesses
While the German Army was undoubtedly at the cutting edge of material and tactical developments, it had not entirely left history behind. It remained, for example, acutely dependent upon horse-drawn logistics. During Operation *Barbarossa* in 1941, it used 750,000 horses within its supply train, with all the accompanying problems of supplying forage and care. In fact, logistics was the true Achilles' heel

of the *Wehrmacht*. In Europe, the nature of the theatre meant that logistical distances were fairly short, but in the vast expanses of the Soviet Union they were quickly stretched to breaking point. *Blitzkrieg* was

designed for quick victory, not for drawn-out campaigns of attrition. Once the *Heer* became spread out holding endless front lines, or was engaged in massive city battles, many of its advantages disappeared.

MISCELLANEOUS *HEER* AND *WAFFEN-SS* DECORATIONS

- Anti-Partisan Badge
- Army Anti-Aircraft Badge
- Army Balloon Observer's Badge
- Army Balloon Observer's Badge: A Comprehensive Study
- Army Parachutist Badge
- Badge for shooting down low-flying aircraft
- Close Combat Clasp
- Commendation Certificate of the Commander-in-Chief of the Army

- Commendation Certificate of the Commander-in-Chief of the Army for Shooting Down Aircraft
- General Assault Badge
- Honour Roll Clasp of the *Heer*
- Infantry Assault Badge
- Marksmanship Lanyards
- Sniper's Badge
- Tank Combat Badge
- Tank Destruction Badge

IRON CROSS DECORATIONS

Award	Date Instituted	Criteria for Award
Iron Cross 2nd Class	1 September 1939	An act of bravery above and beyond the call of duty
Iron Cross 1st Class	1 September 1939	Had already received Iron Cross 2nd Class; 3-5 acts of bravery above and beyond call of duty
Knight's Cross of the Iron Cross	1 September 1939	Had already received Iron Cross 1st Class; multiple, or single important, acts of bravery above and beyond the call of duty
Knight's Cross of the Iron Cross with Oak Leaves	3 June 1940	Had already received the Knight's Cross of the Iron Cross; multiple, or single important, acts of bravery above and beyond the call of duty
Knight's Cross of the Iron Cross with Oak Leaves and Swords	15 July 1941	Had already received the Knight's Cross with Oak Leaves; multiple, or single important, acts of bravery above and beyond the call of duty
Knight's Cross of the Iron Cross with Oak Leaves, Swords and Diamonds	15 July 1941	Had already received Knight's Cross with Oak Leaves and Swords; multiple, or single important, acts of bravery above and beyond the call of duty
Knight's Cross of the Iron Cross with Golden Oak Leaves, Swords and Diamonds	29 December 1944	Had already received Knight's Cross with Oak Leaves, Swords and Diamonds; multiple, or single important, acts of bravery above and beyond the call of duty
Grand Cross of the Iron Cross	1 September 1939	Awarded to staff officers who have made major command decisions with a positive impact upon the war

Kriegsmarine

The Kriegsmarine *was a generally neglected service during the intense rearmament phase of the 1930s. It entered World War II, therefore, with limited resources, although it would quickly make a big impact in the Atlantic theatre with its U-boats.*

The *Kriegsmarine* holds an unusual status in the history of the Third Reich. Hitler was undoubtedly a very land-bound military thinker, and consequently gave little pre-war attention to the development of the German Navy, and never really understood the nature of naval operations. Such is partly understandable. Apart from its northern coastline, Germany is a land-locked nation, and during the rearmament period of the 1930s Hitler's strategic thinking was largely directed towards land campaigns in the East. Yet as the 1930s drew to a close, Hitler came to appreciate that war with France and Britain – both significant naval powers – was becoming more likely, hence he gave belated approval for naval development.

The pre-war situation

The aftermath of World War I had been particularly hard on the German *Kaiserliche Marine* (Imperial Navy). Much of the surviving German *Hochseeflotte* (High Seas Fleet) was scuttled at Scapa Flow in June 1919, and what was left was largely outdated. The Versailles Treaty, as we have seen, placed tight restrictions on naval redevelopment.

Foreign and covert activities meant that the Navy managed to keep its expertise alive and its manpower levels respectable, and also fuelled technical research ('banana freighters' and 'trawlers', for example, were often test beds for future cruisers and minesweepers). During the early 1930s, however, German naval redevelopment became more overt with the commissioning of three new *Panzerschiffe* (armoured ships) – the *Deutschland*, *Admiral Scheer* and *Admiral Graf Spee*.

The possibilities for more dramatic naval rebuilding came under Hitler's chancellorship. Not only did Germany officially reject the Versailles Treaty in 1935 (the foundations of the *Bismarck* and *Tirpitz* were laid down the following year), but in 1938 the Anglo-German Naval Agreement,

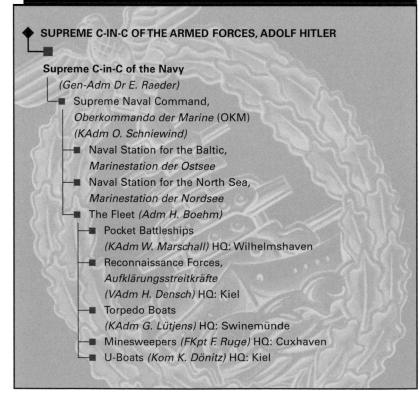

KRIEGSMARINE ORGANIZATION, NOVEMBER 1938

◆ **SUPREME C-IN-C OF THE ARMED FORCES, ADOLF HITLER**

■ **Supreme C-in-C of the Navy**
 (Gen-Adm Dr E. Raeder)
 ■ Supreme Naval Command,
  Oberkommando der Marine (OKM)
  (KAdm O. Schniewind)
  ■ Naval Station for the Baltic,
   Marinestation der Ostsee
  ■ Naval Station for the North Sea,
   Marinestation der Nordsee
  ■ The Fleet *(Adm H. Boehm)*
   ■ Pocket Battleships
    (KAdm W. Marschall) HQ: Wilhelmshaven
   ■ Reconnaissance Forces,
    Aufklärungsstreitkräfte
    (VAdm H. Densch) HQ: Kiel
   ■ Torpedo Boats
    (KAdm G. Lütjens) HQ: Swinemünde
   ■ Minesweepers *(FKpt F. Ruge)* HQ: Cuxhaven
   ■ U-Boats *(Kom K. Dönitz)* HQ: Kiel

then the London Submarine Protocol in 1939, effectively gave Germany the green light to accelerate the construction of a new battle fleet.

In response, Hitler and the naval high command formulated the 'Z-Plan', an ultimately unrealistic long-term plan for equipping the German Navy with a large and cutting-edge surface navy. Most of the vessels on the Z-Plan list never saw their way off the drawing board or out of the shipyard. Germany consequently entered the war far from prepared for naval conflict. The Navy was headed by *Großadmiral* Erich Raeder.

Surface war

The story of the *Kriegsmarine*'s surface war is one of momentary great victories but overall decline and defeat. The Navy entered the early years of World War II with some of the finest battleship types in the world, including vessels already mentioned, and a strong destroyer force. Yet from the outset its limitations when compared with the mass of the Royal Navy were revealed. The *Graf Spee* was scuttled in Montevideo in December 1939, having been trapped by a British naval force, and at Narvik in April 1940 the *Kriegsmarine*'s destroyer force lost 10 vessels to British surface raids.

The German conquest of Western Europe and the operations in the Balkans and Mediterranean opened up new theatres for naval operations, mainly in the form of destroyer, *Schnellboot* (fast boat) and submarine attacks on Allied merchant shipping. German capital ships were also venturing out into Arctic and North

Atlantic waters. On 24 May 1941, in the Denmark Strait, the German battleship *Bismarck* sank the British battlecruiser HMS *Hood* in only a few salvos, the explosive sinking of the ship killing all but three men from the 1418-strong crew. The Royal Navy, bent on vengeance, thereafter deployed major resources to hunt down the *Bismarck*, and on 27 May it was shelled to destruction by two

battleships and two cruisers, her rudder having been disabled in an earlier air attack by Swordfish aircraft.

The destruction of the *Bismarck* was a major propaganda blow to Germany, and Hitler in particular became acutely aware of how vulnerable the major surface ships really were. By 1942, furthermore, the Allies' naval airpower resources were strengthening, and the war was

PERSONNEL IN NAVY (*KRIEGSMARINE*) SERVICE, 1939–45 (ESTIMATED)

Year	Personnel
1939	50,000
1940	250,000
1941	400,000
1942	580,000
1943	780,000
1944	800,000
1945	700,000

ALLIED SHIPPING LOSSES BY CAUSE, 1941

Cause	Number Lost	Gross Tonnage
Submarine	222	777,000 tonnes (765,000 tons)
Mine	129	437,000 tonnes (430,000 tons)
Warship	16	64,000 tonnes (63,000 tons)
Aircraft	30	37,600 tonnes (37,000 tons)
Other	5	8,100 tonnes (8000 tons)

ALLIED SHIPS BUILT AND SUNK, 1942–45

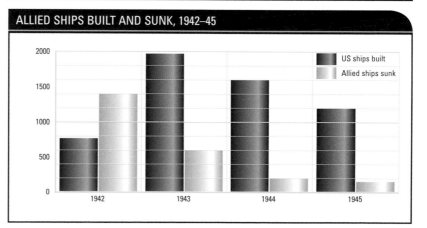

US ships built
Allied ships sunk

revealing that even the largest ships could be undone by airstrikes. For these reasons, the major German capital vessels played no significant role in the rest of the war, apart from diverting Allied naval resources into the far northern theatre. In December 1942, the weakness of German surface operations was revealed when the heavy units *Lützow* (formerly *Deustchland*) and *Admiral Hipper*, escorted by six destroyers, failed to stop an escorted Allied convoy of 14 merchant ships. The dismal results of the Battle of the Barents Sea, as it is known,

infuriated Hitler, who decreed that all German capital ships be decommissioned and scrapped. This order was slackened a little over subsequent weeks, but the damage was done. Raeder resigned, being replaced by the head of the U-boat arm, Karl Dönitz, in January 1943, and the major German warships were consigned to marginal relevance. Apart from the *Scharnhorst*, which went down fighting in one of the last German naval gun battles of the war, most of the other capital vessels were either consigned to humiliating operations as floating anti-aircraft

batteries, shore bombardment vessels, training ships, and hospital or passenger ships, or were even sunk as blockships. The mighty battleship *Tirpitz*, for example, spent two years doing little more than defending itself against Allied air raids or repairing damage, until it was finally wiped out by Lancaster-dropped Tallboy bombs in November 1944. Its loss was a fitting symbol of the general impotence of the German surface fleet to significantly alter the course of the naval war.

U-boat war

In contrast to the surface war, the *Kriegsmarine*'s U-boat war was both wildly successful – for a time – and genuinely influential. Such is indicated by the statement of Prime Minister Winston Churchill, who after the war acknowledged 'The only thing that ever really frightened me during the war was the U-boat peril.'

The U-boat arm went into the war significantly understrength – with fewer than 60 U-boats, mostly of coastal types rather than the long-range Type VII and Type IX submarines – and was largely restricted to coastal operations around northern waters. Two critical developments changed this situation. First, production numbers of U-boats began to climb, although painfully slowly – 58 in 1939; 68 in 1940; 129 in 1941 and 282 in 1942 – with the emphasis shifting to production of the long-range types. (The Type VII became the most numerous type, with 703 examples built.) Second, the German conquest of France in May 1940 brought French coastal bases under German control. Now the

KRIEGSMARINE CAPITAL SHIPS

Battleship/Pocket Battleship	Commissioned	Fate
Admiral Graf Spee	6 Jan 1936	Sunk 17 Dec 1939 in La Plata estuary
Bismarck	24 Aug 1940	Sunk 27 May 1941 in North Atlantic
Gneisenau	21 May 1938	Sunk as blockade ship in May 1945 in Gotenhafen
Scharnhorst	7 Jan 1939	Sunk 25 Dec 1943 at North Cape
Tirpitz	25 Feb 1941	Sunk 12 Nov 1944 in Norway
Heavy Cruiser*	Commissioned	Fate
Admiral Hipper	29 Apr 1939	Scuttled 3 May 1945 at Kiel
Admiral Scheer	12 Nov 1934	Sunk 10 Apr 1945 at Kiel
Blücher	8 June 1937	Sunk 9 Apr 1940 in Oslo Fjord
Deutschland/Lützow	1 Apr 1933	Scuttled 4 May 1945 at Swinemünde
Prinz Eugen	1 Aug 1940	Sunk in post-war atomic tests, Kwajalein atoll
Light Cruiser	Commissioned	Fate
Emden	15 Oct 1925	Blown up 3 Apr 1945 in Heikendorf Bay
Königsberg	17 Apr 1929	Sunk 10 Apr 1940 in Bergen
Karlsruhe	6 Nov 1929	Sunk 9 Apr 1940 at Kristiansand
Köln	15 Jan 1930	Sunk 31 Mar 1945 at Wilhelmshaven
Leipzig	8 Oct 1941	Scuttled 16 Dec 1946 in North Sea
Nürnberg	2 Nov 1935	Scrapped in 1961

* Note that Admiral Scheer and Deutschland/Lützow were until mid-1940 classified as Panzerschiffe (armoured ships), what the Allies would call pocket battleships.

U-boats had direct and easy access straight into the Atlantic, where they could hunt the transatlantic convoys that were so critical to Britain's war effort and very survival. Considering the numbers of U-boats available in the early years of the war, the merchant shipping losses were staggering – more than seven million tonnes (6.9 million long tons) sunk in the Atlantic in 1940 and 1941 alone. And things were about to get worse. From late 1941, the U-boats began to operate in Wolf Packs – groups of U-boats hunting sea lanes together and making attacks in a coordinated fashion. By maximizing the numbers of boats attacking, which further frustrated the Allied escort response, German U-boats sank 6.15 million tonnes (6 million tons) in 1942, aided by easy hunting along the eastern seaboard of the United States when America joined the war in December 1941. There was the very real danger that the Allies could run out of shipping, and Hitler, recognizing the impressive results, gave more backing to submarine production.

And yet, by the end of 1942 fortunes were turning against the U-boats. Allied anti-submarine weapons and tactics were improving, as were detection technologies such as centimetric radar, ASDIC and sonar. The ranges of anti-submarine aircraft extended out into the Atlantic in 1942, and in 1943 closed the mid-Atlantic 'air gap' the U-boats had exploited. Allied codebreaking successes increasingly revealed the details of U-boat operations. In 1942 the *Kriegsmarine* lost 87 submarines, but in 1943 that number leapt to 237, and to 242 the next year. By 1944, manning a submarine became almost a suicide mission, and the U-boat threat had passed.

U-BOAT LOSSES, 1939–45

Year	Losses
1939	9
1940	23
1941	35
1942	87
1943	237
1944	242
1945	151

Total Losses: 784

Luftwaffe

The Luftwaffe *was an integral element in the German* Blitzkrieg, *and Germany undoubtedly produced excellence in both pilots and aircraft. Yet although the German Air Force was tactically sound, it was in the long term strategically ineffective.*

The *Luftwaffe*, unlike the *Kriegsmarine*, caught Hitler's attention from the outset. He appreciated that a powerful combat air arm, allied to focused armoured offensives on the ground, could be decisive in forcing enemies to compliance or defeat. The 1920s and 1930s were a time in which many military theorists, such as the influential Italian Giulio Douhet, were predicting that aerial dominance would become *the* critical element in future warfare.

As we have seen, even under the Versailles Treaty the German armed forces managed to grow the roots of a new air force via civilian companies, but in 1933 the gloves came off and Hitler committed German industry to a major rearmament programme. The *Luftwaffe* officially declared its existence in May 1935, and began to receive machines in significant numbers. In 1938, for example,

Germany produced 5235 aircraft, 3350 of which were combat types. The following year, production figures rose to 8295 aircraft, including 4733 combat types.

Organization

The *Luftwaffe*'s largest organizational body was the *Luftflotte* (Air Fleet), each *Luftflotte* being responsible for a distinct territory. Beneath the *Luftflotten* (which varied in number throughout the war), were the *Fliegerkorps* or *Fliegerdivisionen*, which were sub-divided into *Geschwader* (similar to a British Group or US Wing), then into

Gruppen (Groups) and finally into *Staffeln*, the equivalent of Allied Squadrons and consisting of 9–16 aircraft. The whole *Luftwaffe* came under the OKL as its command HQ.

Narrow focus

Yet there were the seeds of a future problem behind the production figures. Throughout the war, German aircraft production focused principally on single-engined fighters such as the Messerschmitt Bf 109

TOTAL *LUFTWAFFE* AIRCRAFT LOSSES, 1939–45

Aircraft Type	Losses
Combat aircraft	82,258
Transport/reconnaissance aircraft	12,874
Training aircraft	15,428

LUFTWAFFE TOP 20 FIGHTER ACES

Name	Kills
Erich Hartmann	352
Gerhard Barkhorn	301
Günther Rall	275
Otto Kittel	267
Walter Nowotny	258
Wilhelm Batz	237
Erich Rudorffer	224
Heinrich Bär	221
Hermann Graf	212
Heinrich Ehrler	209
Theodor Weissenberger	208
Hans Philipp	206
Walter Schuck	206
Anton Hafner	204
Helmuth Lipfert	203
Walter Krupinski	197
Anton Hackl	192
Joachim Brendel	189
Maximillian Stotz	189
Joachim Kirschner	188

PERSONNEL IN AIR FORCE (*LUFTWAFFE*) SERVICE, 1939–45 (MILLION)

Year	Personnel (million)
1939	0.4
1940	1.2
1941	1.7
1942	1.7
1943	1.7
1944	1.5
1945	1

▶ *LUFTLOTTE* SYSTEM The *Luftwaffe*'s resources were divided into *Luftflotten* (Air Fleets), each *Luftflotte* having its own territory. Here we see the *Luftflotten* at a late stage in the war. In 1940, by contrast, *Luftflotte* 2 was in northern France and Belgium, and was responsible with *Luftflotte* 3 for air operations against Britain. By the end of 1944, *Luftflotte Reich* had became the most demanding air fleet region, as its *Luftwaffe* resources were engaged in a constant battle to defend Germany against Allied air raids.

and Focke-Wulf Fw 190, two-engined ground-attack/heavy fighters like the Messerscmitt Bf 110, and twin-engined medium bombers such as the Dornier Do 17 and Heinkel He 111. What it conspicuously failed to do was develop a long-range bomber force equivalent to those used by the Allies. What the Germans rolled out was a largely tactical air force, one that was excellent in supporting ground forces at a local level or at bombarding front-line targets. What it was not suited to was taking the war to a distant enemy heartland: although its medium bombers were still capable of reducing large sections of a city to rubble, they were never capable of delivering the city-shattering industrial blows of the Allied air offensive.

Victory to defeat

At first this issue was hidden by success in the campaigns of 1939–40. *Luftwaffe* fighters established air superiority against inferior enemy fighter forces in Poland, Scandinavia, the Low Countries and France, giving

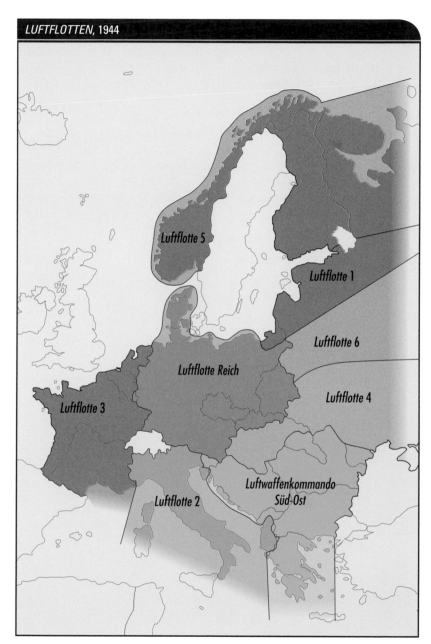

LUFTFLOTTEN, 1944

Luftflotte 5

Luftflotte 1

Luftflotte 6

Luftflotte Reich

Luftflotte 4

Luftflotte 3

Luftwaffenkommando Süd-Ost

Luftflotte 2

the medium and dive bombers a relatively safe environment in which to ply their trade.

Harder lessons were learnt during the infamous Battle of Britain,

Göring's attempt to crush the RAF between July and October 1940 in preparation for an invasion of Britain. The battle was one of the closest-run air wars in history, but the *Luftwaffe* found that its bombers and Ju 87 dive bombers were terribly vulnerable to an organized and well-equipped enemy once the fighter escort turned for home, short on fuel. (Loiter time for fighters over southern Britain was often in the region of only 20 minutes.) Furthermore, in early September Göring switched his attacks from RAF airbases to British cities. Thus began the Blitz, but this gave RAF Fighter Command the reprieve it needed to rebuild, and with Hitler's focus switching to the East, Göring had to admit the first of many defeats.

The campaigns in the Mediterranean and in North Africa both saw the *Luftwaffe* committed in increasingly large numbers, yet there were never enough aircraft to sustain heavy offensives. Allied fighter production totalled 18,566 aircraft in 1941, 30,524 aircraft in 1942, 49,305 in 1943 and 35,187 in 1944. The German figures for those years were 3744 (1941), 5515 (1942), 10,989 (1943) and 26,326 (1944). German output was impressive (the later figures thanks to Speer wresting aircraft production

LUFTFLOTTE COMMANDERS (1939–45)

Luftflotte 1

- Generalfeldmarschall Albert Kesselring (1 Sep 1939–11 Jan 1940)
- Generaloberst Hans-Jürgen Stumpff (11 Jan 1940–10 May 1940)
- General der Flieger Wilhelm Wimmer (11 May 1940–19 Aug 1940)
- Generaloberst Alfred Keller (19 Aug 1940–12 June 1943)
- Generaloberst Günther Korten (12 June 1943–23 Aug 1943)
- General der Flieger Kurt Pflugbeil (23 Aug 1943–16 Apr 1945)

Luftflotte 2

- General der Flieger Hellmuth Felmy (1 Sep 1939–12 Jan 1940)
- Generalfeldmarschall Albert Kesselring (12 Jan 1940–11 June 1943)
- Generalfeldmarschall Wolfram Freiherr von Richthofen (11 June 1943–27 Sep 1944)

Luftflotte 3

- Generalfeldmarschall Hugo Sperrle (1 Sep 1939–23 Aug 1944)
- Generaloberst Otto Dessloch (23 Aug 1944–22 Sep 1944)
- Generalleutnant Alexander Holle (22 Sep 1944–26 Sep 1944)

Luftflotte 4

- Generaloberst Alexander Löhr (1 Sep 1939–20 July 1942)
- Generalfeldmarschall Wolfram Freiherr von Richthofen (20 July 1942–4 Sep 1943)
- Generaloberst Otto Dessloch (4 Sep 1943–17 Aug 1944)
- Generalleutnant Alexander Holle (17 Aug 1944–27 Sep 1944)
- Generaloberst Otto Dessloch (27 Sep 1944–21 Apr 1945)

Luftflotte 5

- Generalfeldmarschall Erhard Milch (12 Apr 1940–9 May 1940)
- Generaloberst Hans-Jürgen Stumpff (9 May 1940–27 Nov 1943)
- General der Flieger Josef Kammhuber (27 Nov 1943–16 Sep 1944)

Luftflotte 6

- Generalfeldmarschall Robert Ritter von Greim (5 May 1943–24 Apr 1945)
- Generaloberst Otto Dessloch (24 Apr 1945–8 May 1945)

Luftflotte Reich

- Generaloberst Hans-Jürgen Stumpff (5 Feb 1944–8 May 1945)

away from Göring's control), but it was dwarfed by Allied capabilities. This is not to say that the *Luftwaffe* did not inflict a cutting toll upon enemy air forces. From June 1941 to May 1945, for example, the Soviet air force lost 106,600 aircraft to all causes, but the vast majority were downed by German fighters. Ground attacks and air combat accounted for 2000 Soviet aircraft in the first few days of *Barbarossa* alone. The most successful German fighter ace of all time, Erich Hartmann, destroyed 352 enemy aircraft in total , all but five of them Soviet machines.

Yet although the Eastern Front was a superb hunting ground for the *Luftwaffe*, the Red Air Force slowly learnt from experience and introduced better tactics, training and aircraft. Combined with massive production increases – in some campaigns in 1944, the local German

FLAKKORPS AREAS OF OPERATION

I. Flakkorps
- Germany (Oct 1939–May 1940)
- France (May 1940–Sep 1940)
- Germany (Sep 1940–Mar 1941)
- Germany (Apr 1941–June 1941)
- Eastern Front, central sector (June 1941–Oct 1944)
- Poland (Oct 1944–Feb 1945)
- Germany (Feb 1945–May 1945)

II. Flakkorps
- Germany (Oct 1939–May 1940)
- France (May 1940–Mar 1941)
- Eastern Front, southern sector (June 1941–Aug 1944)
- Germany (Aug 1944–May 1945)

III. Flakkorps
- France (Feb 1944–Sep 1944)
- Germany (Sep 1944–Dec 1944)
- Ardennes (Dec 1944–Jan 1945)
- Germany & Ruhr pocket (Jan 1945–Apr 1945)

IV. Flakkorps
- Germany (July 1944–May 1945)

V. Flakkorps
- Hungary (Nov 1944–Dec 1944)
- Germany (Dec 1944–May 1945)

VI. Flakkorps
- Western Front (Feb 1945–Mar 1945)
- Northern Germany (Mar 1945–May 1945)

GERMAN COMBAT AIRCRAFT STRENGTH, 1939–45

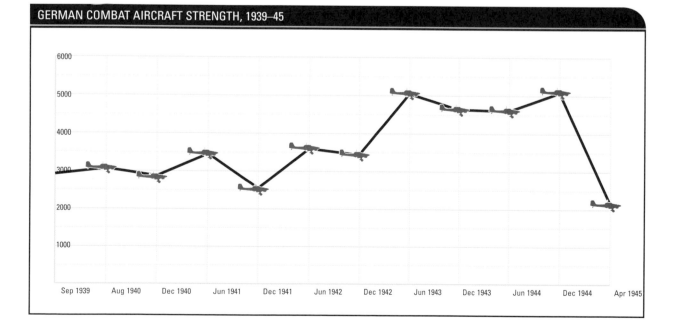

133

air forces were outnumbered by nearly four to one – the balance of air superiority shifted to the Communist forces.

Steadily, the *Luftwaffe*'s strength in every theatre was eroded by daily destruction, even over the Reich itself – from January 1944, US bombers could have round-trip fighter escorts for missions against Germany, and by early 1945 the *Luftwaffe* was losing control over its own country. An important element of the Reich's defence, therefore, became the *Flakkorps* (Anti-Aircraft Corps). The

bulk of anti-aircraft defence in the war was indeed provided by the *Luftwaffe*, being deployed on every major front as well as being thickly clustered around Germany's towns, cities and industrial plants.

Last-ditch defence

In the last months of World War II, as we have seen, German aircraft production efforts were increasingly diverted to jet and rocket aircraft, hoping that the capabilities of these machines would recapture air dominance. Some of these aircraft –

such as the turbojet-powered Messerschmitt Me 262 – were truly threatening planes with astonishing performance for the time (although their endurance was restricted).

Yet the Me 262 and the myriad less successful types were largely just a technical distraction that came too late to have any influence. The *Luftwaffe* had been a rightly feared and highly professional combat arm throughout its existence. Strategic short-sightedness and production inequalities (compared with the Allies) consigned it to defeat.

The Causes and Costs of Defeat

The defeat of Germany in World War II, unlike that of the previous world war, was finally delivered in the very heartland of the Third Reich. The cost of fighting the war had been catastrophic for Germany's army, navy and air force.

One of the questions that military historians periodically toy with is, quite simply, 'Why did Germany lose the war?' The answer cannot be laid at the door of individual German servicemen – the *Wehrmacht* personnel demonstrated conspicuous bravery and tactical intelligence until the very last days of the Reich. (At this point, largely inexperienced and fanatical command elements took over, and Germany was combed through for Hitler Youth or *Volkssturm* personnel.) So at what point, and from what causes, did the fortunes of war finally shift against Hitler?

Tipping points

The conventional point at which victory is considered to have slipped

away from Germany was the Battle of Stalingrad in the winter of 1942/43. Such a view is justified on many levels. First, the scale of the German losses was enormous – the *Wehrmacht* had lost more than 200,000 men, half of them in the city fighting; the remainder were destined for Soviet POW camps, from which few would return.

The loss of a 22-division army profoundly altered the German capability to resist westward Soviet advances, although we should not assume that the Soviets were in a position of unassailable strength or of strategic superiority. Alan Clark has described some of the strengths and weaknesses of the Red Army after Stalingrad:

...the Russians had inherited many of the weaknesses of the previous period. They had brought two and a half million men into uniform since the outbreak of war. They had lost four million trained soldiers. A ruthless standardisation of equipment – two types of trucks, two tanks, three artillery pieces – had allowed them to raise production rates in spite of losing two thirds of their factory space. But of leaders to handle their new army there was a desperate scarcity... The result was that tactical flexibility and speed in exploitation were far below the German standard.

(Clark, 2000)

Clark's observations illustrate how Stalingrad was not necessarily an unequivocal nail in the German coffin, and that the Soviet forces were not poised for inevitable victory.

In fact, a unforeseen and potentially beneficial side-effect for the *Wehrmacht* was that Hitler, physically weakened by the strain of command, temporarily loosened his grip and allowed other talented commanders to come to the fore. Chief amongst them was Erich von Manstein, promoted *Generaloberst* in March 1943 and one of the Third Reich's greatest generals. Manstein, commanding Army Group Don, crushed the spearheads of an offensive by General M.M. Popov's Front Mobile Group, then surrounded Soviet forces in Kharkov. The Soviets were once more on the back foot.

By spring 1943, the fighting had ground to a halt through exhaustion, depletion and the onset of the spring thaw (the infamous *rasputitsa*), which turned all the roads into quagmires. The Soviet Central and Voronezh Fronts occupied a huge bulge in the front line, pivoted around Kursk, and it was here, arguably, that the true future of World War II was set. During a relative four-month lull in operations, both sides began planning their next moves. Against Manstein's proposals, Hitler became fixated on 'nipping off' the Kursk salient in a major combined-arms assault that would become known as Operation *Zitadelle* (Citadel).

When launched on 5 July 1943, *Zitadelle* was the largest land battle in history. Hitler had ordered accelerated production of armour, plus the transfer of many armoured

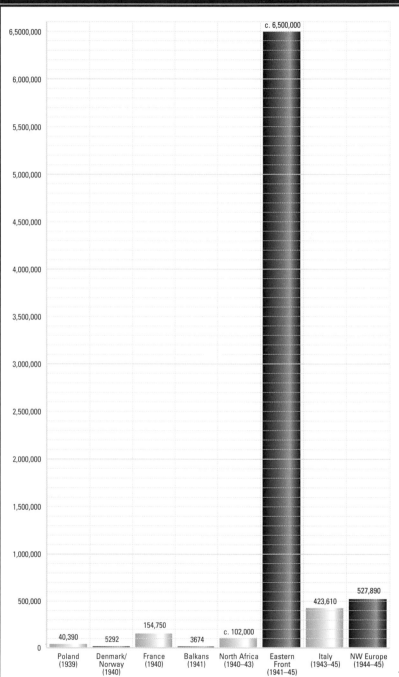

GERMAN GROUND FORCES DEAD, WOUNDED AND MISSING BY CAMPAIGN

Poland (1939)	40,390
Denmark/Norway (1940)	5292
France (1940)	154,750
Balkans (1941)	3674
North Africa (1940–43)	c. 102,000
Eastern Front (1941–45)	c. 6,500,000
Italy (1943–45)	423,610
NW Europe (1944–45)	527,890

PERCENTAGE OF GERMAN SOLDIERS WHO HAD BEEN WOUNDED BY 6 JUNE 1944 (D-DAY)	
Times Wounded	Percentage
Once	35%
Twice	11%
Three times	6%
Four times	2%
More than four times	2%

GERMAN MANPOWER, EASTERN FRONT, 1941–44 (MID-YEAR FIGURES)	
Date	Manpower
1941	3.3 million
1942	3.1 million
1943	2.9 million
1944	3.1 million

units from France to the Eastern Front, so that in total the two German armies used for the offensive (Fourth Panzer Army and Ninth Army) massed 2700 tanks, supported by 1800 aircraft. Combined with 3.3 million men along the whole Eastern Front, Kursk illustrated that the *Wehrmacht* still had fight.

Yet despite the power of the German Kursk offensive, the fact was that the Red Army they faced was even stronger. Soviet tank production ran at double that of the Germans'. Its production of artillery, particularly anti-tank guns and rocket artillery, was even more impressive, with 21,000 anti-tank guns issued directly to infantry regiments and 200 reserve anti-tank regiments waiting in the wings. The period of inactivity during the spring of 1943 was put to use converting the Kursk salient into one of the most heavily defended zones in the world, replete with guns, tanks, minefields, rocket launchers and networks of defensive positions.

Zitadelle was a cauldron for both sides, an epic battle in which two million soldiers and 7000 tanks (4000 Soviet, 3000 German) slugged it out in a battle lasting two weeks. Although the Germans made initial good

penetrations into the salient, over time the advances ground to a halt in the face of will-sapping losses, and by mid-July the Soviets were themselves on the offensive. By 23 July, the German forces were back where they started.

Consequences

Kursk was a cataclysmic defeat for the Germans (although the Soviets lost more armour and men). The exact number of tanks lost is unclear, ranging somewhere between 500 and 900, but hundreds of thousands of men were killed, wounded or captured. The consequences of this defeat, as historian John Keegan here points out, extended beyond local theatre issues:

...these were strategic losses. German tank output, for all Guderian's – and Speer's – efforts, did not approach the thousand per month scheduled for 1943; it averaged only 330. More tanks than that had been lost on several days during Citadel, 160 out of Fourth Army's Panzers having simply broken down on the battlefield. As a result, the central armoured reserve on which the Ostheer *had always thitherto been able to call in a crisis*

was now dissipated and could not be rebuilt out of current production, which was committed to the replacement of normal losses.
(Keegan, 1989)

In contrast, Keegan goes on to point out that Soviet tank production 'would approach 2500 a month in 1944', which meant that the Red Army could increase the numbers of tanks fielded regardless of the heavy costs imposed by German gunners and ground-attack aircraft. 'The main significance of Kursk, therefore, was that it deprived Germany of the means to seize the initiative in the future and so, by default, transferred it to the Soviet Union' (Keegan, 1989).

While Stalingrad had been the tipping point on the Eastern Front – the *Wehrmacht*'s first major defeat against the Soviets, and the limit of its advance – Kursk altered the strategic balance on the Eastern Front irrevocably. From now on, with localized and temporary exceptions, Germany would be fighting a retreat all the way back to the Reich. Furthermore, on 6 June 1944 the Western Allies opened up the second front in France. Now Germany was forced to fight on two major fronts against enemies with awesome combined industrial power.

Hitler – the engineer of defeat?

We have already discussed Hitler's qualities as a military leader, but it is worth exploring further how central he was to the German defeat in World War II, and the costs borne by the *Wehrmacht* for his decisions. The Battle of Kursk just described provides a sharp illustration of his command mindset. Hitler had been ambivalent about *Zitadelle* from the outset, but the defeat (Hitler ordered the cessation of *Zitadelle* on 13 July) simply confirmed that in the future his judgment was king. He defiantly stated, 'That's the last time I will listen to the advice of my General Staff.'

Loss of grip

Hitler had made his fair share of poor command decisions prior to Stalingrad and Kursk. His decision to leave Britain undefeated in 1940 left the Allies with the platform from which the second front could be launched, and from which the United States could prosecute both its air campaign and its later land campaign. In fairness, however, the *Wehrmacht* was not configured for a major amphibious invasion, and such an attempt ran the very real risk of a massacre by the Royal Navy and Royal Air Force in the Channel. Hitler, along with the German General Staff, was probably more culpable in the infamous 'stop order' of May 1940 – an order that Panzer forces advancing towards Dunkirk make a temporary halt to allow following units to close up and ensure that flanks were properly protected. The stop order may have been the right theoretical course, but it essentially allowed the British Army to evacuate intact and fight another day.

Hitler's diversion into the Balkans and North Africa in 1941 was also a serious distraction for, and drain on, German resources. Yet Hitler was probably right when he said, in a directive on 13 December 1940, that it was 'doubly important to frustrate English efforts to establish, behind

the protection of a Balkan front, an air base which would threaten Italy in the first place and, incidentally, the Romanian oilfields.'

These command mistakes are debatable, but as the war progressed some of his failures were less ambiguous. The declaration of war on the United States in late 1941 was industrially suicidal – Germany could never compete with US war production capabilities.

Hitler's diversion of Panzer forces from Army Group Centre in the Ukraine during the first months of Operation *Barbarossa* arguably saved Moscow. The disasters of operations into southern Russia and the Ukraine have already been noted, and after these Hitler's grip on both tactical and strategic realities

steadily disintegrated. His aversion to relinquishing ground resulted in the virtual destruction of entire armies, and increasing alienation from his military commanders. Blinded to reason, he spent his last weeks of command ordering about divisions that scarely existed, except on paper.

Paying the price

Every German campaign, even the successful ones, added significantly to the death toll on the German forces. Some 13,000 troops died in Poland, 43,000 in France, 60,000 in Italy, 128,000 in Northwest Europe, and, incredibly, more than two million on the Eastern Front. The German armed forces had delivered a uniquely futile sacrifice.

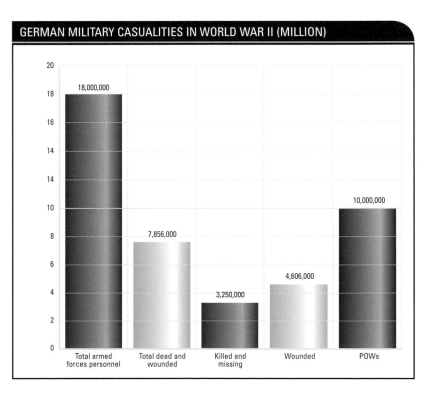

GERMAN MILITARY CASUALITIES IN WORLD WAR II (MILLION)

CHAPTER 7

Racial Policy

The Third Reich is not only remembered for dragging the world into global conflict. It is also burned into memory for the Holocaust, possibly the greatest crime against humanity in recorded history.

Hitler was a passionate anti-Semite, which was not uncommon in post-World War I Europe. Yet Hitler combined his vehement racial theories with actual power: the German army's conquest of foreign lands allowed the Nazis to unleash a systematic programme of extermination. In only a few years, six million Jews were murdered, along with hundreds of thousands of gypsies, homosexuals, Soviet POWs and other people who did not fit the Nazis Aryan model.

How and why the Holocaust occurred are not simple questions to answer. One of the most complicated issues is the level of complicity of the German people in a horrifying exercise in mass murder.

◼ Polish Jews are rounded up for deportation in a district of Warsaw. More than 90 per cent of Poland's Jewish population was killed by the Nazis.

Persecution and Extermination

The Nazi persecution of the Jews gained new, state-sanctioned vitality when Hitler took office in 1933. Although the extermination camps were some years away, early legislation tightened the screws on all aspects of Jewish life.

Hitler rose to power in a society that, although deemed civilized and sophisticated, still retained strong undercurrents of anti-Semitism. Such prejudice had centuries-old roots in Europe, but in Germany it often coalesced around feelings that the small Jewish population enjoyed affluence by virtue of a 'parasitic' relationship with German society. Historian Geoff Layton expands:

The Jews became easy scapegoats for the discontent and disorientation felt by many people as rapid industrialisation and urbanisation took place. The Jewish community

was easily identifiable because of its different traditions, and became the focus of envy because it was viewed as privileged. In 1933, for example, although Jews comprised less than 1 per cent of the German population, they composed more than 16 per cent of lawyers, 10 per cent of doctors and 5 per cent of editors and writers.

(Layton, 2000)

The Jews were, therefore, a visible and distinct community that attracted social envy and ideological hostility. Hitler turned those forces into outright persecution, steadily stripping Jews of their civic rights.

From positions of influence, they would become pariahs in their own country by 1939.

Legalizing persecution

It is hard for us today to understand how the German people accepted the anti-Jewish legislation passed by the Nazi government. Yet as well as bearing in mind the widespread anti-Semitic context outlined above, we should also acknowledge that the road to the Holocaust was gradualist – it occurred little by little over a period of around nine years (1933–42), so society adjusted to the policies one at a time.

Add to this fact the apparent benefits Hitler brought to the German economy, plus the effects of Nazi propaganda, and the acceptance of persecution is a little more understandable. (There was also the fear of standing up to the authorities – it took a brave individual to speak out under the shadow of a *Gestapo* prison).

Yet although the overall process was gradualist, there was no doubt that Hitler was set on rigorously pursuing an anti-Jewish agenda. In 1933 alone, there was a raft of legislation attacking Jewish civil rights. As we have seen, the Law for the Restoration of the Professional Civil Service removed Jews from civil service employment; later that same

JEWISH CITIZENS RESIDENT IN GERMANY, 1933

Nationality	Number
Austrian	4647
British	532
Czech	4275
Dutch	1604
German	400,935
Hungarian	2280
Latvian	827
Lithuanian	903
Polish	56,480
Romanian	2210
Soviet	1650
Turkish	753
US	536
Misc European	1692
Misc non-European	398
Stateless	19,746

JEWISH EMIGRATION FROM GERMANY, 1937–39

State	1937	1938	1939
Austrian *Gaue*	–	1193	1915
Baden	624	950	654
Bavaria	776	1547	1169
Bremen	59	189	141
Hamburg	429	1620	2187
Hesse	386	566	381
Prussia	4248	9393	14,671
Saxony	104	229	496
Württemberg	350	600	442
Other parts of the Reich	179	274	650

Data source: Tim Kirk, The Longman Companion to Nazi Germany *(Longman, 1995)*

NAZI JUSTIFICATIONS FOR EUTHANASIA PROGRAMME

The following excerpt is taken from Karl Bareth and Alfred Vogel, *Erblehre und Rasenkunde für die Grund- und Hauptschule* (Heredity and Racial Science for Elementary and Secondary Schools), 2nd edition (Bühl-Baden: Verlag Konkordia, 1937). It was intended to explain to children why mentally or physically disabled people were a burden on the state.

Hereditary illness places the state under a great burden: The cost to the state per day is:

- *For a normal pupil: ⅛ Reich Mark*
- *For a backward pupil: 1½ Reich Marks*
- *For a mentally ill pupil: 2⅖ Reich Marks*
- *For the blind or deaf pupil: 4 Reich Marks*

In 1932, one German city listed the following expenses:

- *A person on a small pension: 433 Reichmarks*
- *An unemployed person on welfare: 500 Reichmarks*
- *Costs for someone mentally ill: 1944 Reichmarks*

The total extra costs for caring for those hereditary illnesses in 1930 were about 1 billion Reich Marks, and 350 million Reich Marks went to handling such cases during the 1933/34 Winter Relief Program.

To protect the healthy population from the dangers of hereditary illness and weakness, the National Socialist State enacted the Law for the Prevention of Offspring with Hereditary Illnesses on 14 July 1933. Under this law, the genetically inferior are sterilized for the following diseases:

1. *Backward mentality*
2. *Schizophrenia*
3. *Manic depression*
4. *Epilepsy*
5. *St. Vitus' Dance*
6. *Blindness*
7. *Deafness*
8. *Major physical deformity*
9. *Severe alcoholism*

MAJOR ANTI-SEMITIC LAWS IN GERMANY, 1933–38

Date	Law	Terms
7 April 1933	Law for the Restoration of the Professional Civil Service	Bans Jews from the German civil service
7 April 1933	Law Regarding Admission to the Bar	Peoples of non-Aryan descent denied access to the Bar
25 April 1933	Law Against the Crowding of German Schools and Institutions of Higher Learning	The numbers of 'non-Aryan' Germans within an educational establishment had to be lower than those of 'pure' German pupils
15 September 1935	Law for the Protection of German Blood and German Honour	Marriage or 'extramarital intercourse' between Jews and non-Jews is forbidden. Jews are forbidden to fly the Reich and national flag and to display Reich colours
15 September 1935	Reich Citizenship Law	Stripped Jews of their German citizenship and rights
14 November 1935	First Supplementary Decree to the Reich Citizenship Law	Clarified the conditions of the Reich Citizenship Law (see box p. 142)
17 August 1938	Second Decree for the Implementation of the Law Regarding Changes of Family Names	Jews whose names did not conform to the Guidelines on the Use of Given Names were forced to adopt an additional given name – 'Israel' in the case of males and 'Sarah' in the case of females

month (April) the Law Against the Overcrowding of German Schools and Universities restricted Jews to 1.5 per cent of the educational population, and they were banned from admission to the Bar. In July, Jewish migrants from territories such as Russia and Poland were stripped of citizenship; from October, Jews could no longer be journalists.

Similar legislation continued throughout 1934 and 1938, most of it

SELECTED ARTICLES OF FIRST SUPPLEMENTARY DECREE TO THE REICH CITIZENSHIP LAW, NOVEMBER 14, 1935

On the basis of Article 3, Reich Citizenship Law, of September 15, 1935 (RGBl I, page 1146) the following is ordered:

Article 1.
(1) Until additional regulations regarding citizenship papers are issued, all subjects of German or kindred blood who had voting rights in the Reichstag elections at the time the Citizenship Law came into effect shall, for the time being, possess the rights of Reich citizens. The same shall be true of those to whom the Reich Minister of the Interior, in conjunction with the Deputy of the Führer, has given preliminary citizenship.
(2) The Reich Minister of the Interior, in conjunction with the Deputy of the Führer, can withdraw preliminary citizenship.

Article 2.
(1) The regulations in Article I are also valid for Reich subjects of mixed Jewish blood.
(2) An individual of mixed Jewish blood is one who is descended from one or two grandparents who were fully Jewish by race, insofar as he or she does not count as a Jew according to Article 5, Paragraph 2. One grandparent is considered as full-blooded if he or she belonged to the Jewish religious community.

Article 3.
Only the Reich citizen, as bearer of full political rights, possesses the right to vote in political affairs or can take public office. The Reich Minister of the Interior, or any agency empowered by him, can make exceptions during the transition period, with regard to occupying public offices. The affairs of religious organizations will not be affected.

Article 4.
(1) A Jew cannot be a citizen of the Reich. He has no right to vote in political affairs, he cannot occupy a public office.
(2) Jewish civil servants will retire as of 31 December 1935. If these civil servants served at the front in the World War, either for Germany or her allies, they will receive in full, until they reach the age limit, full pension to which they were entitled according to the last salary they received; they will, however, not advance in seniority. After reaching the age limit, their pensions will be calculated anew, according to the last salary they received, on the basis of which their pension was calculated.
(3) The affairs of religious organizations will not be affected.
(4) The employment status of teachers in Jewish public schools remains unchanged until new regulations for the Jewish school systems are issued.

designed to expel Jews from public positions or respected vocations. They were excluded from service in the German armed forces, and were dismissed from all public offices from November 1935. By the end of 1936, Jews could no longer practise as doctors, dentists, lawyers, notaries or teachers (of 'Aryan' pupils). More fundamental general legislation was the Reich Citizenship Law, which essentially stripped Jews of their German civil rights (putting them beyond the protection of the law), and the Law for the Protection of German Blood and German Honour, which forbade intermarriage or sexual relations between Jews and non-Jews.

Losing their country

Steadily the Jews were being squeezed out of German society. Furthermore, in 1938 Hitler switched his focus to Jewish businesses and assets. 'Aryanization' laws in March 1938 liquidated many Jewish firms, and in April all Jewish assets worth more than 5000 Reichsmarks had to be registered with the state, so that they could be used by Göring's Four-Year Plan office. In November 1938, a huge 'compensation fee' of 1000 million Reichsmarks was imposed on the German Jewish community, to be collected through liquidated assets,

LOCATIONS OF MAJOR CONCENTRATION AND EXTERMINATION CAMPS, 1939–45*

KEY
■ Extermination camps
■ Concentration camps

* Shows 1939 borders

and in February 1939 Jews were even required to surrender their precious metals and jewellery.

Under such heavy policies, it is little wonder that thousands of Jews chose to flee Germany for territories abroad. The fortunate ones put sea between them and Germany, going to Britain and the United States. Less fortunate were those who went to

▲ **THE NETWORK OF TERROR The German concentration camps were located mainly in Germany and Poland, although there were camps as far west as France and Belgium, and as far south as Italy and the Balkans. The pure extermination camps were located exclusively in Poland, where they could more effectively dispose of the Jews of Poland and Eastern Europe and were hidden from the eyes of the regular German population. Most of the other concentration camps were labour camps, although mass executions did take place there, and the labour and living conditions were so severe that they killed hundreds of thousands of people without the need for bullets or gas.**

LIST OF PRINCIPAL NAZI CONCENTRATION, HOLDING AND EXTERMINATION CAMPS

Camp Name	Country (today)	Camp Type	Years	Camp Name	Country (today)	Camp Type	Years
Amersfoort	Netherlands	Prison and transit camp	1941–45	Klooga	Estonia	Labour camp	1943–44
Arbeitsdorf	Germany	Labour camp	1942	Lager Sylt (Alderney)	Channel Islands	Labour camp	1943–44
Auschwitz-Birkenau	Poland	Extermination and labour camp	1940–45	Langenstein-Zwieberge	Germany	Buchenwald sub-camp	1944–45
Banjica	Serbia	Concentration camp	1941–44	Le Vernet	France	Internment camp	1939–44
Bardufoss	Norway	Concentration camp	1944– ?	Majdanek (KZ Lublin)	Poland	Extermination camp	1941–44
Belzec	Poland	Extermination camp	1942–43				
Bergen-Belsen	Germany	Collection point	1943–45	Malchow	Germany	Labour and transit camp	1943–45
Berlin-Marzahn	Germany	First a 'rest place' then labour camp	1936– ?	Maly Trostenets	Belarus	Extermination camp	1941–44
Bolzano	Italy	Transit camp	1944–45	Mauthausen-Gusen	Austria	Labour camp	1938–45
Bredtvet	Norway	Concentration camp	1941–45	Mittelbau-Dora	Germany	Labour camp	1943–45
Breendonk	Belgium	Prison and labour camp	1940–44	Natzweiler-Struthof	France	Labour camp; Nacht und Nebel camp	1941–44
Breitenau	Germany	First a 'wild' camp, then labour camp	1933–34, 1940–45	Neuengamme	Germany	Labour camp	1938–45
Buchenwald	Germany	Labour camp	1937–45	Niederhagen	Germany	Prison and labour camp	1941–43
Chelmno (Kulmhof)	Poland	Extermination camp	1941–43, 1944–45	Oranienburg	Germany	Collective point	1933–34
				Osthofen	Germany	Collective point	1933–34
Crveni krst	Serbia	Concentration camp	1941–45	Plaszów	Poland	Labour camp	1942–45
Dachau	Germany	Labour camp	1933–45	Ravensbrück	Germany	Labour camp for women	1939–45
Falstad	Norway	Prison camp	1941–45	Risiera di San Sabba (Trieste)	Italy	Police detainment camp	1943–45
Flossenbürg	Germany	Labour camp	1938–45				
Grini	Norway	Prison camp	1941–45	Sachsenhausen	Germany	Labour camp	1936–45
Gross-Rosen	Poland	Labour camp; Nacht und Nebel camp	1940–45	Sajmiste	Serbia	Extermination camp	1941–44
KZ Herzogen-busch (Vught)	Netherlands	Prison and transit camp	1943–44	Salaspils	Latvia	Labour camp	1941–44
				Sobibór	Poland	Extermination camp	1942–43
Hinzert	Germany	Collective point and sub-camp	1940–45	Soldau	Poland	Labour; transit camp	1939–45
				Stutthof	Poland	Labour camp	1939–45
Janowska (Lwów)	Ukraine	Ghetto; transit, labour, and extermination camp	1941–43	Theresienstadt (Terezín)	Czech Republic	Transit camp and ghetto	1941–45
Jasenovac	Croatia	Extermination camp	1941–45	Treblinka	Poland	Extermination camp	1942–43
Kaiserwald (Mezaparks)	Latvia	Labour camp	1942–44	Vaivara	Estonia	Concentration and transit camp	1943–44
Kaufering/Landsberg	Germany	Labour camp	1943–45	Warsaw	Poland	Labour and extermination camp	1942–44
Kauen (Kaunas)	Lithuania	Ghetto and internment camp	?	Westerbork	Netherlands	Collective point	1940–45

other mainland European countries, ones that Hitler's forces would later occupy in 1940.

Note also that Jews were not the only people being singled out by Hitler's racial excesses. Gypsies and blacks were also victims of persecutory legislation.

Violence and 'euthanasia'
The anti-Jewish laws of the 1930s were still a long way from the gas chambers of Auschwitz, but there were signs of a violent destiny for the Jews. Attacks by members of the Nazi Party, SA and SS against Jews and Jewish shops escalated steadily,

the perpetrators having the reassurance that there would be little or no legal comeback from such actions. The violence reached its pre-war apogee on 9 November 1938, following the murder of a German diplomat by a Polish Jew in Paris. In a state-ordered night of mayhem, 91 Jews were murdered, more than 200 synagogues were burned and 7500 Jewish businesses were ransacked. *Kristallnacht* ('Night of the Broken Glass') was followed by mass arrests of Jewish men, who were sent to Germany's burgeoning concentration camp system.

The violence was thuggish and horrifying, but it was not the meticulously planned slaughter that would later emerge. Yet there were still disquieting indicators of the ruthlessness of Nazi thinking.

Nazi ideology was obsessed with the idea of physical and hereditary 'health', and of keeping the Aryan people 'pure'. From that perspective, mental and physical disabilities were seen as a burden on both state and posterity. In August 1939, a Nazi directive from the Minister of the Interior ordered physicians and maternity staff to report cases of disabilities in babies and children under three. From the following October, parents were coerced into bringing the children to what were ostensibly specialist pediatric centres – in fact, the children were killed there by lethal injection or even by starvation.

This was just the beginning of the Nazi 'euthanasia' programme. Over time, the age group for selection was extended up to 17 years old, resulting in the murder of some 7000 mentally and physically disabled children. In October 1939, however, the programme was relabelled *Aktion* T4 (Action T4), and took the killing to a new scale. A far broader and more comprehensive classification system – which included patients with conditions such as epilepsy and dementia – required more efficient killing methods. In response, six gassing centres were developed at secret locations, and between January 1940 and August 1941 some 70,273 people were executed there in fake shower blocks filled with carbon monoxide gas. These killings were a haunting indicator of what was to come. Public knowledge of the programme led to its cessation in theory in the summer of 1941, but killing still continued in various covert ways throughout the rest of the war. Soon Germany would also have the means of mass execution.

Einsatzgruppen

In September 1939, German forces invaded Poland. In the wake of the regular forces trawled the *Einsatzgruppen* (Task Forces), SS murder squads charged with cleansing the territory of Jews and other 'undesirables'. The *Einsatzgruppen* were also deployed heavily in the Soviet Union and Baltic states following *Barbarossa* in June 1941. Their methods were as brutal as they were effective – in total it is estimated that the *Einsatzgruppen* murdered one to two million people. Entire territories were combed of Jews – men, women, children, babes in arms – who were herded into remote locations and shot, beaten or tortured to death, often with the help of local police and collaborators. For example, in the Babi Yar ravine near Kiev in the Ukraine, *Einsatzgruppe* C murdered 33,000 Jews in two days at the end of September 1941. A report from *Einsatzkommando* 3 (a detachment of an *Einsatzgruppe*) listed in detail the dates, locations and numbers of Jews murdered in

WANNSEE CONFERENCE, 20 JANUARY 1942 – PARTICIPANTS LISTED IN OFFICIAL MINUTES OF MEETING	
Participant	Position/Department
SS-*Obergruppenführer* Reinhard Heydrich	Chief of the RSHA and *Reichsprotektor* of Bohemia-Moravia
Dr Josef Bühler	Government of the General Government
Dr Roland Freisler	Reich Ministry of Justice
SS-*Gruppenführer* Otto Hofmann	Race and Resettlement Main Office
SA-*Oberführer* Dr Gerhard Klopfer	NSDAP Chancellery
Ministerialdirektor Friedrich Wilhelm Kritzinger	Reich Chancellery
SS-*Sturmbannführer* Dr Rudolf Lange	Deputy Commander of the SS in Latvia
Reichsamtleiter Dr Georg Leibbrandt	Reich Ministry for the Occupied Eastern Territories
Dr Martin Luther	Foreign Office
Gauleiter Dr Alfred Meyer	Reich Ministry for the Occupied Eastern Territories
SS-*Gruppenführer* Heinrich Müller	Chief of *Amt* IV (*Gestapo*), Reich Main Security Office (RSHA)
Erich Neumann	Director, Office of the Four-Year Plan
SS-*Oberführer* Dr Karl Eberhard Schöngarth	SD, assigned to the General Government
Dr Wilhelm Stuckart	Reich Ministry for the Interior
SS-*Obersturmbannführer* Adolf Eichmann	Head of *Referat* IV B4 of the *Gestapo*, recording secretary

Lithuania in 1941 – the final tally came to 37,346.

Not all Jews were murdered of course – there were simply too many for immediate execution, and the SS killing squads were not sufficient in number. Instead, hundreds of thousands of Jews were swept into city ghettos, where they would live on the edge of starvation until the Germans decided their fate.

The actions of the *Einsatzgruppen* must have been centrally approved by Hitler. Even back in January 1939 Hitler had told the *Reichstag* that a war would mean 'the extermination of the Jewish race in Europe'. Yet for all the massive death tolls inflicted by the *Einsatzgruppen*, there were many in the Nazi upper echelons searching for an even more effective solution to the 'Jewish problem'. In a warped sympathy, the SS leadership recognized that spending hours machine-gunning women and infants, or making men dig their own graves before shooting them, was emotionally exhausting, so it looked for a more industrial killing method.

The Final Solution

Die Endlösung (The Final Solution) was the ultimate programme for the

---

EXTRACT FROM THE JÄGER REPORT

The following are just two pages from a six-sheet document listing the killings of Jews in Lithuania by *Einsatzkommando* 3, written by the commander of the liquidation squad. The final total of executions listed on sheet six was 137,346.

2.10.41	Zagare	633 Jews, 1,107 Jewesses, 496 Jewish children (as these Jews were being led away a mutiny rose, which was however immediately put down; 150 Jews were shot immediately; 7 partisans wounded)	2,236
4.10.41	Kauen-F.IX	315 Jews, 712 Jewesses, 818 Jewish children (reprisal after German police officer shot in ghetto)	1,845
29.10.41	Kauen-F.IX	2,007 Jews, 2,920 Jewesses, 4,273 Jewish children (mopping up ghetto of superfluous Jews)	9,200
3.11.41	Lazdijai	485 Jews, 511 Jewesses, 539 Jewish children	1,535
15.11.41	Wilkowiski	36 Jews, 48 Jewesses, 31 Jewish children	115
25.11.41	Kauen-F.IX	1,159 Jews, 1,600 Jewesses, 175 Jewish children (resettlers from Berlin, Munich and Frankfurt am main)	2,934
29.11.41	Kauen-F.IX	693 Jews, 1,155 Jewesses, 152 Jewish children (resettlers from from Vienna and Breslau)	2,000
29.11.41	Kauen-F.IX	17 Jews, 1 Jewess, for contravention of ghetto law, 1 Reichs German who converted to the Jewish faith and attended rabbinical school, then 15 terrorists from the Kalinin group	34
EK 3 detachment in Dunanberg in the period 13.7-21.8.41:		9,012 Jews, Jewesses and Jewish children, 573 active Comm.	9,585
EK 3 detachment in Wilna: 12.8-1.9.41 City of Wilna		425 Jews, 19 Jewesses, 8 Comm. (m.), 9 Comm. (f.)	461
2.9.41 City of Wilna		864 Jews, 2,019 Jewesses, 817 Jewish children (sonderaktion because German soldiers shot at by Jews)	3,700
		Total carried forward	99,084

12.9.41	City of Wilna	993 Jews, 1,670 Jewesses, 771 Jewish children	3,334
17.9.41	City of Wilna	337 Jews, 687 Jewesses, 247 Jewish children and 4 Lith. Comm.	1,271
20.9.41	Nemencing	128 Jews, 176 Jewesses, 99 Jewish children	403
22.9.41	Novo-Wilejka	468 Jews, 495 Jewesses, 196 Jewish children	1,159
24.9.41	Riesa	512 Jews, 744 Jewesses, 511 Jewish children	1,767
25.9.41	Jahiunai	215 Jews, 229 Jewesses, 131 Jewish children	575
27.9.41	Eysisky	989 Jews, 1,636 Jewesses, 821 Jewish children	3,446
30.9.41	Trakai	366 Jews, 483 Jewesses, 597 Jewish children	1,446
4.10.41	City of Wilna	432 Jews, 1,115 Jewesses, 436 Jewish children	1,983
6.10.41	Semiliski	213 Jews, 359 Jewesses, 390 Jewish children	962
9.10.41	Svenciany	1,169 Jews, 1,840 Jewesses, 717 Jewish children	3,726
16.10.41	City of Wilna	382 Jews, 507 Jewesses, 257 Jewish children	1,146
21.10.41	City of Wilna	718 Jews, 1,063 Jewesses, 586 Jewish children	2,367
25.10.41	City of Wilna	1,776 Jewesses, 812 Jewish children	2,578
27.10.41	City of Wilna	946 Jews, 184 Jewesses, 73 Jewish children	1,203
30.10.41	City of Wilna	382 Jews, 789 Jewesses, 362 Jewish children	1,553
6.11.41	City of Wilna	340 Jews, 749 Jewesses, 252 Jewish children	1,341
19.11.41	City of Wilna	76 Jews, 77 Jewesses, 18 Jewish children	171
19.11.41	City of Wilna	6 POW's, 8 Poles	14
20.11.41	City of Wilna	3 POW's	3
25.11.41	City of Wilna	9 Jews, 46 Jewesses, 8 Jewish children, 1 Pole for possesion of arms and other military equipment	64

extermination of European Jewry. Pinning down the exact moment when it was decided to murder all the Jews in occupied Europe is difficult. Certainly practical arrangements began back in the early summer of 1941, when Göring ordered Reinhard Heydrich, overseen by Himmler, to prepare a detailed proposal for achieving the Final Solution. A special commission was established

to implement Operation *Reinhard*, the murder of Polish Jewry, and from September 1941 the first pure extermination camps began to emerge in Poland. Previously, concentration camps had been primarily used as forced labour centres and places for the incarceration of political prisoners. The new camps – such as Treblinka, Chelmno, Sobibór, Majdenek and

▼ **GHETTO CENTRES The ghettos played a fundamental role in the Holocaust, concentrating Jewish populations in confined urban centres, from where they could be more efficiently processed. While living in the ghettos, the Jews suffered high mortality rates from starvation and disease, and they also provided the Germans with a dense seam of free labour.**

GHETTOS IN OCCUPIED EUROPE, 1939–45*

KEY

■ Ghetto established 1939–May 1941

■ Ghetto established June 1941–1943

■ Ghetto established 1944

* Shows 1939 borders

Belzec – were pure extermination centres, designed for the industrial-scale killing of thousands of Jews by using specially designed gas chambers, disguised as shower blocks. The notorious Auschwitz-Birkenau complex also contained an extermination centre, although it should be noted that Auschwitz comprised three major camps, only one of which, Auschwitz II (Birkenau), was a death camp. The first experimental gassing of inmates at Auschwitz, using Zyklon-B cyanide gas, occurred on 3 September 1941, after which there were regular trials (usually on Soviet POWs) to refine the process.

The Wannsee Conference

While the techniques of mass murder were being modelled, Heydrich was nearing the end of his planning process for the destruction of Europe's Jews. It culminated in the so-called Wannsee Conference, a meeting headed by Heydrich at Wannsee in the Berlin suburbs. (See p. 145 for a list of the attendees.)

The purpose of the conference was nothing less than the discussion of the Final Solution, and the minutes of the meeting have survived. The Wannsee Protocol, as the final document was called, used veiled language to propose the total eradication of Jews in Europe. Essentially, Jews from all parts of the Greater German Reich were to be ghettoized, then deported to labour and/or extermination camps, where they would meet their end by gas, exhaustion or starvation. One key section of the protocol ran as follows:

Under proper guidance, in the course of the final solution the Jews are to be allocated for appropriate labour in the East. Able-bodied Jews, separated according to sex, will be taken in large work columns to these areas for work on roads, in the course of which action doubtless a large portion will be eliminated by natural causes.

The possible final remnant will, since it will undoubtedly consist of the most resistant portion, have to be treated accordingly, because it is the product of natural selection and would, if released, act as the seed of a new Jewish revival (see the experience of history.)

In the course of the practical execution of the final solution, Europe will be combed through from west to east.

In the Wannsee Protocol, 'emigration' or 'evacuation' act as euphemisms for deportation and murder. Heydrich here proposes that the Jews are either killed through the 'natural causes' of forced labour, or from other means not defined but already understood by those present. Some Holocaust deniers have gone on to claim that the Wannsee Protocol certainly outlines a forced labour programme but not a plan for mass extermination.

Yet there seems no doubt that in the minds of the Nazi hierarchy this was exactly what was intended. Robert Ley, who was present at Wannsee, later told a conference in May 1942 that 'It is not enough to isolate the Jewish enemy of mankind, the Jews have to be exterminated.' Equally transparently, in October 1943 Himmler, who would have overall authority for the Final Solution, talked

MASS EXTERMINATIONS IN THE DEATH CAMPS

Camp	Commencement Date for Mass Killings	Main Method of Extermination	Estimated Death Toll
Chelmno	7 December 1941	Gas vans	320,000
Auschwitz-Birkenau	September 1941	Zyklon-B gas	1,400,000
Belzec	17 March 1942	Carbon monoxide gas	600,000
Sobibór	March 1942	Carbon monoxide gas	250,000
Treblinka	23 July 1942	Carbon monoxide gas	870,000
Majdanek	October 1942	Carbon monoxide and Zyklon-B gas	360,000
Stutthof	June 1944	Zyklon-B gas	65,000

NUMBERS OF DEATHS IN BUCHENWALD CONCENTRATION CAMP, 1937–45

Date	Deaths
1937	48
1938	771
1939	1235
1940	1772
1941	1522
1942	2898
1943	3516
1944	8644
January to March 1945	13,056
March to 11 April 1945	913
Total	34,375

TOTAL NUMBERS DEPORTED TO AUSCHWITZ-BIRKENAU, BY ETHNICITY	
Ethnicity	Number
Jews	1,000,000
Poles	70–75,000
Gypsies	21,000
Soviet POWs	15,000
Others	10–15,000

AUSCHWITZ-BIRKENAU – SYSTEM OF VISUAL CLASSIFICATION	
Indentifying Symbol	Meaning
Red triangles	Political prisoners
Green triangles	Criminal prisoners
Black triangles	'Asocial' – included Gypsies
Purple triangles	Prisoners of belief, e.g. Jehovah's Witnesses, Pacifists
Pink triangles	Homosexuals
Red and yellow Star of David	Jewish prisoners

with a group of SS officers in occupied Poland:

I want to speak here before you in all openness about a very sensitive subject. Amongst us it should be talked about quite openly, but despite this it should never be discussed in public. I mean the evacuation of the Jews, the extermination of the Jewish people... Most of you know what it means when 100 corpses are lying together, when 500 are lying there, or 1000 are lying there. To have seen that through while doing so – leaving aside exceptions owing to human weakness – to have maintained our integrity, that has made us hard. This is an unwritten and never-to-be written page of glory in our history.

This chilling insight into the Nazi mentality demonstrates how the Final Solution was openly pursued.

The European Holocaust

Today it is difficult to comprehend the scale of the Holocaust. The combination of extreme racial prejudice and industrial methods of killing systematically destroyed more than six million people, most of them between 1942 and 1945.

For the Nazis to achieve their goals of stripping Germany and occupied Europe of its Jews, the process of collection and killing had to be conducted with industrial rigour. The darkest example of this objective in action can be seen in a typical gassing operation, such as was used in all the major extermination camps. Deported Jews would arrive by rail in cattle cars, having spent days on the train with no food and water – transit alone killed thousands of individuals. On arrival, they were herded off the train and passed through a selection process in which Nazi 'doctors' distinguished between those who would work, and those who would go to the gas chambers (women, children and the elderly were almost always in the latter category). Those selected for gassing were moved straight to the execution block, where they were told to strip naked and prepare themselves for a shower or delousing. Great care was taken to maintain the illusion that nothing insidious awaited them. They were then herded into the gas chamber, where they would be executed either by Zyklon-B gas (delivered in the form of pellets dropped through holes in the roof) or by carbon monoxide gas. The deaths of several hundred people could be watched through an observation glass in the door, and the whole killing process took some 15–20 minutes.

Once silence prevailed, the doors were opened and the gas was allowed to disperse. Then the *Sonderkommando* (Special Unit) – Jewish prisoners forced to assist in the killing process – faced the hideous task of removing all the bodies for cremation. They were also responsible for removing any gold teeth from the corpses, this gold

ESTIMATES OF HOLOCAUST DEATH TOLL, BY NATIONALITY

Country	Jewish Population	Estimated Killed
Austria	185,000	65,000
Belgium	65,700	28,900
Bohemia-Moravia	118,310	71,150
Denmark	7800	60
Estonia	4500	2000
Finland	2000	7
France	350,000	77,320
Germany	214,000	200,000
Greece	77,380	67,000
Hungary	800,000	596,000
Italy	44,500	7680
Latvia	95,000	80,000
Lithuania	168,000	143,000
Luxembourg	3000	1950
Netherlands	140,000	100,000
Norway	1700	762
Poland	3,300,000	3,000,000
Romania	342,000	287,000
Slovakia	88,950	71,000
USSR	3,020,000	1,100,000
Yugoslavia	78,000	63,300

ESTIMATED PERCENTAGE OF JEWISH POPULATION KILLED, BY COUNTRY

Country	Percentage killed
Austria	35%
Belgium	45%
Bohemia-Moravia	60%
Bulgaria	0%
Denmark	0.8%
Estonia	44%
Finland	0.3%
France	22%
Germany	93%
Greece	87%
Hungary	74%
Italy	17%
Latvia	84%
Lithuania	85%
Luxembourg	55%
Netherlands	71%
Norway	45%
Poland	91%
Romania	84%
Slovakia	80%
USSR	36%
Yugoslavia	81%

eventually being melted down and turned into an additional source of Reich revenue. All the Jews' belongings were also processed in separate facilities, many SS men building considerable wealth through robbing the valued possessions of the deceased.

Although killing hundreds of thousands of people was an art many of the camps seemed to perfect, the greatest 'challenge' remained body disposal. Cremation was always the preferred method, either via crematoria or, more crudely, in huge open pits. Auschwitz-Birkenau, when it reached the point of maximum efficiency in 1942 and 1943, could gas and cremate up to 20,000 people a day. Those who had escaped gassing were in no sense reprieved – they were typically worked, starved or tortured to death.

Death toll

Space here does not allow us to explore the full horror of the concentration camp experience. Even those people sent to labour camps rather than extermination centres, still suffered appallingly and lived short, brutal lives at the mercy of violent, dehumanized individuals. What is truly horrifying is how effective the Final Solution was in terms of its overall objectives. The estimated six million Jews who were murdered included three million Poles, 1.1 million Soviets, 596,000. Hungarians and 287,000 Romanians. Other countries' Jewish populations suffered much fewer deaths, but as a percentage of the total national Jewish population the death toll of the Holocaust reveals the 'success' of the Nazi plan. Greece, for example, was stripped of 87 per cent of its Jewish population, the Netherlands of 71 per cent, Slovakia of 80 per cent and Germany itself of 36 per cent. Poland, with its total Jewish population of 3.3 million, suffered a unique level of horror – 91 per cent of its Jews were murdered. Hitler nearly triumphed in eradicating Jews as a presence in Europe. In addition, 224,000 Sinti and Roma had also been murdered by 1945.

Complicity

The peak of extermination camp activity was in 1942/43. After that, the changing fortunes of war disrupted the efficient transit of Jews to the gas chambers, and by late 1944 there was also the increasing panic amongst the Germans that their crimes were about to be discovered. Such fears did not, however, stop the murders – if anything there seemed

to be a desparate desire to eradicate the surviving Jews as potential witnesses. When the Soviets approached Poland in 1944, and then Germany in 1945, the concentration camp guards sometimes simply torched entire housing blocks with the prisoners inside, or forced the inmates on torturous marches deeper into Germany, executing all who fell by the wayside.

With the liberation of the camps, the wider world was stunned by what had occurred. As well as the obvious culpability of the Nazi leadership and the SS, the question remained as to

the level of complicity amongst the general European population. The fact remains that the sheer logistics of deportation were achieved only through the assistance of civilian authorities and accomplices. Sometimes this assistance was forced, but sometimes it came willingly – Germany was not the only nation with anti-Semitic tendencies. Moreover, in the East especially, civilian personnel and local police frequently worked alongside the Germans in direct murder actions. Holocaust guilt does not lie purely on the shoulders of the Germans.

AUSCHWITZ – KEY DATES

25 January 1940
Decision is made to construct concentration camp near Oswiecim, Poland. This will be Auschwitz.

20 May 1940
First prisoners arrive at the camp.

1 March 1941
Heinrich Himmler inspects Auschwitz and orders the expansion of Auschwitz I to hold 30,000 prisoners, plus the construction of an additional camp near Birkenau.

3 September 1941
The first gassing takes place in Auschwitz, killing 850 people with Zyklon-B gas.

15 February 1942
The first Jews arrived in Auschwitz, from Upper Silesia. They are gassed immediately upon arrival.

29 January 1943
The Reich Central Office for Security orders all Gypsies living in Germany, Austria, Bohemia, and Moravia to be deported to Auschwitz. The first arrive at Auschwitz on

26 February, where they are housed in Section B-IIe of Auschwitz-Birkenau. The last of 20,000 Gypsies transported to the camp are murdered by 2 August 1944.

7 October 1944
Jewish prisoners of the Sonderkommando (Special Unit) stage a revolt, destroying Crematorium IV and killing some guards. The revolt is crushed by the SS.

25 November 1944
Heinrich Himmler orders the destruction of the Auschwitz-Birkenau gas chambers and crematoria, as the Soviet Army approaches from the east.

18–27 January 1945
The SS evacuates prisoners from Auschwitz. Some 15,000 prisoners die on the subsequent 'death march', and thousands more are killed in the concentration camps to which they are relocated.

27 January 1945
Soviet troops liberate Auschwitz – there are 7000 prisoners remaining in the camp.

CHAPTER 8

Social Policy

Nazi policy-making was as much about social engineering as it was about practical government and administration. Hitler saw that the relations between state and identity had to be reconstructed if Nazi ideology was to permeate through every sector of society.

A central component of Nazi social policy was its focus on youth and the education of the young. Hitler's perspective was very future-oriented; hence the young embodied the promise of long-term fulfilment of his ambitions. Yet as the war progressed, every element of society was drawn into the Nazi remit. Women not only took on an increasing role in the labour force but were also burdened with Nazi expectations of fertility and motherhood. In the later years of the Third Reich, old men were drawn out of retirement into active military service. Everyone, it seemed, had their part to play in Germany's new National Socialist adventure.

German youths carry a vaulting horse during a gymnastics festival in the late 1930s. The Nazis were determined to prove the superiority of the Germanic peoples through gymnastics and other types of physical displays.

Youth Organizations

Hitler's youth organizations were principally tools of indoctrination, vehicles for turning a malleable young person into someone imbued with Nazi ideology, destined to serve the Third Reich in both youth and adulthood.

A useful insight into the Nazi perspective on youth comes from the pen of Baldur von Schirach, *Reichsjugendführer* (Reich Youth Leader) from 1933. In the photo-collection book *Adolf Hitler,* published in 1936, Schirach pays homage to the *Führer's* talents for inspiring the German youth:

Our youth pays homage to the Führer in all parts of the Reich. Today Adolf Hitler belongs to an inflamed and captivated youth which rejoice over him and serve him... Adolf Hitler bred a whole Nation to service an idea. The 10-year-olds are, with just as much awareness, carriers of his work and harbingers of his will as are the 30- and 40-year-olds. Yes, the younger ones feel especially strong bonds with the person of the Führer because they feel with the infallible certainty of their instinct that the Führer dedicated his thoughts and concerns especially toward them.

They know he is serving the future which they themselves are.
(Translated from Quinn, 1978)

Through the sycophantic prose, Shirach nevertheless expresses a certain truth about the Third Reich. There did seem to be much backing for Hitler and the Nazi Party amongst the German youth. If we look at Nazi youth-organization membership from 1923 to 1939, the upward curve is impressive. In 1923 there were 1200 members of Nazi youth organizations, but 107,000 in 1932. In the first year of Hitler's rule as Chancellor, the membership figure climbed astronomically to 2,292,000, and in 1939 it stood at 7,728,000.

Youth organizations

There were four principal Nazi youth organizations – two for boys, two for girls – all arranged by age spectrum. For boys aged 10 to 14, the first port of call was the *Deutsches Jungvolk* (German Young People), after which

they could go into the *Hitlerjugend* (Hitler Youth; HJ) until the age of 18. The parallel organizations for the girls were the *Jungmädelbund* (League of Young Girls) for the younger age bracket, then the *Bund Deutscher Mädel* (League of German Girls; BDM) for the older girls.

Paramilitary training

The Nazi youth organizations were certainly not simple places for young people to meet and chat. Nor were they places in which they expanded their cultural horizons. In 1939, Hitler clearly stated what he wanted from the youth of Germany:

A violently active dominating, intrepid, brutal youth – that is what I am after. Youth must be all those things. It must be indifferent to pain. There must be no weakness or tenderness in it. I want to see once more in its eyes the gleam of pride and independence of the beast of prey. Strong and handsome must

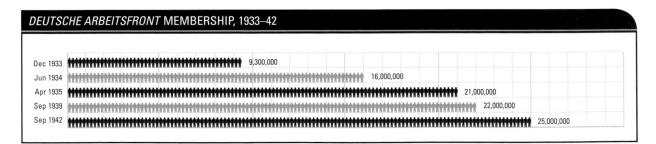

DEUTSCHE ARBEITSFRONT MEMBERSHIP, 1933–42

Dec 1933	9,300,000
Jun 1934	16,000,000
Apr 1935	21,000,000
Sep 1939	22,000,000
Sep 1942	25,000,000

ROBERT LEY

■ **Robert Ley, the head of the Deutsche Arbeitsfront (DAF).**

Birth:	15 February 1890
Death:	25 October 1945
Place of birth:	Niederbreidenbach, Hesse
Place of death:	Nuremberg (by suicide)
Education:	Graduate in Chemistry
Employment:	Employed by IG Farben in 1920
Military service:	Combat pilot in World War I
NSDAP member:	1923
Major political positions:	1925 – Gauleiter to Southern Rhineland District
	1928 – Elected to Prussian Landtag
	1930 – Elected to Reichstag
	1932 – Reich Organization Leader
	1933 – Head of the German Labour Front (DAF)

my young men be. I will have them fully trained in all physical exercises. I intend to have an athletic youth – that is the first and the chief thing. In this way I shall eradicate the thousands of years of human domestication. Then I shall have in front of me the pure and noble natural material. With that I can create the new order.

Hitler's desire to inculcate a violent nature in German youth is quite astonishing. His emphasis on hard physicality expressed itself directly in the programmes offered by the HJ and other such groups. Prior to 1935, the HJ focused on hearty outdoor activities such as hiking, camping and competitive sports, but from 1935 and the reintroduction of conscription the training became much more military in focus. Standard pastimes included rifle marksmanship, practising fieldcraft and camouflage, and visits to military bases. Physical weakness was utterly disdained, and

many a frail boy spent years victimized and bullied by both staff and other boys alike.

The organization of the HJ also started to reflect arms of service realities. Three sub-branches of the HJ were the *Motor-HJ*, *Marine-HJ* and the *Flieger-HJ*. These focused, respectively, on training for boys who were interested in motor vehicles, maritime training and flying. In turn, these provided the foundations for skills that would be useful in the Panzer and mechanized divisons, the *Kriegsmarine* and the *Luftwaffe*.

There were numerous other minor units, with specialisms ranging from communications to anti-aircraft defence duties.

During the war, the military training took an even more overt form in the *Wehrertüchtigungslager der Hitlerjugend* (Military Service Competency Camps for the Hitler Youth). Established in March 1942, the *Wehrertüchtigungslager* delivered a three-week infantry combat training course to boys aged 16 to 18, conducted by serving *Wehrmacht* or *Waffen-SS* personnel.

NAZI PARTY SCHOOL AND FURTHER EDUCATION SYSTEM

Type of School	Age Range	Notes
Nationalpolitische Erziehungsanstalten (NPEA or NAPOLA; National Political Educational Institutes)	10–18	Military-style education for pupils destined for the armed forces
Adolf Hitler Schulen (AHS; Adolf Hitler Schools)	12–18	NSDAP schools for potential Party leaders
Ordensgsburgen (Regulatory Institutions)	about 25	Additional ideological training for AHS graduates
Langemarck Schools	15+	18-month university entrance course for underprivileged students

Pre-war training in the female youth organizations was largely stripped of military connotations, although the obsessive insistence on physical exercise was retained. It seems that the overarching policy of the BDM was to produce 'healthy' young women, doubtless with an eye to future breeding stock for the German nation – one unflattering interpretation of the BDM abbreviation was *Bald Deutsche Mutter* ('Soon [to be] a German mother'). During the war years, however, more BDM girls became acquainted with military training, particularly with small arms, anti-aircraft teams, and even Panzerfausts, but this was largely incidental rather than official.

Apart from a militaristic education, the Nazi youth organizations fairly diligently avoided any sort of substantial intellectual or academic pursuits. Bearing in mind the following statement from Hitler in 1939, it is not hard to see why:

I will have no intellectual training. Knowledge is ruin to my young men. I would have them learn only what takes their fancy. But one thing they must learn – self-command! They shall learn to overcome the fear of death, under the severest tests. That is the intrepid and heroic stage of youth. Out of it comes the stage of the free man, the man who is the substance and essence of the world, the creative man, the god-man.

Hitler here mythologizes the anti-intellectual, someone for whom physical labour and martial training dominate over mere learning.

More will be said about education below, but we should recognize that there was both a synergy and a tension between school education and the education received in the HJ. The tension was between standard school intellectual pursuits and the physical priorities of a Nazi education. The synergy, however, came from the fact that many teachers also became HJ leaders. In 1938, the total number of full-time HJ leaders was 7000, but in addition there were also 720,000 part-time leaders – these positions were often filled by teachers, who in return took HJ principles back with them into the regular classroom.

Forced membership

As with many elements of so-called Nazi success stories, the fact needs separating from the propaganda. In terms of the HJ, the incentives – both positive and negative – to join became extremely coercive as time went on. Schirach had initially proclaimed that 'no boy will be forced into the Hitler Youth', but a law passed in March 1939 made membership compulsory for 10- to 18-year-olds. Yet still significant volumes of youth remained outside, and they faced further 'incentives' to join.

First, apart from the Catholic youth leagues, the Nazis banned all competing youth organizations, meaning that the young person would

TOTAL NAZI YOUTH ORGANIZATION MEMBERSHIP, 1923–39

Date	1923	1924	1925	1926	1927	1928
Number	1200	2400	5000	6000	8000	10,000

Date	1929	1930	1931	1932	1933	1934
Number	13,000	26,000	63,700	107,000	2,292,000	3,577,000

Date	1935	1936	1937	1938	1939
Number	3,943,000	5,437,000	5,879,000	7,031,000	7,728,000

NAZI YOUTH ORGANIZATION MEMBERSHIP BY ORGANIZATION, 1932–39

Organization	Age Range	1932	1933	1934	1935	1936	1937	1938	1939
Bund Deutscher Mädel	14–18	19,244	243,750	471,944	569,599	873,127	1,035,804	1,448,264	1,502,571
Deutsches Jungvolk	10–14	28,691	1,130,521	1,457,304	1,498,209	1,785,424	1,884,883	2,064,538	2,137,594
Jungmädelbund	10–14	4656	349,482	862,317	1,046,134	1,610,316	1,722,190	1,855,119	1,923,419
Hitler Jugend	14–18	55,365	568,288	786,000	829,361	1,168,734	1,237,078	1,663,305	1,723,886

feel increasingly ostracized from his peers if he did not join their ranks. More forcible incentives could come from school – teachers might give extra homework and physically harder discipline to those who stayed outside the HJ. By the late 1930s, there was a clear official sense that consciously opting out of the Nazi youth groups was both a sign of weakness and politically suspect. The following was a statement issued by the German government to young people on 3 May 1941:

The Hitlerjugend *(HJ) come to you today with the question: why are you still outside the ranks of the HJ? We take it that you accept your Führer, Adolf Hitler. But you can only do this if you also accept the HJ created by him. If you are for the Führer, therefore for the HJ, then sign the enclosed application. If you are not willing to join the HJ, then write us that on the enclosed blank.*

There is a threat in this document – those who chose to stay outside of the HJ would have to declare their decision to do so, with the implicit recognition that their decision would be registered and mean that they were not 'for the Führer'.

Propaganda

Yet there were positive incentives to joining the Nazi youth groups. For many, the outdoor adventures, smart uniforms, military training and camaraderie were easily attractive. Nazi youth propaganda was also glamorous and noble. The Nazi Party presented films that dignified the Party youth and presented their

UNIT STRUCTURES – *HITLER JUGEND*

Unit Title	Structure
Kameradschaft	10–15 boys
Schar	3 Kameradschaften; 50–60 boys
Gefolgschaft	3 Scharen; 150–190 boys
Unterbann	4 Gefolgschaften; 600–800 boys
Bann	5 Unterbanne; about 3000 boys
Oberbann	5 Banne; about 15,000 boys
Gebiet	about 75,000 boys; 223 Banne were divided into 42 Gebiete
Obergebiet	about 375,000 boys; 42 Gebiete were divided into 6 Obergebiete

RANKS OF THE NAZI YOUTH ORGANIZATIONS

Hitler Jugend
- Reichsjugendführer
- Stabsführer
- Obergebietsführer
- Gebietsführer
- Hauptbannführer
- Bannführer
- Oberstammführer
- Stammführer
- Hauptgefolgschaftsführer
- Obergefolgführer
- Gefolgschaftsführer
- Oberscharführer
- Scharführer
- Oberkameradschaftsführer
- Kameradschaftsführer
- Oberrottenführer
- Rottenführer
- Hitlerjunge
- Jungzugführer
- Jungenschaftsführer
- Pimpf

Deutsches Jungvolk
- Jungbannführer
- Unterbannführer
- Fähnleinführer

Bund Deutscher Mädel
- Reichsführerin
- Obergauführerin
- Hauptmädelführerin
- Untergauführerin
- Mädelringführerin
- Mädelgruppenführerin
- Mädelscharführerin
- Mädelschaftsführerin
- Mädel

Jungmädelbund
- Jungmädeluntergauführerin
- Jungmädelringführerin
- Jungmädelgruppenführerin
- Jungmädelscharführerin
- Jungmädelschaftsführerin
- Jungmädel

experience as a stirring epic. One such film, shown in 1933, was *Hitlerjunge Quex* ('Hitler Youth Quex'; 'Quex' was the nickname of the protaganist of the movie). The film tells the story of HJ member Heini Völker, who escapes a hard upbringing to find solidarity and meaning within the HJ. Heini eventually dies fighting the Communists while protecting his HJ comrades, reinforcing the message that devotion to country and comrades was more important than anything else, even family. (Heini's father was an alcoholic Communist.) Most of all, young Germans, like all youth, would have the desire to belong, and that sense of belonging was most visibly expressed in the HJ and similar groups. As Stephen Roberts, an historian who visited Germany during the 1930s, observed: 'children wanted to join the HJ. To be outside Hitler's organization was the worst form of punishment.'

Labour service

It was, of course, not long before the Nazi leadership realized that youth organizations could provide a rich manpower resource. The *Landdienst* (Land Service), for example, used German youth workers for agricultural labour, such as collecting harvests. The period of duty typically lasted six weeks, and was concentrated in the summer. Historian Alan Dearn explains the economic and ideological benefits of the *Landdienst* for the Nazi regime and the economy:

UNIT STRUCTURES – *BUND DEUTSCHER MÄDEL*

Unit Title	Structure
Mädelschaft	10–15 girls
Mädelschar	3–4 Mädelschaften; 50–60 girls
Mädelgruppe	3–4 Mädelscharen; 150–190 girls
Mädelring	4–6 Mädelgruppen, 600–800 girls
Untergau	5 Mädelringe; about 3000 girls
Gau	5 Untergaue; about 15,000 girls
Obergau	5 Gaue; about 75,000 girls
Gauverband	5 Obergaue; about 375,000 girls

LAW ON THE HITLER YOUTH, 1 DECEMBER 1936

The future of the German Nation depends upon its youth, and German youth shall have to be prepared for its future duties.

Therefore the Government of the Reich has prepared the following law which is being published herewith:

1. All of the German youth in the Reich is organized within the Hitler Youth.

2. The German Youth besides being reared within the family and school, shall be educated physically, intellectually, and morally in the spirit of National Socialism to serve the people and community, through the Hitler Youth.

3. The task of educating the German Youth through the Hitler Youth is being entrusted to the Reich Leader of German Youth in the NSDAP. He is the 'Youth Leader of the German Reich'. The position of his office is that of a higher governmental Agency with its seat in Berlin, and is directly responsible to the Führer and the Chancellor of the Reich.

4. All regulations necessary for the execution and completion of this law will be issued by the

Führer Chancellor of the Reich.
Berlin, 1 December 1936

The Führer and Chancellor of the Reich
Adolf Hitler

The Secretary of State and Chief of the Reich Chancellery
Dr. Lammers

*By 1942 this had become
compulsory, and was of enormous
benefit to the German economy.
In that year, 600,000 boys and
1.4 million girls were sent off for
six weeks during their summer
holidays to bring in the harvest.
However, in addition to its economic
value, Hitler Youth Landdienst also
often had the more sinister purpose
of promoting the imperialist aims of
the Reich.* (Dearn, 2006)

In regard to his last point, Dearn
goes on to explain how BDM girls,
after the age of 16, were often sent
away on a *Pflichtjahr* (Duty Year) of
agricultural or domestic service, with
many of them being consigned to
colonized or occupied territories. This
posting was essentially part of
Germany's attempt at social
engineering. During their term of
posting, the girls would often help
manage land that had been taken
from the indigenous population, or
support the *Volksdeutsche* population
in settling the land.

Note that for young Germans
turning 18, the *Reichsarbeitsdienst*
(Reich Labour Service; RAD) was
often the next step in terms of their
labour service to the Third Reich.
RAD service became compulsory in
June 1935, and for the young men this
meant a further nine months of sweat
and toil before they could enter the
military. RAD service for young
women did not become compulsory
until 1939. By 1942, not only were girls
obliged to undergo six months of RAD
service, but they then had to perform
six months of war duties, such as
working in armaments factories.

War service
With the outbreak and exigencies of
World War II, the manpower of the
Nazi youth organizations was
increasingly channelled into combat
support roles. This employment was
given further impetus by a steady
drop in the age of conscription,
which fell to 17 in 1943 (it had been
19 in 1940), and RAD service was
dropped for eligible young men. In
March 1945, the emergency facing
the Reich led to that conscription age
dropping even further, to 15. At this
stage of the war, young German
men might find themselves serving
in the *Volkssturm* (established on
25 September 1944), a *Wehrmacht*
formation that was actually under the
Party leadership of local *Gauleiter*.
A select few might find themselves
serving in the 'Werewolves',
Himmler's guerrilla organization that
specialized in sabotage and
assassination activities. Whatever
the case, thousands of boys would be
killed defending the Reich, some
fighting with fanatical bravery,
although thousands more had the
good sense to surrender once the
bullets started flying.

There were several other types of
direct military service open to the
Hitler Youth members. From spring
1943, HJ boys aged 15 to 17 were
utilized as flak auxiliary troops –
200,000 during the course of the war
– assisting anti-aircraft crews during
Allied bombing raids in tasks from
handling ammunition to manning
searchlights, and later operating the
guns themselves. Thousands of BDM
girls also found themselves in similar
roles later in the war. Note also that
the young flak crews could be sent
away from home to perform their
duties, typically to the major cities
that were receiving a daily
hammering from the Allied bombers.

If not taking part in air defence, the
youth members might be employed in
firefighting squads or helping out (in
the case of girls) at feeding centres
for people made homeless by air
raids. The military training and direct
combat experience gained by Hitler
Youth organization members made
them naturally appealing to the
armed forces once they reached
conscription age. Competition
between the *Wehrmacht* and the SS
to recruit the young men was fierce,
although the latter had an advantage
in its ties with the Party. The ferocity
with which some HJ boys fought at
the end of the war signifies that
Hitler's ambition to breed a violent
youth was at least partly realized.

PERCENTAGE OF MAJOR CITIES DESTROYED BY ALLIED BOMBING	
City	Area Destroyed (%)
Berlin	33
Bremen	60
Cologne	61
Dortmund	54
Dresden	59
Duisburg	48
Düsseldorf	64
Essen	50
Frankfurt am Main	52
Hamburg	75
Hanover	60
Kassel	69
Mannheim	64
Munich	42
Nuremberg	51
Stuttgart	46
Wuppertal	94
Würzburg	89

ARBEITSGAUE OF THE REICHSARBEITSDIENST (REICH LABOUR SERVICE; RAD)

Number	Arbeitsgaue	HQ	Number	Arbeitsgaue	HQ
I	Ostpreußen	Königsberg	XXI	Niederrhein	Düsseldorf
II	Danzig-Westpreußen	Danzig	XXII	Hessen-Nord	Kassel
III	Wartheland-West	Posen	XXIII	Thüringen	Weimar
IV	Pommern-Ost	Köslin	XXIV	Moselland	Koblenz
V	Pommern-West	Stettin	XXV	Hessen-Süd	Wiesbaden
VI	Mecklenburg	Schwerin	XXVI	Württemberg	Stuttgart
VII	Schleswig-Holstein	Kiel	XXVII	Baden	Karlsruhe
VIII	Brandenburg-Ost	Frankfurt/Oder	XXVIII	Franken	Würzburg
IX	Brandenburg-West	Berlin-Lankwitz	XXIX	Bayern-Ostmark	Regensburg
X	Niederschlesien	Liegnitz	XXX	Bayern-Hochland	München
XI	Mittelschlesien	Breslau	XXXI	Köln-Aachen	Köln
XII	Oberschlesien	Oppeln	XXXII	Westmark	Metz
XIII	Magdeburg-Anhalt	Magdeburg	XXXIII	Alpenland	Innsbruck
XIV	Halle-Merseburg	Halle/Saale	XXXIV	Oberdonau	Linz
XV	Sachsen	Dresden	XXXV	Niederdonau	Wien
XVI	Westfalen-Nord	Münster	XXXVI	Südmark	Graz
XVII	Niedersachsen-Mitte	Bremen	XXXVII	Sudetenland-West	Teplitz-Schönau
XVIII	Niedersachsen-Ost	Hannover	XXXVIII	Böhmen-Mähren	Prag
XIX	Niedersachsen-West	Oldenburg	XXXIX	Süd-Ostpreußen	Zichenau
XX	Westfalen-Süd	Dortmund	XL	Wartheland-Ost	Litzmannstadt

Education

Given Hitler's preoccupation with youth, it was natural that the education system would be manipulated to suit Nazi ends. Education from the primary years through to university was governed along ideological lines.

Ostensible responsibility for the education system of the Third Reich fell to Bernhard Rust, the Minister of Science, Education and Culture. Rust was known as an indecisive and easily manipulated man (he had actually been dismissed from teaching positions in 1930 following accusations of having molested a female pupil). Technically, the whole system of state education continued as normal on a structural level, apart from Rust's ministry taking central authority in 1934, but on an ideological level there was distinct interference.

Schools and teachers

Teachers who did not follow Nazi orthodoxy in their teaching methods and content were unlikely to last long in the Third Reich. Jewish teachers were dismissed from 1933, and the remaining teachers were monitored by Nazi officials for their political reliability. The pupils themselves could denounce a teacher to the authorities for anti-Nazi teaching, and headmasters were appointed by outside Nazi agencies, running their schools along Party lines. The curricula and syllabuses of courses were vetted for content by the Ministry of Education, and written to emphasize Nazi perspectives on race, history and science.

The result was a general conformity to Nazi ideology amongst the teaching profession, reinforced by pressure to join the *Nationalsozialistischer Lehrbund* (National Socialist Teachers League; NSLB). By 1937, a total of 97 per cent of all teachers in the Reich were members of the NSLB.

Alongside state schools, the Nazis also established their own Party schools. The *Nationalpolitische Erziehungsanstalten* (National Political Education Institutes; NAPOLA), were designed for 10- to 18-year-old boys and focused on providing a military-style education (they were run by the SS). The *Adolf Hitler Schulen* (Adolf Hitler Schools; AHS), of which there were 12 by the end of 1943, were meant as training centres for the future German elite. Aimed at 12- to 18-year-old boys, the AHS delivered more of the same – physical training took up more than 75 per cent of every teaching day. Finally, for AHS graduates and men who had spent time in the RAD and/or armed forces, there were the *Ordensburgen* (Castles of Order), boarding institutions typically aimed at 25- to 30-year-olds, and essentially intended as elite finishing schools for producing Germany's leaders.

In reality, the Nazi schools tended to deliver a dreadful quality of education. In fact, any German school pupil could expect a skewed agenda of inaccurate racial science and contorted interpretations of history.

Universities

The universities were no more immune from Nazi control than the schools. The higher education equivalent of the NSLB was the *Nationalsozialistischer Deutscher Dozentenbund* (National Socialist German University Lecturers League; NSDDB), which all lecturers were obliged to join – membership benefits included regular sessions of ideological instruction from Party officials. Students were also required to join an NSDAP body, the *Nationalsozialistischer Deutscher Studentenbund* (National Socialist German Students League; NSDSB), which not only included political reeducation but also time working in an SA camp and four months of labour service.

Nazi anti-intellectualism had a noticeable impact upon university attendance. In 1932, the number of students in higher education stood at 127,580. By 1939 that number had slumped dramatically to 56,477. The arts were muscled out in favour of 'hard' topics such as engineering, and the colleges became intellectually stunted institutions.

STUDENTS IN HIGHER EDUCATION, 1918–43

Year	Students
1918	46,180
1920	115,633
1922	120,557
1924	100,751
1926	95,255
1928	111,582
1930	129,708
1932	127,580
1934	92,622
1936	64,482
1937	58,325
1939	56,477
1941	40,968
1943	61,066

NUMBER OF UNIVERSITY STUDENTS BY DISCIPLINE, WINTER SEMESTER 1935–36

Sector	Men	Women
Agriculture and Forestry	2030	36
Aircraft Construction	229	2
Architecture	3565	62
Chemistry	2765	271
Dentistry	4100	749
Education	6133	1088
Electrical Engineering	1921	1
Engineering	2701	2
Evangelical Theology	4113	138
Humanities	7409	2633
Law	8026	175
Mathematics and Natural Sciences	3797	782
Medicine	20,556	3818
Mining and Steelworking	461	–
Pharmacy	2193	510
Roman Catholic Theology	4654	5
Social and Economic	4591	514
Veterinary Science	1534	12
Other	660	178

Data source: Tim Kirk, The Longman Companion to Nazi Germany (Longman, 1995)

Women

Nazi attitudes to women were focused on issues such as reproduction and motherhood. The necessities of war, however, meant that women increasingly took on roles traditionally practised by men.

We have already seen something of how women in the Third Reich were treated in terms of employment and in youth organizations. Yet although women could be found serving Germany in duties ranging from manufacturing weapons to working on anti-aircraft gun teams, the Nazi attitude towards women changed little throughout the period.

Breeding a nation

After all else, Hitler and the Nazi hierarchy promoted the belief that the core responsibility of German women was reproduction. In a speech given in 1934, Hitler stated: 'What the man gives in courage on the battlefield, the woman gives in eternal self-sacrifice, in eternal pain and suffering. Every child that a woman brings into the world is a battle, a battle waged for the existence of her people.' The last sentence is the hub of Hitler's thoughts on gender. Women, in his mind, were part of a breeding equation – quite simply, they had to produce enough children to fuel the Reich's growth and dominance. To that end, Nazi ideology eulogized the healthy, attractive, vital woman, while simultaneously insisting that women belonged in a separate sphere of existence.

From some contemporary accounts, there may well have been a distinct male agenda in promoting reproductive vitality. In 1939, Heinrich Himmler spoke to the leaders of the BDM, and after the event its chief, Utta Rudiger, recalled:

He said that in the war a lot of men would be killed and therefore the nation needed more children, and it wouldn't be such a bad idea if a man, in addition to his wife, had a

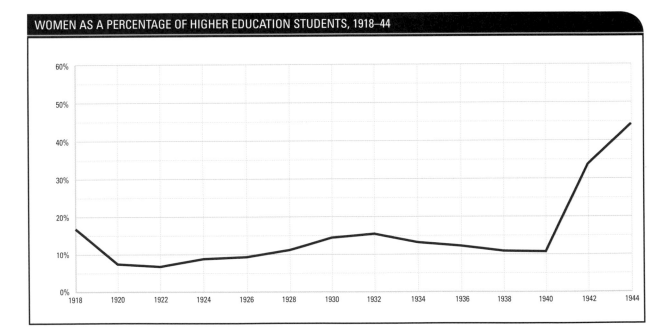

WOMEN AS A PERCENTAGE OF HIGHER EDUCATION STUDENTS, 1918–44

girlfriend who would bear his children. And I must say, all my leaders were sitting there with their hair standing on end.

Himmler was also behind the establishment of the *Lebensborn* (Fount of Life) programme established in 1935. Under this programme,

Himmler developed special fertility and maternity centres throughout Germany, and later the occupied territories, dedicated to the selective breeding of SS men with good 'Aryan' specimens of womanhood, often from the ranks of the BDM. In addition, thousands of children, those deemed to conform to Nazi physical models,

were snatched from the occupied territories and adopted by 'racially trustworthy' German families to be raised for the Reich's service.

Birth rates
A concern for Hitler was the persistent long-term decline in German birth rates – 1.6 million in 1920, but only 990,000 in 1932. General improvements in health care reduced infant mortality figures (see graph below), but the government also delivered legislation aimed at increasing the overall number of births. A Marriage Loan was introduced in 1933 – an average interest-free loan of 600 Reichsmarks was paid to newly-weds, with a deduction of 25 per cent of the amount to be repaid for every child produced by the family. Packaged with tax benefits for couples with dependent children, such measures

---

HITLER – EXTRACT OF SPEECH TO NSDAP WOMEN'S ASSOCIATION, SEPTEMBER 1934

The proclamation 'emancipation of women' was created by Jewish intellectuals. If the man's world belongs to the realm of the State, his struggle and the commitment of his strength to serving the community, then we can perhaps say that the woman's world is a smaller world. For the woman's world is her husband, family, children and home. What would happen in the greater world if there was no one to look after the smaller world? The greater world cannot survive without the stability of the smaller world. We do not believe that women should interfere in the world of man. We believe that it is natural for these two worlds to remain separate.

INFANT MORTALITY, 1925–40 (DEATHS IN FIRST YEAR OF LIFE, PER 1000 BIRTHS)

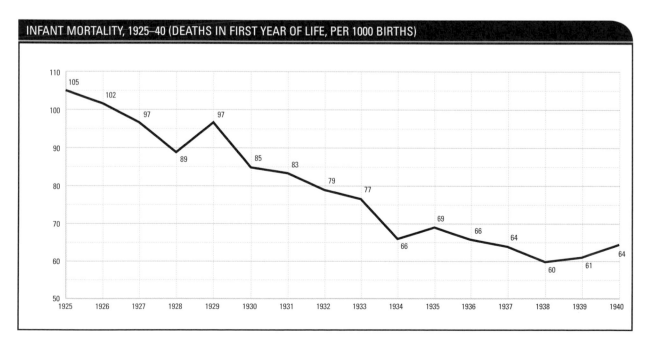

did seem to have a marginal effect on raising birth rates – 1,198,350 children were born in 1934.

Yet although there were financial advantages to child-rearing, and ideological praise – medals were awarded to women with especially large families – the Nazis never really achieved their goals of having women produce more than one or two children. Furthermore, by 1939 there were still one million single women in Germany, plus 5.4 million childless women.

Wartime conditions did not aid either opportunities for conception or the desire to produce many children. Vast swathes of German manhood disappeared into the armed services. Women found themselves channelled increasingly into agriculture and industry as labourers – by September 1944, there were 14.9 million women in munitions production alone. Industrial conscription for women was technically levied from 1943, and yet a large number of exemption conditions produced only an additional 500,000 workers. Such is partly explained by the general Nazi reluctance to allow women into the 'male sphere', despite all they had to offer the war effort.

Strength through Joy

The Kraft durch Freude *(Strength through Joy; KdF) organization was the Nazi Party's attempt to rationalize and control Germany's leisure hours. Although it had its failings, it did provide leisure benefits to millions of Germans.*

The KdF was an offshoot of the DAF, and was essentially a precautionary measure to defuse working-class discontent on account of low wages and long working hours. By filling the workers' leisure hours, furthermore, the Nazi Party had opportunities to deliver indoctrination and also to develop, through encouraging fitness activities, a fit and healthy populace. Fostering opportunities to travel around Germany (see below) was also part of a programme to break down old class and regional barriers, and encourage national unity.

Bankrolling leisure
The KdF provided a broad range of subsidized entertainments for the masses, including theatre performances, concerts, sports facilities and training, German and foreign holidays, and even a car-purchase scheme.

Total funds supplied to the KdF amounted to 56 million Reichsmarks between 1933 and 1936 alone, although in a sense the workers paid for much of the entertainment through payroll deductions or contributions for their employers.

Membeship of the KdF came automatically with that of the DAF, and by 1935 there were consequently a total of 35 million KdF members.

Travel
The KdF's holiday programmes were amongst its most popular benefits. Travel in Germany had been fuelled by the economic expansion of the 1930s, particularly the growth of the German railway network (see data, left). The KdF also invested in a series of cruise liners and international holiday resorts, providing the opportunities for foreign travel to a populace not used to straying beyond its borders. In 1938 alone, 180,000 KdF members went on foreign cruises, while 50 per cent of the working population had national holidays.

Note, however, that the cruises were generally the preserve of the

Year	Kilometres	Miles
1933	53,816	33,439
1934	53,871	33,474
1935	54,331	33,760
1936	54,458	33,839
1937	54,522	33,878
1938	62,942	39,110
1939	72,656	45,146
1940	75,553	46,946
1941	78,257	48,627
1942	78,730	48,920
1943	78,879	49,013
1944	75,763	47,077

LENGTH OF RAILWAY TRACK, *DEUTSCHE REICHSBAHN*, 1933–44

KRAFT DURCH FREUDE STATEMENT ON THE KDF-WAGEN (VOLKSWAGEN), 1 AUGUST 1938

As of 1 August 1938, the great savings programme for the People's Car 'Strength Through Joy' will commence. I hereby state the conditions under which every working person can acquire an automobile.

1. Each German, without distinction of class, profession, or property can become the purchaser of a Volkswagen.

2. The minimum weekly payment, including insurance, will be 5 marks. Regular payment of this amount will guarantee, after a period which is yet to be determined, the purchase of a Volkswagen. The precise period will be determined upon the beginning of production.

3. Application for the Volkswagen savings programme can be made at any office of the German Labour Front and of 'Strength Through Joy', where further details can also be obtained. Factories and shops can submit collective orders.

A Volkswagen for every German – let that be our aim. That is what we hope to achieve. Will all of you help in that goal; it shall be our way of saying 'thank you' to the Führer.

better-off middle classes, who could afford the extra costs. For example, 28 Reichsmarks would purchase a week hiking in the Harz mountains. A two-week cruise to Italy, by contrast, set the bar much higher at 155 Reichsmarks. Foreign destinations, which were also accessible by rail, included Portugal, Norway (for skiing holidays), Libya, Madeira, Finland, Bulgaria and Turkey. The Baltic coast was another popular KdF holiday destination, with some major resorts built at key beauty spots.

Cruise control

The cruise ships were meant to illustrate the elimination of class distinctions, yet even on board the passengers were reminded of the social pecking order. The prime cabins aboard the ship, set on the upper levels, were generally reserved for Party officials, and there were frequent reports of these officials drinking excessively and fraternizing with female passengers,

against the official cruise policy. (Ironically, Robert Ley himself had a terrible reputation for misbehaviour aboard the cruise ships.) As an additional touch, the *Gestapo* would include covert agents on the passenger list, there to spy on the holidaymakers.

The People's Car

The Nazi attempt to provide the workers of Germany with their own vehicles left a lasting legacy in the form of the Volkswagen Beetle. The initial aim was for the car maker Ferdinand Porsche to produce a car that would sell for under 1000 Reichsmarks, but the project came under KdF control when this ambition

fell short of reality. Known first as the *KdF-Wagen* (KdF-Car), then the *Volkswagen* (People's Car), the car was technically available to workers through an instalment payment scheme (see document above). Some 340,000 workers paid up to a quarter of their weekly wages into the plan, but in 1939 all vehicle production was turned over to military control, and so the workers simply lost their investment into the government coffers.

The failed *Volkswagen* scheme was a particularly stinging blow for the workers, yet overall their commitment to Germany's stability suggests that at least some of KdF's entertainment brought approval.

CHAPTER 9

Culture, Religion and Ideology

As we have seen throughout this book, the Nazi regime despised intellectualism on many levels, not least for its supposed enfeebling of the martial spirit. This attitude tipped over into Nazi policies on the arts and culture in general, producing a tightening of restrictions on what was classified as 'permissible' or 'degenerate'.

Any cultural expression that clashed with Nazi ideology was prohibited, a policy that not only produced some ludicrous intellectual contortions but also placed the Third Reich in an uneasy relationship with organized religion and the German churches.

At its best, German culture became characterized by bland, unspiring art, predictable cinema and clichéd books. At its worst, Nazi culture revealed itself in book burnings, prohibited art lists and the imprisonment and death of men and women of faith.

Javelin throwers Tilly Fleischer and Luise Krüger accept gold and silver medals for Germany at the Berlin Olympics. The bronze was won by Polish athlete Maria Kwasniewska, who refused to offer the Nazi salute. Saluting in the foreground is Theodor Lewald, President of the Organizing Committee of the Berlin Olympic Games.

Sport

The Nazi obsession with sport was part of its general policy towards creating a physically healthy society. In the 1936 Olympics, the racial baggage that came with that policy was severely tested.

Sport and fitness permeated society during the years of the Third Reich. Nazi sports programmes were part and parcel of youth organizations and many businesses – factories would often stop work for half an hour for the employees to perform fitness routines – and five million Germans were awarded their National Sports

MEDALS WON BY GERMANY, 1936 BERLIN OLYMPICS

Athletics	Medal	Team/Athlete
Men		
4 x 100m Relay	Bronze	Team
4 x 400m Relay	Bronze	Team
Long Jump	Silver	Luz Long
Shot	Gold	Hans Woellke
	Bronze	Gerhard Stöck
Hammer	Gold	Karl Hein
	Silver	Erwin Blask
Javelin	Gold	Gerhard Stöck
Women		
100m	Bronze	Käthe Krauß
80m Hurdles	Silver	Anny Steuer
High Jump	Bronze	Elfriede Kaun
Discus	Gold	Gisela Mauermayer
	Bronze	Paula Mollenhauer
Javelin	Silver	Luise Krüger

Swimming	Medal	Team/Athlete
Men		
200m Breaststroke	Silver	Erwin Sietas
Highboard Diving	Bronze	Hermann Stork
Water Polo	Silver	Team
Women		
100m Freestyle	Bronze	Gisela Arendt
200m Breaststroke	Silver	Martha Geneger
4 x 100m Freestyle	Silver	Team
Highboard Diving	Bronze	Käthe Köhler

Boxing	Medal	Team/Athlete
Flyweight	Gold	Willy Kaiser
Featherweight	Bronze	Josef Miner
Welterweight	Silver	Michael Murach
Light-heavyweight	Silver	Richard Vogt
Heavyweight	Gold	Herbert Runge

Weightlifting	Medal	Team/Athlete
Lightweight	Bronze	Karl Jansen
Middleweight	Silver	Rudolf Ismayr
	Bronze	Adolf Wagner
Light-heavyweight	Silver	Eugen Deutsch
Heavyweight	Gold	Joseph Manger

Greco-Roman Wrestling	Medal	Team/Athlete
Bantamweight	Bronze	Jakob Brendel
Welterweight	Silver	Fritz Schäfer
Middleweight	Silver	Ludwig Schweickert
Heavyweight	Bronze	Kurt Hornfischer

Freestyle Wrestling	Medal	Team/Athlete
Bantamweight	Bronze	Johannes Herbert
Lightweight	Silver	Wolfgang Ehrl
Light-heavyweight	Bronze	Erich Siebert

Fencing	Medal	Team/Athlete
Team Foil	Bronze	Team
Team Sabre	Bronze	Team
Individual Foil (women)	Silver	Helene Mayer

Modern Pentathlon	Medal	Team/Athlete
Individual	Gold	Gotthard Handrick

Certificates through the KdF. There were definite health benefits to the nation: in 1910 the average life expectancy of an adult German was 45–48, but by 1939 that number had risen to 60–63, mainly through reductions in coronary illnesses, strokes and cancers. Conversely, there was a signal increase in the rates of physical injury, especially amongst the young and amongst older people forced to exert themselves beyond their limits during compulsory physical testing.

Yet physical fitness was also an instrument of ideological indoctrination. Jewish or Gypsy athletes were removed from professional sport by their own governing bodies (those ejected include boxer Johann Trollman, tennis champion Daniel Prenn and high-jumper Gretel Bergmann), and from 1935 German sports clubs delivered racial doctrine classes during the month of October, dedicated to proving the physical superiority of the German people over Jews, blacks and Slavs. In 1932, this world view seemed confirmed when

Canoeing	Medal	Team/Athlete
1000m Kayak Singles K1	Silver	Helmut Cämmerer
10,000m Kayak Singles K1	Gold	Ernst Krebs
1000m Kayak Pairs K2	Silver	Team
10,000m Kayak Pairs K2	Gold	Team
1000m Canadian Singles C1	Bronze	Erich Koschik
10,000m Folding Kayak Singles K1	Bronze	Xaver Hörmann
10,000m Folding Kayak Pairs F2	Silver	Team

Rowing	Medal	Team/Athlete
Single Sculls	Gold	Gustav Schäfer
Double Sculls	Silver	Team
Coxless Pairs	Gold	Team
Coxed Pairs	Gold	Team
Coxless Fours	Gold	Team
Coxed Fours	Gold	Team
Coxed Eights	Bronze	Team

Yachting	Medal	Team/Athlete
Olympic Monotype	Silver	Werner Krogman
International Star	Gold	Team
8m Class	Bronze	Team

Cycling	Medal	Team/Athlete
1000m Time Trial	Bronze	Rudolf Karsch
1000m Sprint	Gold	Toni Merkens
2000m Tandem	Gold	Team

Equestrian	Medal	Team/Athlete
Three-day Event	Gold	Ludwig Stubbendorf
Three-day Event – Team	Gold	Team
Grand Prix (dressage)	Gold	Heinz Pollay
	Silver	Friedrich Gerhard
Grand Prix (dressage) – Team	Gold	Team
Grand Prix (jumping)	Gold	Kurt Hasse
Grand Prix (jumping) – Team	Gold	Team

Shooting	Medal	Team/Athlete
Rapid-fire Pistol	Silver	Heinz Hax
Free Pistol (50m)	Silver	Erich Krempel

Gymnastics	Medal	Team/Athlete
Men		
Individual Combined Exercises	Gold	Alfred Schwarzmann
	Bronze	Konrad Frey
Team	Gold	Team
Parallel Bars	Gold	Konrad Frey
	Bronze	Alfred Schwarzmann
Floor	Bronze	Konrad Frey
Horse Vault	Gold	Alfred Schwarzmann
	Bronze	Matthias Volz
Horizontal Bar	Silver	Konrad Frey
	Bronze	Alfred Schwarzmann
Rings	Bronze	Matthias Volz
Pommel Horse	Gold	Konrad Frey
Women		
Team	Gold	Team

Others	Medal	Team/Athlete
Handball	Gold	Team
Hockey	Silver	Team

German boxer Max Schmeling beat African-American heavyweight champion Joe Louis. Then, in a rematch on 22 June 1938, Louis put Schmeling (who was no racist, it should be pointed out) down in the first round, a result that saw the unfortunate Schmeling marginalized on his return home.

Berlin Olympics

In 1936, Germany was given the opportunity to showcase its physical talents, and its economic regeneration, by hosting the Olympic Games, despite international controversy over the country's racial agenda. The Berlin Olympics was a spectacular event, the opening ceremony including the release of 20,000 carrier pigeons and the *Hindenburg* airship circling over the *Sportpalast* stadium.

In the surrounding city, persecutory laws were temporarily relaxed. The pomp and noise, however, masked sinister racial issues at play. To appease international opinion, the German athletes included some Jewish representatives, including the half-Jewish fencing champion Helene Mayer, who won silver. (Mayer gave the Nazi salute when receiving her medal from Hitler.) In total, Germany took 33 gold medals during the games, and was placed top in the medals table. While the placing seemed to vindicate, for the Nazis, National Socialist racial theory, there were other more contradictory signs. African-Americans won 14 medals. The remarkable Jesse Owens took gold in the 100m and 200m sprints, the long jump, and as part of the US 4 x 100m relay team. Predictably, Hitler refused to shake hands or present medals to any black athletes.

Rallies

The Nazi Party rallies were not just occasions for the gathering of the faithful. They were a key ingredient in Nazi power projection to the wider population.

NSDAP rallies – known as *Parteitage* (Party Days) – began in Munich in 1923, and over the next 16 years swelled to become events of national importance. They combined mass gatherings of Party officials and military ceremonies with almost religious fervour and ritual – typical practices included the consecration of Nazi flags and tremendously picturesque torchlit processions, all framed by towering swastikas and Nazi eagles.

The first three rallies were held at Munich, Nuremberg and then Weimar respectively, but from 1929 onwards the rallies settled in Nuremberg as their home, where they eventually reached unbelievable levels of majesty and theatricality. Held in a complex of rally grounds designed by Paul Ludwig Troost and Albert Speer, and choreographed by the Propaganda Minister Joseph Goebbels, the rallies became events

NUREMBERG RALLIES, 1923–39		
Year Held	*Event*	*Programmatic Title*
1923 (January)	1st Party Congress	–
1923 (September)	'German Day' Rally	–
1926	2nd Party Congress	Refounding Congress
1927	3rd Party Congress	Day of Awakening
1929	4th Party Congress	Day of Composure
1933	5th Party Congress	Rally of Victory
1934	6th Party Congress	Rally of Unity and Strength
1935	7th Party Congress	Rally of Freedom
1936	8th Party Congress	Rally of Honour
1937	9th Party Congress	Rally of Labour
1938	10th Party Congress	Rally of Greater Germany
1939	11th Party Congress (cancelled)	Rally of Peace

lasting an entire week and – in the case of the 1938 rally – attended by more than one million people.

Stage management

Dramatic presentation was key to the rallies, which were filmed for public viewing. The 1934 rally, for example (the first of the rallies to last an entire week), was filmed by the director Leni Riefenstahl, who essentially produced a three-hour episode in Hitler worship entitled *Triumph des Willens* ('Triumph of the Will'). (See the next section for more on Riefenstahl and her films.)

At the 1936 rally, more than 300,000 Party members and spectators listened to Hitler in the huge *Zeppelinfeld* (Zeppelin Field). Speer introduced a particularly dramatic note with his 'Cathedral of Light' effect – 130 searchlights ringing the stadium, which at night projected their beams straight up to form a wall of light around the arena. From 1936, militarism became more of a keynote. Having rejected the Versailles Treaty, Hitler was now free to display his military hardware in the open, and there were endless displays, including infantry marching, tank formations and *Luftwaffe* fly-pasts.

The final Nuremberg rally, which took place on 5–12 September 1938, received international coverage. More importantly, it projected confidence before Hitler took the German people to war.

NUREMBERG RALLY PROGRAMME, 1938

Monday, 5 September – Greetings
- *Press meeting*
- *Reception for Hitler at Nuremberg City Hall*

Tuesday, 6 September – Opening of Party Congress
- *Hitler reviews Hitler Youth flags*
- *Official opening of the Party Congress – Speeches by Rudolf Hess, Julius Streicher, Adolf Wagner*
- *Imperial Crown Jewels presented to Hitler*
- *Exhibition Kampf in Osten ('Struggle in the East') opens to attendees – Speech by Alfred Rosenberg*
- *Presentation of National Prizes for Art and Science – Speeches by Alfred Rosenberg, Adolf Hitler*

Wednesday, 7 September – *Deutsche Arbeitsfront* (DAF) day
- *DAF parade – Speeches by Konstantin Hierl and Adolf Hitler*
- *DAF parade through Nuremberg*
- *Party Congress continues – Speeches by Alfred Rosenberg, Erich Hilgenfeldt and Adolf Wagner*

Thursday, 8 September – Day of Fellowship
- *Athletic competitions*
- *Party Congress continues – Speeches by Fritz Todt and Dr Otto Dietrich*
- *Torchlight parade*

Friday, 9 September – Day of the Leaders
- *Party Congress continues – Speeches by Konstantin Hierl, Walter Darré and Max Amann*
- *Presentation by National Socialist Women's Association – Speech by Gertrude Scholtz-Klink*
- *Review of political leaders on the Zeppelinfeld – Speeches by Robert Ley and Adolf Hitler*

Saturday, 10 September – Hitler Youth Day
- *Review of the Hitler Youth – Speeches by Rudolf Hess and Adolf Hitler*
- *Committee meeting of DAF – Speeches by Robert Ley and Hermann Göring*
- *Final athletic games*
- *Party Congress continues – Speeches by Robert Ley, Fritz Reinhardt and Joseph Goebbels.*

Sunday, 11 September – Day of the SA and SS
- *Mass meeting – Speeches by Viktor Lutze and Adolf Hitler*
- *Parade through Nuremberg*
- *Meeting of political leadership – Speech by Rudolf Hess*

Monday 12 September – Armed Forces Day
- *Review and mass presentation of the Army – Speech by Adolf Hitler*
- *Closing ceremony – Speech by Adolf Hitler*

Cinema and the Arts

The Nazis completely remodelled the relationship between art and wider German society. 'Art for art's sake' was no longer tolerated – instead, art had to either serve the interests of propaganda or promote the ideological outlook of the Party.

It is no coincidence that Germany between 1918 and 1933 experienced an extraordinary fertility in the fields of visual, dramatic and literary arts. The experience of war for millions of men, plus the loosening of the old Prussian social orders, led artists and thinkers to explore the boundaries of artistic expression. This was the period of writers such as Heinrich Mann, Erich Maria Remarque and Erich Kästner, of musicians such as Arnold Schönberg and Kurt Weill, of architects such as Walter Gropius (founder of the Bauhaus movement) and Ludwig Mies van der Rohe, and of artists like Ernst Ludwig Kirchner and Max Beckman. The Weimar period was one of great experimentalism, with movements such as Expressionism, Cubism, Surrealism, Dadaism and post-Impressionism challenging social norms of what constituted art, and often attacking the class structures that had led the world into the previous war.

Nazi culture

Such discordant art forms were certainly not 'popular' in the sense of being universally appreciated, but to Hitler and the Nazis they were socially dangerous. For the Nazis, art in all its forms had to inspire and embolden the people, not create introspective reflection. He believed,

mistakenly, that movements such as Dadaism and Cubism were Bolshevik inventions, with subversive potential, and instead favoured art that expressed 'heroic realism' and embodied values such as community, militarism, physical

health and unity of purpose. Nazi art should be masculine and promote the connection between *Blut und Boden* (Blood and Soil) that was believed to lie at the heart of German nationhood. Society had to be shown as either domestically

MAJOR MOVIES SHOWING IN GERMAN CINEMAS, 1933

Title	Director	Genre
Carmen	Lotte Reiniger	Animation
Der Choral von Leuthen	Carl Froelich, Arzén von Cserépy	War/History
Der Deutsche Reichstag zu Nürnberg	–	Documentary
Don Quichotte	Georg Wilhelm Pabst	Drama
F.P.1	Karl Hartl	Drama/Aviation
I.F.1 ne répond plus	Karl Hartl	Drama/Aviation
Flüchtlinge	Gustav Ucicky	Historical
Gretel zieht das große Los	Carl Boese	Comedy
Hans Westmar. Einer von vielen. Ein deutsches Schicksal aus dem Jahre 1929	Franz Wenzler	Nazi propaganda
Hitlerjunge Quex	Hans Steinhoff	Nazi propaganda
Hitlers Aufruf an das deutsche Volk	–	Hitler address
Ich und die Kaiserin	Friedrich Hollaender	Musical comedy
Lachende Erben	Max Ophüls	Romantic comedy
Liebelei	Max Ophüls	Romantic drama
Meisterdetektiv	Franz Seitz	Comedy
Morgenrot	Vernon Sewell, Gustav Ucicky	War
Der Page vom Dalmasse-Hotel	Victor Janson	Comedy
S.A.-Mann Brand	Franz Seitz	Propaganda
S.O.S. Eisberg	Arnold Fanck	Survival drama
S.O.S. Iceberg	Tay Garnett	Survival drama
Der Sieg des Glaubens	Leni Riefenstahl	Documentary
The Testament of Dr. Mabuse	Fritz Lang	Crime drama
Der Tunnel	Curtis Bernhardt	Drama
Viktor und Viktoria	Reinhold Schünzel	Musical comedy
Was Frauen träumen	Géza von Bolváry	Romantic comedy
Zwei gute Kameraden	Max Obal	Comedy

harmonious, unified in family, work and home, or illustrating the courage and power of armed service (anything considered defeatist was prohibited).

Moreover, from 1933 Hitler had the instrument to enforce his artistic preferences – the Reich Chamber of Culture, or *Reichskulturkammer*. Headed by Joseph Goebbels, and hence controlled by his powerful Ministry of Propaganda, the *Reichskulturkammer* extended its reach over all aspects of German cultural life through seven main departments:

– *Reichskammer der bildenden Künste* (Fine Arts)
– *Reichsfilmkammer* (Film)
– *Reichsmusikkammer* (Music)
– *Reichspressekammer* (Press)
– *Reichsrundfunkkammer* (Radio)
– *Reichsschriftumskammer* (Literature)
– *Reichstheaterkammer* (Theatre)

With such a powerful new official instrument, the *Führer* could set about reshaping the cultural life of the country.

Film

Although the Nazis were culturally reactionary, they were not averse to new media. Film is a case in point. Goebbels in particular recognized the propaganda utility of cinema, with its direct access to a mass public audience. The appetite for cinema was certainly growing – in 1933 there were 245 million visits to German cinemas, but in 1942 that figure rose to more than one billion.

Much cinematic output, especially during the war, was given over to news footage and strictly controlled versions of how the war was progressing. Yet Goebbels also realized the distraction value of regular entertainment, and so the Third Reich saw a healthy output of standard feature films. The *Reichsfilmkammer* had a direct say over the content of films made in Germany, and it also had controlling influence over the film studios. There were four major film studios in Nazi Germany, which although privately owned between 1933 and 1942, had the Ministry of Propaganda as the majority shareholder. Furthermore, once in power the Nazis moved to eliminate the large numbers of talented Jewish and liberal actors, directors, producers and scriptwriters from the industry, individuals who were often responsible for the high international regard achieved by German cinema during the Weimar period. Notable names driven into exile include Fritz Lang, Fritz Kortner and Marlene Dietrich. Eventually, in 1942, the German film industry was nationalized.

From 1933 to 1945, a total of 1363 feature films were produced in Germany. Most of them are lost to history, consisting of the standard fare of period dramas, comedies, adventures, musicals etc. Yet in addition to familiar escapist cinema, the Nazi era also yielded films with more conspicuous ideological or propaganda content. (Approximately

LENI RIEFENSTAHL – FILMS

Films as Actress	Translation	Year
Wege zu Kraft und Schönheit – Ein Film über moderne Körperkultur	Ways to Strength and Beauty	1926
Der Heilige Berg	The Holy Mountain	1926
Der Große Sprung	The Great Leap	1927
Das Schicksal derer von Habsburg	The Destiny of the Habsburgs	1928
Die weiße Hölle vom Piz Palü	The White Hell of Pitz Palu	1929
Stürme über dem Mont Blanc	Storm Over Mont Blanc	1930
Der weiße Rausch – neue Wunder des Schneeschuhs	The White Ecstasy	1931
Das Blaue Licht	The Blue Light	1932
S.O.S. Eisberg	S.O.S. Iceberg	1933
Tiefland	Lowlands	1954

Films as Director	Translation	Year
Das Blaue Licht (Co-director: Bela Balazs)	The Blue Light	1932
Der Sieg des Glaubens	Victory of Faith	1933
Triumph des Willens	Triumph of the Will	1934
Tag der Freiheit: Unsere Wehrmacht	Day of Freedom: Our Armed Forces	1935
Olympia, Part 1 known as Fest der Völker Part 2 as Fest der Schönheit	Festival of the Nations Festival of Beauty	1938
Tiefland	Lowlands	1954
Impressionen unter Wasser	Underwater Impressions	2002

14 per cent of films produced between 1933 and 1945 in Germany had a direct political message.) In terms of propaganda features, few directors in history have surpassed the achievements of Leni Riefenstahl. The actress and director is known for her epics of Nazi idealism, particularly *Triumph des Willens* and also *Olympia*, which covered the Berlin Olympics of 1936. Known for both their veneration of Hitler and of the human body, these films were ideologically contorted, but well crafted, and gave Riefenstahl a dubious fame in posterity.

Many other propaganda movies assaulted the Nazis' 'axis of evil' – Communism and Judaism. *Hitlerjunge Quex*, mentioned earlier, *SA-Mann Brand* and *Hans Westmar* depicted noble Nazi heroes struggling against the Communist rabble. Far more insidious were the twisted anti-Jewish films such as *Der ewige Jude* ('The Eternal Jew'), *Die Rothschilds* and *Jud Süss*. The eponymous Jew of the latter was depicted as such a vile character by actor Veit Harlan that Harlan was

actually imprisoned for war crimes in 1945 (the film was sometimes shown to SS units as motivation prior to anti-Jewish operations in the occupied territories). Although Harlan was finally exonerated in 1949,

there is no doubt that such films worked to harden the cement of anti-Semitism in Germany, and aid wider society turn a blind eye to the unfolding terrors of the Holocaust.

Degenerate art

As already noted, the heroic realism favoured by the Nazis meant that much of what we today class as great art fell under the category of 'degenerate'. Those not on the approved list included Van Gogh, Gauguin, Matisse, Picasso and Cézanne, and in their place came monotonous art of Aryan specimens practising sport, soldiers gathered around the *Führer*, or peasants happily working the land.

To make clear to the public what was degenerate and what was

STATISTICS ON *KRAFT DURCH FREUDE* FOR PERIOD 1933–38, GIVEN IN THE PUBLICATION *DAS DANKEN WIR DEM FÜHRER*	
Structures improved by KdF:	6000 factory courtyards
	17,000 canteens and lounges
	13,000 showers and changing rooms
	800 community buildings
	1200 sports facilities
	200 swimming pools
	Crew quarters in 3500 ships
Visitors to KdF art galleries:	2.5 million
Audiences at KdF concerts:	5.6 million
Audiences at KdF theatre productions:	22 million
Cabaret/variety performances:	40,000 shows
KdF holidaymakers:	20 million (since 1934)
Number of domestic vacation trips:	60,000
Distance travelled by KdF trains:	2.16 million km (1.3 million miles)
Number of KdF cruise ships:	9
Major cruise desinations:	Norway, Majorca, Italy

ARTISTS CLASSIFIED AS PRODUCING 'DEGENERATE' WORK AT THE *ENTARTETE KUNST* (DEGENERATE ART) EXHIBITION IN 1937		
Artist	Lifespan	Notes
Mark Chagall	1887–1985	Painter, inspired by Jewish traditions
Max Ernst	1891–1976	Painter, one of the founders of Surrealist movement
Wassily Kandinsky	1866–1944	Painter and art theorist, pioneered abstract art
Paul Klee	1879–1940	Artist, influenced by Cubism and Surrealism
Ernst Ludwig Kirchner	1880–1938	Expressionist painter and printmaker
Emile Nolde	1867–1956	Expressionist painter and graphic artist
Franz Marc	1880–1916	Expressionist painter and printmaker
Edvard Munch	1863–1944	Symbolist/Expressionist painter and printmaker
Max Beckman	1884–1950	Painter, draughtsman, printmaker, sculptor, writer
Otto Dix	1891–1969	Realist painter and printmaker

approved, the Nazis put on several exhibitions illustrating the difference. German galleries were purged of more than 12,000 examples of 'decadent' art, and selected works were displayed at the *Entartete Kunst* (Degenerate Art) exhibition in Munich in July 1937. (It subsequently toured several other locations in Germany.) Visitors flocked to the exhibition, but to ensure that they went away with the right message the authorities painted slogans alongside the artworks, such as 'An insult to German womanhood' and 'German farmers – a Yiddish view'. A nearby exhibition entitled *Grosse deutsche Kunstausstellung* (Great German Art Exhibition) presented approved artworks depicting heroic Stormtroopers and rural idylls. The ideological lesson might have been somewhat lost on the public, however, as the exhibition of degenerate art received three-and-a-half times more visitors than its approved counterpart.

The consequence of Nazi interference in the visual arts was that art became lifeless and monotonous. Artists who infringed regulations issued by the *Reichskammer der bildenden Künste* could have their works confiscated or could themselves be arrested by the *Gestapo*. German fine art thus entered something of an historical dead zone.

Literature

Not only fine art suffered under the tightening fist of Nazi rule. Literature also appeared quickly in the crosshairs of Nazi policing. Louis Snyder notes:

ART LOOTED BY THE NAZIS DURING WORLD WAR II

Figures derived from evidence presented during the Nuremberg Trials; these figures are probably not complete but give some indication of the scale of Nazi looting:

- 21,903 works of art
- 5281 paintings, pastels, water colors, drawings
- 684 miniatures, glass and enamel paintings, illuminated books and manuscripts
- 583 sculptures, terracottas, medallions, and plaques
- 2477 articles of furniture of art historical value
- 583 textiles (tapestries, rugs, embroideries, Coptic textiles)
- 5825 objects of decorative art (porcelains, bronzes, faience, majolica, ceramics, jewelry, coins, art objects with precious stones)
- 1286 East Asiatic artworks (bronzes, sculpture, porcelain, paintings, folding screens, weapons);
- 259 artworks of antiquity (sculptures, bronzes, vases, jewellery, bowls, engraved gems, terracottas).

MAJOR GERMAN LITERARY, POLITICAL AND PHILOSOPHICAL WORKS, 1918–43

Year	Author	Title	Translation
1918	Heinrich Mann	Der Untertran	Man of Straw
1919	Franz Kafka	In der Strafkolonie	In the Penal Colony
1922	Ludwig Wittgenstein	Tractatus Logico-Philosophicus	
	Oswald Spengler	Der Untergang des Abendlandes	The Decline of the West
1924	Thomas Mann	Der Zauberberg	The Magic Mountain
1925	Frank Kafka	Der Process	The Trial
	Hans Grimm	Volk ohne Raum	People without Space
	Adolf Hitler	Mein Kampf, Vol. 1, Eine Abrechnung	A Reckoning
1926	Franz Kafka	Das Schloß	The Castle
	Adolf Hitler	Mein Kampf, Vol. 2, Die Nationalsozialistische Bewegung	The National Socialist Movement
1929	Alfred Döblin	Berlin Alexanderplatz	
	Erich Kästner	Emil und die Detektive	Emil and the Detective
	Erich Maria Remarque	Im Westen nichts Neues	All Quiet on the Western Front
1930	Thomas Mann	Mario und der Zauberer	Mario and the Magician
	Alfred Rosenberg	Der Mythus des 20. Jahrhunderts	The Myth of the 20th Century
1932	Hans Fallada	Kleiner Mann, was nun?	What Now, Little Man?
1936	Thomas Mann	Joseph in Ägypten	Joseph in Egypt
	Klaus Mass	Mephisto	
1939	Ernst Junger	Auf den Marmorklippen	On Marble Cliffs
	Thomas Mann	Lotte in Weimar	
1943	Robert Musil	Der Mann ohne Eigenschaften	The Man Without Qualities

LOCATION OF MAJOR BOOK BURNINGS, 1933

DENMARK

■ KIEL

■ ROSTOCK
■ GREIFSWALD

■ KÖNIGSBERG

USSR

■ HAMBURG

POLAND

HOLLAND

■ HANOVER   ■ BERLIN
■ BRUNSWICK
■ MÜNSTER
■ GÖTTINGEN
■ HALLE
■ KÖLN   ■ MARBURG   ■ LEIPZIG   ■ DRESDEN
■ BONN   ■ BRESLAU

■ FRANKFURT
■ DARMSTADT
■ WORMS   ■ WÜRZBURG
■ MANNHEIM   ■ NUREMBERG   CZECHOSLOVAKIA
■ KARLSRUHE

FRANCE

AUSTRIA

▲ PURGING LITERATURE Although the book burnings in 1933 achieved their greatest visibility in Berlin, they occurred in numerous towns and cities across Germany. Those authors whose works ended up on the bonfires included Erich Maria Remarque, Thomas Mann, Albert Einstein, Marcel Proust, Jack London, Lion Feuchtwanger, Helen Keller and Sigmund Freud (see table, previous page). The burnings were officially promoted by the Nazi Party. During the burnings, Joseph Goebbels made the pronouncement that 'These flames not only illuminate the end of the old era, they also light up the new.' Note, however, that the burnings were downplayed in the German media, the Nazis being sensitive to accusations of barbarism.

Literature was the branch of art most seriously affected by the Nazis' coming to power. Hitler sensed that the written word could be dangerous for his regime. After 1933 more than 2,500 writers, including Nobel Prize winners, left Germany either voluntarily or under duress. Within a short time German literature, which had won global acclaim, was reduced to a level of boredom that the German public found distasteful.

(Snyder, 1998)

LANDMARK NAZI ARCHITECTURAL PROJECTS

Building	Translation	Architect	Location	Opened	Function
Tempelhof Airport	–	Frnst Sagebiel	Berlin	1934	Civilian airport
Ehrentempel	Honour Temples	Paul Ludwig Troost	Munich	1935	Memorial
Reichsluftfahrtministerium	Air Ministry Building	Ernst Sagebiel	Berlin	1936	Government building
Olympiastadion	Olympic Stadium	Werner March/Albert Speer	Berlin	1936	Sports stadium
Zeppelinfeld	Zeppelin Field	Albert Speer	Nuremberg	1937	Nazi Party rally ground
Propagandaministerium	Propaganda Ministry	Albert Speer	Berlin	1937	Government building
Wehrmacht HQ	–	Albert Speer	Berlin	1937	Armed Forces HQ
Haus der deutschen Kunst	House of German Art	Paul Ludwig Troost	Munich	1937	Art gallery
Kanzlei des Führers	Hitler's Chancellery	Troost/Speer	Berlin	1938	Government building
Nürnberger Kongreßhalle	Nuremberg Congress Hall	Albert Speer/ Ludwig and Franz Ruff	Nuremberg	1938	Congress Hall
Prora	–	Dr Robert Ley/ Erich Putlitz	Rügen	1939	Resort complex

The new hostility to literature was physically manifested in May 1933, when students were encouraged forcibly to purge bookshops and libraries of any works considered inimical to Nazi ideology.

Anti-war, Jewish, Communist and abstract works were particular targets, and the action ended with huge book burnings, thousands of volumes going up in smoke on the Unter den Linden in Berlin alone. The international condemnation of the burnings signalled a new awareness of the nature of the Nazi regime.

By 1939, German publishing was effectively nationalized, with all stages of the production process – writing, editing, publishing, bookselling – controlled by Goebbels' offices. Hitler's *Mein Kampf* became the bestselling title (six million copies sold by 1940), but the remainder of German literature of the time consisted of deadeningly formulaic National Socialist epics or poetry, emphasizing martial spirit, community and racial superiority.

Architecture

Hitler's anti-intellectualism did not extend to architecture, which he saw as a potent means for expressing state power and influence over the population. (Hitler himself had originally wanted to train as an architect.) In essence, Nazi architecture was retrospective rather than innovative. It looked back to classical Greek and Roman models combined with the grand ornamentation of neo-classical and baroque styles. Through revisiting these models, the Third Reich, in Hitler's view, could project timeless strength, aided by creating buildings on a massive scale and imbuing them with a certain Germanic austerity.

In terms of architects, two names dominate the landscape of the Third Reich – Paul Ludwig Troost and Albert Speer. Prior to his death in March 1934, Troost was Hitler's personal favourite architect (he actually began work for the Nazi Party back in the 1920s). Troost's early commissions included the renovation and refurbishment of the

Reich Chancellery residence in Berlin and the Nazi Party headquarters in Munich. New-build projects included the *Haus der deutschen Kunst* (House of German Art) in Munich, a rather stark, linear affair fronted by an imposing rank of columns.

Albert Speer

Troost was involved in numerous other public building projects around Germany, but with his death came the need to find someone capable of filling his shoes. Here Albert Speer enters the picture, the man who would most enduringly represent the architecture of the Third Reich.

Albert Speer was a sound figure for the Nazis. Born in 1905, he had studied architecture and graduated to become an assistant at the Berlin Technical College. He was also a Nazi Party member from 1931 and a member of the SS from 1932. Speer's Nazi credentials and abilities as an architect had already caught Hitler's attention. In May 1933, Speer was given responsibility for the technical features of the Nazi Party rally at

Tempelhof Field. The huge success of the rally was in large part down to Speer's theatrical genius, with thousands of Nazi flags, torchlit parades and the 'Cathedral of Light' searchlight effect leaving an impression that few would forget, including Hitler.

Commissions now came thick and fast for Speer, especially after Troost's death. He completed Troost's work on the Reich Chancellery, and designed the great *Zeppelinfeld* at Nuremberg, capable of seating some 300,000 people in a strident marble arena. Speer also reshaped Werner March's *Olympiastadion* in Berlin to meet with Hitler's preferences by adding a bold stone exterior.

With numerous public design projects behind him, including the *Wehrmacht* HQ and the Propaganda Ministry building, both in Berlin, Speer was appointed as General Architectural Inspector of the Reich in 1937. Hitler wanted Speer to reshape Berlin to become the greatest capital city in the world, the centre of the *Germania* empire. Speer planned the *Welthauptstadt Germania* (World Capital Germania) in exhaustive detail. The plans included a triumphal arch 99m (325ft) high, a 150,000-person capacity Great Hall, plus cinemas, hotels, spas, luxury restaurants and lashings of public buildings, all arranged around two north-south and east-west axes, the former alone measuring 4.8km (3 miles). The visionary city, however, would remain but a dream, and Berlin itself would eventually be a ruin.

Radio and Newsprint

Mass media – which in the 1930s and 1940s meant radio and newspapers – was integral to spreading the Nazi message. Once the radio and press media were under Nazi control, the public knowledge of foreign affairs was easily manipulated.

Radio, apart from in the poorest sectors of German society, had a presence similar to that of television today. By 1939, a total of 70 per cent of German households had their own radio set, and most of the major towns and cities in Germany by 1941 had between 65 and 80 per cent of the population tuned in to the radio at some point during the week. Some cities went even higher – Stuttgart, for instance, had listening figures of 87 per cent in 1941, and Kiel boasted 85 per cent.

Such impressive radio listening figures were due in a large part to Nazi efforts to make cheap radios available to the masses. Realizing the propaganda potential of being able to speak directly into people's homes, Goebbels worked with industry to ensure that radio sets were both affordable and accessible. The first model, known as '30. Januar', sold for 78 Reichsmarks, but for subsequent models the price came down. In qualification, however, it should be noted that every household with a radio had to pay a 2-Reichsmark annual radio tax.

The radio not only brought news and current affairs stories to the German public, it also provided the welcome distractions of music and comedy. Being such a powerful medium, however, it was inevitable that radio would soon come under Nazi control.

In a speech in 1933, dedicated purely to the subject of radio, Goebbels eulogized the power of the radio while also sending out an ambiguous message about its value as a popular tool of entertainment and a vehicle for political education:

We do not seek to use the radio purely for a partisan agenda. We want to allow entertainment, popular arts, games, comedy and music. But everything should have a relationship to present conditions. Everything should speak of our great reconstruction, or at least not stand in its way. Most important, it is necessary to centralize all radio activities, and put spiritual values ahead of technical ones, to introduce the leadership principle, to provide a clear world perspective, and to present this perspective in different ways.

Goebbels seems to give with one hand, only to take away with the other. He initially reassures that the radio will not become a monotone political mouthpiece, but then states that radio output will be 'centralized' according to Nazi values.

Control

The first element in controlling German radio was the establishment of the *Reichsrundfunkkammer* in 1933, headed by Eugen Hadamowsky. An insight into Goebbels' intentions for radio comes from a report written by Hadamowsky in August 1933:

We National Socialists must demonstrate enough energy and enthusiasm coupled with lightning speed to impress Germany and the whole world. Party comrade Dr Goebbels ordered me on 13 July to purge the German radio of influences that were opposed to our cause. I can now report that the work has been done thoroughly.

All radio output was monitored and controlled centrally, and Goebbels also took measures to ensure that the people were listening, particularly to Hitler's speeches, which were broadcast on an infuriatingly regular basis. Employers or civic officials in charge of anywhere with large concentrations of people – factories, offices, restaurants, town squares etc – were ordered to install loud

speakers to provide the broadcasts to a captive audience. Entire workplaces would often come to a halt just to listen to a speech from their *Führer*.

Content

Outside of direct political transmissions, radio broadcasts were the traditional mix of content, although all approved or inflected along Nazi lines. In terms of music, the Nazi filtering system was a little more sophisticated than with some other art forms, and largely reflected Hitler's personal tastes. Out went Meyerbeer and Mendelssohn – they were Jews, after all – and the experimentalism of the acclaimed Paul Hindemith was branded as degenerate. In came the stirring power of Wagner and Richard Strauss – indeed, for a time Strauss

---

LYRICS OF THE HORST WESSEL LIED

Original
Die Fahne hoch! Die Reihen fest geschlossen!
SA marschiert mit mutig-festem Schritt.
Kameraden, die Rotfront und Reaktion erschossen,
Marschieren im Geist in unseren Reihen mit.
Die Straße frei den braunen Bataillonen.
Die Straße frei dem Sturmabteilungsmann!
Es schau'n aufs Hakenkreuz voll Hoffnung
   schon Millionen.
Der Tag für Freiheit und für Brot bricht an!
Zum letzten Mal wird nun Appell geblasen!
Zum Kampfen steh'n wir alle schon bereit!
Bald flattern Hitlerfahnen über Barrikaden.
Die Knechtschaft dauert nur noch kurze Zeit!
Die Fahne hoch! Die Reihen fest geschlossen!
SA marschiert mit ruhig-festem Schritt.
Kameraden, die Rotfront und Reaktion erschossen,
Marschieren im Geist in unseren Reihen mit.

English translation
The flag is high! The ranks are tightly closed!
The SA marches with a brave, strong pace.
Comrades whom the Red Front and Reaction shot dead
March in spirit amongst our ranks.
The streets are free for the brown battalions;
The streets are free for the SA man!
Already millions are looking to the swastika,
   filled with hope;
The day of freedom and bread is dawning.
The alert has sounded for the final time!
We are all prepared to fight!
Soon Hitler's flags will flutter over the barricades.
Our servitude will not last much longer now!
The flag is high! The ranks are tightly closed!
The SA marches with a calm, strong pace.
Comrades whom Red Front and Reaction shot dead
March in spirit amongst our ranks.

GERMAN NEWSPAPER TITLES, 1918–35

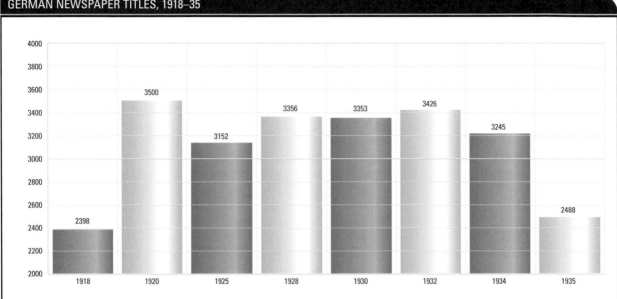

MAJOR NAZI NEWSPAPERS, 1935, WITH CIRCULATION FIGURES

Title	Translation	Location	Circulation
Der Angriff	The Attack	Berlin	95,000
Der Mitteldeutsche	The Midlands	Magdeburg	103,100
Der Stürmer	The Stormer	Nuremberg	450,000
Nationalzeitung	National Times	Essen	140,600
Rheinische Landeszeitung	Rhine Gazette	Düsseldorf	166,200
Völkischer Beobachter	People's Times	Munich/Berlin	400,700
Westdeutscher Beobachter	West German Observer	Cologne-Aachen	187,300
Westfälische Landeszeitung	Westphalian Times	Dortmund	171,800

was head of the *Reichsmusikkammer*. Much popular music was frowned upon. Regional folk tunes were permitted, but the decadent import that was Jazz was seen as corrupting, especially of the young, to whom its rhythms most strongly appealed.

One major problem for the Nazis, however, was the intrusion of foreign radio broadcasts into German homes. The problem with the ideologically biased Nazi radio programming was that it soon bored its listeners. Goebbels recognized this fact himself in a speech to radio executives:

At all costs avoid being boring. You must help to bring forth a nationalist art and culture which is truly appropriate to the pace of modern life and to the mood of the times. You must use your imagination, an imagination which is based on sure foundations and which employs all means and methods to bring to the ears of the masses the new attitude, in a way which is modern, up-to-date, interesting and appealing.

Goebbels' concerns were not borne out in the realities of programming, and so millions of Germans furtively tuned into transmissions from the British Broadcasting Corporation (BBC) and even propaganda broadcasts from the Soviet Union (in the later war years). Realizing this to be the case, the Nazis made listening to foreign radio broadcasts a criminal offence, and although thousands of people were indeed convicted and sentenced to concentration camps for this offence (1500 in 1939 alone), millions more persisted in the privacy of their own homes. Sometimes they did not have a choice – the Soviets later pioneered methods of cutting directly into German radio shows.

In balance, the Germans also pushed Nazi content around the world, riding on the back of short-wave radio technology. German propaganda messages not only went out to the occupied territories but also as far afield as the United States, South America and Asia.

Newspapers

The other strand of the mass media the Nazis sought to control was newspapers. From 1933, any newspapers with socialist or Communist credentials were closed down under the Decree for the Protection of the People and State, and those that remained came under the *Reichspressekammer*'s control. Yet the press situation remained a challenge for the Nazis, as when they took office there were 4700 newspapers in circulation, mostly local and regional titles.

One of the most insidious early measures passed against the German press was the Editors Law of 4 October 1933. This piece of legislation made editors responsible for content – an implicit threat that was combined with Propaganda Ministry directives on what sort of content could be published.

Via the *Deutsches Nachrichtenburo* (German News Bureau; DNB), journalists and editors were given daily briefings from the Propaganda Ministry, with clear instructions on what stories could be covered, and how. Those who could not attend the briefings were given their instructions via telegrams or the mail. Furthermore, all Jewish or liberal editors or journalists had to be removed from the papers, part of the

MUSICIANS AND COMPOSERS APPROVED BY THE THIRD REICH		
Name	*Date*	*Profession*
Anton Bruckner	1824–1896	Composer
Elly Ney	1882–1968	Pianist
Hans Pfitzner	1869–1949	Composer
Herbert von Karajan	1908–1989	Conductor
Ludwig van Beethoven	1770–1827	Composer
Richard Wagner	1818–1883	Composer
Richard Strauss	1864–1949	Composer

Nazi attempt to create a 'racially pure' press.

Buying the press

The Nazis did have newspapers of their own. These included the *Völkischer Beobachter* ('People's Times'), which had been running since 1921, and the fairly disreputable and salacious *Der Stürmer* ('The Stormer'). Between them, these two titles had a circulation of more than 800,000 in 1935. Yet in the early months of Nazi power, such papers still held only 2.5 per cent of the total market, so more drastic action was required to bring the press under Nazi control.

The second major strand in Nazi press relations, therefore, was the literal acquisition of newspapers. In 1933 alone, the Nazis purchased 27 titles with a 2.7-million readership, and many more would follow. In 1939, 69 per cent of German newspapers were concentrated under Nazi ownership, but by 1944 that figure was at a monopolistic 82 per cent. In addition, the Nazi Party also scooped up printers and distribution networks, enabling them to control every stage of the newspaper

PERCENTAGE OF HOUSEHOLDS LISTENING TO RADIOS, 1941 (SELECTED CITIES)	
City	*Percentage*
Augsburg	73
Berlin	78
Bremen	75
Cologne	67
Danzig	68
Dortmund	71
Dresden	78
Düsseldorf	72
Essen	61
Frankfurt am Main	77
Halle	81
Hamburg	75
Hanover	79
Kiel	85
Königsberg	80
Leipzig	80
Magdeburg	80
Mannheim	73
Munich	77
Nuremberg	76
Stettin	71
Stuttgart	87
Wuppertal	67

production process. Nazi control over the press simply resulted in bad, prejudiced journalism that people were increasingly reluctant to read. Even in the pre-war years, the Nazis' measures dramatically affected the numbers of newspapers in circulation – there were around 1000 fewer papers in 1935 compared with 1932. The only paper that retained a modicum of independence was the *Frankfurter Zeitung* (Frankfurt Newspaper), which on account of its international reputation and its place amongst the German elite was even permitted to make delicate criticism of the National Socialist regime.

Faith and Religion

Hitler's private opinion of Christianity was low – he saw it as weak and Jewish-influenced, whereas he wanted a militaristic and anti-Semitic people. Yet he could not entirely alienate millions of believers.

There is no doubt that Hitler was essentially opposed to the practice of Christianity. Yet Germany's long traditions of Catholicism, and its place as the historical centre of the Protestant Reformation, meant that it was a presence he could not openly attack (that attention was the preserve of the Jewish faith, of course). His chosen course, therefore, was a mixture of skewed theology, de facto persecution and begrudging tolerance.

Toleration and theology

It is easy to see why Hitler was antagonistic towards Christianity. Here was a faith that not only had Jewish roots and scriptures (the Old Testament) but also promoted ideas of conciliation, love of enemies, kindness, mercy and forgiveness – all of which notions were anathema to Nazi ideologies of war, violence, hard hearts and racial enmity.

At first, however, the Nazis seemed to buy into a much modified version of Christianity, emphasizing racial and heroic notes at the expense of its gentler doctrines, aided by support from many of the churches, who believed Hitler had rescued German faith from the clamp of Bolshevism. The Nazi Party Programme even expressed support for the practice of 'positive Christianity'.

The Catholic Church, disturbed by a potential loss of authority and the erosion of its influence in Germany, signed a concordat with the Nazis in 1933. This act, as much an attempt to calm international opinion as to protect domestic Catholicism, ostensibly protected the practice of the Catholic faith in Gemany, including the integrity of Catholic schools and youth groups.

At the same time as Hitler was promoting tolerance, he was also attempting to reshape core Christian theology to match his own world view, aided by Nazi theologians such as Professor Ernst Bergmann. Among his books, several of which ended up on the Catholic list of banned titles, Bergmann published *Die 25 Thesen der Deutschreligion* ('The Twenty-five Points of the German Religion'), a work of breathtakingly imaginative theology that amongst its premises claimed that Christ was not Jewish but Nordic, Adolf Hitler was the new messiah and that the Old Testament was no longer considered part of scripture. Bergmann also argued that 'Either we have a German God or none at all.' The construction of a new German neo-pagan religion based on Nordic deities rather than the Christian god, termed the *Deutsche Glaubensbewegung* (German Faith Movement) and headed by 'Reich Bishop' Ludwig Müller, rankled with Germany's regular Christians, who saw the Nazi religious charade for what it was. Once German Christians felt direct evidence of Nazi moral failings with the onset of war in 1939, and the persecution of the Jews, there was a backlash amongst elements of the church.

Resistance and persecution

It has to be acknowledged that resistance to Nazism from German Christians was minor. In fact, as the figures on this page show (see left), the numbers of people leaving organized faith during the Nazi era were high, especially during the pre-war years when many Germans did indeed find a new faith in the *Führer*.

NUMBERS OF PEOPLE IN GERMANY LEAVING ORGANIZED FAITH, 1932–44			
Date	Catholic	Protestant	Total
1932	52,000	225,000	277,000
1933	34,000	57,000	91,000
1934	27,000	29,000	56,000
1935	34,000	53,000	87,000
1936	46,000	98,000	144,000
1937	104,000	338,000	442,000
1938	97,000	343,000	440,000
1939	95,000	395,000	490,000
1940	52,000	160,000	212,000
1941	52,000	195,000	247,000
1942	37,000	105,000	142,000
1943	12,000	35,000	47,000
1944	6000	17,000	23,000

The principal resistance came in the form of the *Bekenntniskirche* (Confessional Church), headed by Pastor Martin Niemöller. The *Bekenntniskirche*'s declared intention was to keep the Protestant faith pure, and distant from the influence of the *Deutsche Glaubensbewegung*. Some 7000 Protestant pastors signed a declaration saying that Christianity and Nazism were not compatible. This extraordinary act of bravery was to cost them dear.

During the 1930s and the war years, Hitler's policy of tolerance towards the orthodox churches gradually shifted to targeted persecution. The Confessional Church members were destined for concentration camps and/or execution. Niemöller, for example, spent seven years in such camps before his release.

Other Protestant resisters were involved in more active subversion of the Nazi state. The theologian Dietrich Bonhoeffer was another member of the *Bekenntniskirche* who became involved in anti-Nazi espionage and plots against Hitler. He was eventually arrested in April 1943, and after two years in *Gestapo* prisons and concentration camps was finally executed on 9 April 1945.

Nor was religious resistance only confined to the Protestants. During the 1930s and early 1940s, the Catholic Archbishop of Münster, Clemens Galen, railed against Nazi racial laws and euthanasia programmes. His prominence in the Catholic Church prevented his immediate extirpation, but following the July Bomb Plot in 1944 he finally disappeared into Dachau concentration camp, where he was brutalized but survived the war.

Hundreds of other members of the clergy served peace instead of war during the Nazi era, expressing their beliefs with acts ranging from proclaiming their faith to rescuing Jews from certain death. The fact remains, however, that in the main, religious believers were a compliant body for the Nazis, or at least one that hid its true voice.

Mythology and Symbolism

The Nazi Party had an especially keen eye for symbolism, realizing that powerful imagery was integral to cohesive political and social movements. It consequently created one of the most memorable systems of iconography in history.

Although, as we have seen, Hitler had little time for orthodox religion, his political views did contain spiritual overtones. Hitler's beliefs centred around ideas of messianic destiny; of the power of *Blut und Boden* (Blood and Soil); and on the concept of racial purity. Nazi rituals were akin to high church ceremonies.

Some pro-Nazi thinkers and even Party members began to explore Nordic paganism as a form of Germanic replacement for the Christian faith. Yet while some scholars have attempted to forge

NORSE MYTHOLOGY, KEY FIGURES AND PLACES IN NAZI NEO-PAGANISM	
Figure	*Meaning*
Wotan/Odin	Norse warrior king, celebrated for being a military archetype.
Thor	Norse god of thunder and son of Wotan/Odin. Also celebrated for his martial qualities.
Race of giants	A race of Norse giants, enemies of the gods, whom some Nazis saw as archetypes of the enemies with which they struggled, particularly at the end of the war.
Magni and Modi	These sons of Thor were both warrior gods, and together they represented the ideal of total war, expressing ferocity in battle and a complete lack of weakness that appealed to the Nazi mentality.
Jarnsaxa	A giantess who became a god through marriage to Thor. Could represent the status of women in the Third Reich – important but inferior.
Valhalla and Asgard	Asgard was the home of the Norse gods, and Valhalla the 'heaven' within Asgard – the place for fallen warriors. Both places had martial connotations, and so were more stirring to the Nazis when compared with Christian notions of heaven.

substantial links between Nazism and pagan or even occult practices, the link should not be taken too far. Hitler actually frowned on overt occultism, and some mystics such as Friedrich Bernhard Marby were even dispatched to concentration camps for more extreme attempts to revive old German religions.

Yet while the Nazis may have opposed outright pagan religiosity, they were intensely interested in the symbolism and legends of antiquity.

The Aryan mythology often revolved around ideas of a lost ancestral centre, or historical patterns of racial destiny, mixed with pseudo-religious imagery. The *Thule Gesellschaft* (Thule Society), for example, was a nationalistic and anti-Semitic organization formed in the early post-World War I years. It was named after a mythical Nordic country and used mystical symbols in its iconography, including the swastika. Its quest to define the spiritual and

geographical homeland of the Aryan race attracted several thousand members, including Nazi Party authorities such as Rudolf Hess and Alfred Rosenberg.

Ritual images

Looking at Nazism for signs that it was an organized religion or cult are misguided. What was certain, however, was that the Nazis had a deeply spiritual relationship to their symbolism. The SS, for example, relied heavily on runic symbols in its insignia, with uniform collars and hats bearing symbols for death, victory, fidelity and so on (see table on opposite page).

By far the most definable emblem of Nazi ideology, however, was the *Hakenkreuz* ('Hook Cross', or swastika). Although the swastika has come to be identified with the Nazi era, it is actually a symbol of great antiquity. It is first seen in decorative arts in Persia back in the fourth millennium BC, and was subsequently used as a religious symbol in ancient Greece, India and Japan.

The Nazis adopted the swastika as their official emblem – often combined with the German eagle – because of its connections with the Aryan Indians and the perceived associations of racial purity (on account of the Indian caste system). Whatever the philosophy, the swastika was wielded with powerful national pride by the Nazis, and was treated as virtually a sacred motif of nationhood. Ultimately, Nazi symbolism was largely about style over substance, but both Goebbels and Hitler realized that the former was often what motivated people.

SWASTIKA FLAG VARIATIONS

Image	Flag	Example
	45° black swastika, set on a white disc	NSDAP flag
	45° black swastika, set in a white lozenge	Hitler Youth flag
	45° black swastika, set in a white outline	Tail marking on *Luftwaffe* aircraft
	45° black swastika, outlined by white and black lines, set on a white disc	German War Ensign (used by the *Kriegsmarine*)
	Upright black swastika, outlined by white and black lines, set on a white disc	Adolf Hitler's personal standard
	45° swastikas in gold, silver, black, or white; often set on or being held by an eagle	Numerous military badges and flags
	Upright swastika with curved arms, described in white outline on black background, forming a circle	Emblem of *Waffen-SS Nordland* Division

NAZI SYMBOLISM

Image	Symbol	Origins	Nazi Meaning and application
	Hakenkreuz (Swastika)	Uncertain – prevalent across Indo-European cultures from the Bronze Age	National flags and offical emblem of NSDAP
	Sonnenrad ('Sunwheel' Swastika)	Old Norse symbol for the sun	Divisional sign for Waffen-SS divisions Wiking and Nordland
	Eagle	Roman Empire	Represented Nazi Party (when looking to right) and Nazi Germany (when looking to left)
	Totenkopf (Death's Head)	Ancient; eighteenth-century European military symbol	Used by SS as official badge
	Sig rune	Ancient/medieval Germanic alphabets	Symbolized victory. Two side by side became the official emblem of the SS
	Opfer rune	Ancient/medieval Germanic alphabets	Symbolized self-sacrifice. Used in SA Sports Badge for War Wounded
	Odal rune	Ancient/medieval Germanic alphabets	Symbolized family and racial cohesion. Used by the SS Race and Settlement Department
	Ger rune	Ancient/medieval Germanic alphabets	Symbolized faith. Alternative divisional sign for Waffen-SS Division Nordland
	Heilszeichen	Ancient/medieval Germanic alphabets	Symbolized success. Used on SS Death's Head ring
	Wolfsangle (Wolf's Hook)	Medieval German	Symbolized liberty. Early motif of NSDAP and used by Waffen-SS Division Das Reich
	Toten rune	Ancient/medieval Germanic alphabets	Symbolized death, hence used on official SS documents alongside date of death
	Tyr rune	Ancient/medieval Germanic alphabets	Symbolized leadership in battle. Used on SS grave markers
	Eif rune	Ancient/medieval pagan Germanic alphabets	Symbolized enthusiasm, passion. Worn by SS adjutants in the 1930s
	Hagall rune	Ancient/medieval Germanic alphabets	Symbolized fidelity (to Nazi cause). Featured on SS Death's Head ring

Bibliography

Books

Bishop, Chris. *Order of Battle: German Panzers in WWII.*
St Pauls, MN: Zenith Press, 2008.

Bishop, Chris. *Order of Battle: Germany Infantry in WWII.*
St Pauls, MN: Zenith Press, 2008.

Burleigh, Michael. *Germany Turns Eastward.*
London: Pan Books, 2002.

Carr, William. *Hitler – A Study in Personality and Politics.*
London: Edward Arnold, 1986.

Dearn, Alan. *The Hitler Youth 1933–45.* Oxford:
Osprey Publishing, 2006.

Deighton, Len. *Blitzkrieg – From the Rise of Hitler to the Fall of Dunkirk.*
Fakenham: Book Club Associates, 1979.

Evans, Richard J. *The Third Reich in Power 1933–1939 – How the
Nazis Won Over the Hearts and Minds of a Nation.*
London: Penguin Books, 2006.

Grunberger, Richard. *A Social History of the Third Reich.*
London: Phoenix, 2005.

Kirk, Tim. *The Longman Companion to Nazi Germany.*
Harlow: Longman Group Limited, 1995.

Layton, Geoff. *Germany: The Third Reich 1933–45.*
London: Hodder & Stoughton, 2000.

Lucas, James. *Germany Army Handbook 1939–1945.*
Stroud: Sutton Publishing, 1998.

Overy, Richard. *The Penguin Historical Atlas of the Third Reich.*
London: Penguin Books, 1996.

Quinn, Carl Underhill. *Adolf Hitler – Pictures from the Life of the Führer.*
New York: Peebles Press, 1978.

Rees, Laurence. *The Nazis – A Warning From History.*
London: BBC Worldwide, 2002.

Snyder, Louis L. *Encyclopedia of the Third Reich.*
Ware: Wordsworth Edition Limited, 1998.

Trevor-Roper, Hugh. *Hitler's Table Talk 1941–1944.*
London: Phoenix Press, 2000.

Useful web sites

Axis History Factbook – http://www.axishistory.com
Feldgrau.com – http://www.feldgrau.com
United States Holocaust Memorial Museum – http://www.ushmm.org
German Police in World War II – http://www.germanpolice.org
The Nizkor Project – http://www.nizkor.org

Glossary

Abteilung – Battalion/Detachment
Admiral (Adm) – Admiral
Anschluss – Union with Austria, March 1938
Arbeitsgaue – Divisional Work Districts
Armee – Army
Armeegruppe – Army Group
Auftragstaktik – Mission-oriented Tactics
Ausbildungs – Training
Autobahn – Motorway
Bataillon – Battalion
Befehlshaber der Ordnungspolizei (BDO)
– Chief of the Order Police
Bekenntniskirche – Confessional Church
Bergpolizei – Mountain Police
Blitzkrieg – Lightning War
Blockwart – Block Warden
Blut und Boden – 'Blood and Soil'
Bodenständige – Static
Bund Deutscher Mädel (BDM)
– League of German Girls
**Chef der Deutschen Polizei im Reichsministerium
des Innern** – Chief of the German Police in the
Reich Ministry of the Interior
Christliches Landvolk
– Christian Agrarian Party
Der Stürmer – 'The Stormer' (newspaper)
Deutsche Arbeitsfront (DAF)
– German Labour Front
Deutsche Glaubensbewegung
– German Faith Movement
Deutsches Jungvolk – German Young People

Deutsches Nachrichtenburo (DNB)
– German News Bureau
Deutschnationale Volkspartei (DNVP)
– German National People's Party
Die Endlösung – 'The Final Solution'
Dienststelle Ribbentrop – Ribbentrop Bureau
Dienstverpflichtung – Compulsory service
Division – Division
Einsatzgruppen – Task Forces (mobile death
squads)
Einsatzkommando – Sub-unit of an Einsatzgruppen
Eisenbahnpolizei – Railway Police
Entartete Kunst – Degenerate Art
Ersatz – Replacement
Ersatzheer – Replacement Army
Fallschirmjäger – Paratroops
Feld-Division (Luftwaffe)
– Field Division (Luftwaffe) (from 1943)
Feldgendarmerie – Field Police
Feldgerichtsabteilung – Court-Martial Department
Feldheer – Field Army
Feldjäger – Sharpshooters
Festung – Fortress
Flakkorps – Anti-Aircraft Corps
Fliegerdivision – Air Division
Flieger-HJ
– Hitler Youth Paramilitary Aviation Enthusiasts
Fliegerkorps – Air Corps
Frankfurter Zeitung
– 'Frankfurt Newspaper' (newspaper)
Fregattenkapitän (Fkpt) – Captain (junior)

Freikorps – Free Corps
Fremdarbeiter – Foreign Workers
Führerbunker – Hitler's bunker
Führerkanzlei – Führer Chancellery
Führerprinzip – Leadership Principle
Gastarbeitnehmer – Guest Workers
Gau – District
Gauleiter – District Leader
Gebiet der Kriegsverwaltung
– Military Administrative Zone
Gebietskommissar –Area leader
Gebirgsjäger – Mountain Light Infantry
Gefechtsgebiet – Combat Zone
Geheime Feldpolizei (GFP) – Secret Field Police
Geheime Staatspolizei (Gestapo)
– Secret State Police
Generaladmiral (Gen-Adm) – General-Admiral
(equivalent to an Army Colonel-General)
Generalbevollmächtigter für den Arbeitseinsatz
– General Plenipotentiary for Labour Deployment
Generalbezirke – General Regions
Generalfeldmarschall – Field Marshal
Generalgouvernement
– General Government (of Central Poland)
Generalkommissar – Commissar general
Generalmajor – Major-General
Generaloberst – Colonel-General
Germania – latin term for Germany. *Welthauptstadt*
('World Capital') Germania was the name Adolf
Hitler gave to the projected renewal of the
German capital Berlin, part of his vision for the

future of Germany after the planned victory in World War II.

Geschwader – Group (RAF); Wing (USAAF)
Gleichschaltung – Coordination
Großadmiral – Grand Admiral
Großdeutsches Reich – Greater Germany
Gruppe – Wing (RAF); Group (USAAF)
Hafenpolizei – Harbour Police
Hakenkreuz – 'Hook Cross', Swastika
Hauptamt Ordnungspolizei
 – Order Police Headquarters
Hauptgebiete – Main Districts
Hauptkommissar – Commissar captain
Hauptmann – Captain
Haus der deutschen Kunst
 – House of German Art (Munich)
Heeresgruppe – Army Group
Heimatsgebiet – Home Zone
Heiliges Römisches Reich deutscher Nation
 – Holy Roman Empire of the German Nation
Herrenvolk – Master Race
Hilfspolizei (Hipo) – Auxiliary Police
Hilfswillige ('Hiwis') – Voluntary Assistants
Hitlerjugend (HJ) – Hitler Youth
Hochseeflotte – High Seas Fleet
Höchste SS- und Polizeiführer (HöSSPF)
 – Supreme SS and Police Leader
Höherer SS- und Polizeiführer (HSSPF)
 – Higher SS and Police Leader
Jagdpolizei – Game Conservation Police
Jäger – Chasseur, Light (of infantry)
Jungmädelbund – League of Young Girls
Junker – landowner
Kaiserlich – Imperial
Kaiserliche Marine – Imperial Navy
Kampfgruppe – Battle Group
Kapitän zur See (KptzS) – Captain of the Sea
Kasernierte Polizei – Barrack Police
KdF-Wagen – 'KdF-Car' (later the Volkswagen)
Kommandeure der Orpo
 – Commanders of the Order Police
Kommodore (Kom) – Commodore
Kompanie – Company
Konteradmiral (KAdm) – Rear-Admiral
Korps – Corps
Kraft durch Freude (KdF) – 'Strength through Joy'
Kreis – Local Council
Kreisgebiete – Area Districts
Kreisleiter – County Leader
Kreispolizeibehörde
 – City/County Police Authority
Kriegsmarine – (German) Navy
Kriminalpolizei (Kripo) – Criminal Police
Kristallnacht – 'Night of the Broken Glass'
Landdienst – Land Service
Länder – States, Provinces
Landesinspekteur – Regional Inspector
Landespolizeibehörde – Regional Police Authority
Landtag – Provincial Parliament
Lebensborn – 'Fount of Life'
Lebensraum – 'Living Space'
Luftflotte – Air Fleet
Luftwaffe – (German) Air Force
Luftwaffe-Feld Division
 – Luftwaffe Field Division (to 1943)
Militärinternierte – Military Internees, POWs

Militärverwaltung – Military Administration
Minister für Kirchenfragen
 – Minister for Church Affairs
Motorisierte Infanteriedivision
 – Motorized Infantry Division
Nationalpolitische Erziehungsanstalten (NAPOLA)
 – National Political Education Institutes
**Nationalsozialistische Deutsche Arbeiterpartei
(NSDAP)** – National Socialist German Workers
Party
**Nationalsozialistischer Deutscher Dozentenbund
(NSDDB)** – National Socialist Germany University
Lecturers League
**Nationalsozialistischer Deutscher Studentenbund
(NSDSB)** – National Socialist German Students
League
Nationalsozialistischer Lehrbund (NSLB)
 – National Socialist Teachers League
NS Rechtswahrerbund – Nazi Lawyers Association
Oberkommando der Luftwaffe (OKL)
 – Luftwaffe High Command
Oberkommando der Marine (OKM)
 – Naval High Command
Oberkommando der Wehrmacht (OKW)
 – Armed Forces High Command
Oberkommando des Heeres (OKH)
 – Army High Command
Oberst – Colonel
Olympiastadion – Olympic Stadium, Berlin
Operationsgebiet – Operations Zone
Ordnungspolizei (Orpo) – Order Police
Ortsgruppenleiter – Local Group Leader
Ortspolizeibehörde – Local Police Authority
Ostarbeiter – Eastern Workers
Osthilfe 'Help for the East'
Panzergrenadier – Motorised infantry
Panzerschiff – Armoured Ship, Pocket Battleship
Parteikanzlei – Party Chancellery
Parteitage – Party Days (Rallies)
Pflichtjahr – Duty Year (BDM)
Polizei Abschnitt – Police Sector
Polizei Gruppe – Police Group
Polizeiverwaltungsbeamten – Administrative Police
Polizeivollzugsbeamten – Uniformed Police
Raum – Space
Regierungspräsident – Government President
Regiment – Regiment
Reichsarbeitsdienst (RAD) – Reich Labour Service
Reichsbank – Reich Bank
Reichsbevollmächtiger – Reich Plenipotentiary
Reichsfilmkammer – Reich Chamber for Film
Reichsgau – Administrative district created in
areas annexed by Nazi Germany
Reichsheer – Reich Army
Reichsjugendführer – Reich Youth Leader
Reichskammer der bildenden Künste
 – Reich Chamber for Fine Arts
Reichskommissariat – Reich Commission
Reichskulturkammer – Reich Chamber of Culture
Reichsleiter – Reich Leader
Reichsleitung der NSDAP
 – Reich Leadership of the NSDAP
Reichsmarine – Reich Navy
Reichsministerium für die besetzen Ostgebiete
 – Reich Ministry for the Occupied Eastern
Territories

Reichsmusikkammer – Reich Chamber for Music
Reichspressekammer
 – Reich Chamber for the Press
Reichsrundfunkkammer
 – Reich Chamber for Radio
Reichsschriftumskammer
 – Reich Chamber for Literature
Reichssicherheitshauptamt (RSHA)
 – Reich Main Security Office
Reichstag – German parliament in Berlin
Reichstatthalter – Reich Governors
Reichstheaterkammer – Reich Chamber for Theatre
Reichswehr – Reich Defence Forces
Reviere Polizei – Precinct Police
Rückwartiges Gebiet – Rear Area
Schnellboot – Fast Boat
Schutzmannschaften der Ordnungspolizei
 – Detachments of Order Police
Schutzstaffel (SS) – Security Squad
Schwarze Reichswehr – Black Reichswehr
Sicherheitsdienst (SD) – Security Service
Sicherheitspolizei (Sipo) – Security Police
Sonderkommando – Special Unit
Sonderpolizei – Special Police
Sportpalast – Winter sports stadium in Berlin
SS- und Polizeiführer (SSPF)
 – SS and Police Leader
SS-Oberabschnitt Führer
 – SS Leader of the Main Districts
SS-Polizei Regiment – SS Police Regiment
Staffel – Squadron
Sturmabteilung (SA) – Assault Detachment/Storm
Detachment
Technische Nothilfe – Technical Emergency Service
Thule Gesellschaft – Thule Society
Truppenamt – Troop Office (Schwarze Reichswehr)
übergangsheer – Transitional Army
Untermenschen – Sub-humans
Vizeadmiral (VAdm) – Vice-Admiral
Volk – People
Völkischer Beobachter
 – 'People's Times' (newspaper)
Volksdeutsche – Ethnic Germans
Volksgemeinschaft – People's Community
Volksgerichtshof – People's Court
Volksgrenadier – People's Grenadier
Volkssturm – People's Militia
Volkswagen – People's Car
Vorläufige Reichsheer – Provisional Army
Vorläufige Reichsmarine – Provisional Navy
Vorläufige Reichswehr
 – Provisional Defence Forces
Waffen-SS – Armed SS
Wehrertüchtigungslager der Hitlerjugend
 – Military Service Competency Camps for the
Hitler Youth
Wehrkreis – Military District
Wehrmacht – (German) Armed Forces
Wehrwirtschaft – War Economy
Welthauptstadt Germania
 – 'World Capital Germania'
Zellenleiter – Cell Leader
Zeppelinwiese – Zeppelin Field (Nuremberg)
Zivilarbeiter – Civilian Workers
Zug – Platoon

Index